D1569946

THE INTERREGNUM OF DESPAIR

☆ ☆ ☆ ☆ ☆

THE
INTERREGNUM
OF DESPAIR

Hoover, Congress, and the Depression

JORDAN A. SCHWARZ

UNIVERSITY OF ILLINOIS PRESS
Urbana · Chicago · London

© 1970 by the Board of Trustees of the University of Illinois.
Manufactured in the United States of America.
Library of Congress Catalog Card No. 78–113768.
252 00112 5

To my wife Linda

PREFACE

The events of 1929–1933, like many of the ideas of Herbert Hoover, did not logically belong with the epochs either immediately preceding or following them. For the most part, President Hoover and the Hoover years were not in complete accord with the precepts of the New Era or in rebellion against them; likewise, the man and his era had some continuity with the New Deal but did not anticipate it. Hoover and the Hoover years do not belong to any mainstream of recent American history. The man and his era are symbols of transition, confusion, and uncertainty. Rather, one of the best ways to understand this period is to study the national forum where problems of the times were both confronted and ignored. Congress in this turbulent period became the reluctant vehicle for an orderly and coherent transmogrification in the relationship between the federal government and the economy.

This is a study of the congressional response to the Great Depression. It is concerned with congressional attitudes and actions on the major economic and social problems of the pre–New Deal depression years. Accordingly the president becomes a somewhat secondary figure in this narrative. He often opposed or unwillingly supported such legislative departures as the first peacetime federal expansion of private capital investment, the most progressive peacetime tax law in American history, and the first federal unemployment relief act.

But, in fairness to Hoover, much of what the 72nd Congress legislated went against the conventional wisdom of most legislators. Most of Congress preferred the responsive or inert legislative function desired by Hoover. Most lawmakers ignored the struggle of economic philosophies between the president who sought recovery by priming the investment pump and senators like Robert F. Wagner who sought relief by priming the employment pump; desperation or political opportunism usually governed legislative decisions. In this book, the term "progressive" denotes a desire for federal action against depression unemployment and "conservative" identifies resistance to such legislative activity. That the progressives had more momentum by 1933 is not a tribute to any philosophical change; it is best explained by the prevailing fear of inaction. The necessity for action against the depression worked great changes in the government-economy relationship in 1932 and set a political pattern for the New Deal.

My greatest debt is to the archivists who collect, organize, and make available to historians documents upon which our research is based. They are unsung heroes in the writing of history. Their numbers, unfortunately, are too few for such great and growing tasks. Perhaps it is in the historians' interest to give more attention to archival needs. I have been assisted by too many for individual mention here, but as a group they were unfailingly courteous and helpful to me and I appreciate their efforts.

Also, I owe a special expression of gratitude to William E. Leuchtenburg of Columbia University who often went beyond mere university responsibilities to give me his time, editorial attention, and intellectual inspiration; he has been an ideal mentor. John A. Garraty of Columbia sponsored the master's essay which grew into this book. Robert E. Burke of the University of Washington offered many valuable suggestions on smoothing the manuscript's rough edges. I have enjoyed the professional stimulation of my colleagues at Northern Illinois University and have profited from the ideas of Paul A. Carter, J. Carroll Moody, and Carl P. Parrini who read parts of the manuscript. Of course, I cannot shift the responsibility for anything in these pages to the above people. My thanks to Mrs. Darla Woodward, Mrs. Janis Merritt, and other Department of History typists for their aid. My mother, Mrs. Helen Schwarz Pearl, gave me my first awareness of the drama and significance of the period about which I write. My wife Linda has shared the whole experience of writing this book; only she knows how great an acknowledgment is due to her. Finally, two beautiful little people named Orrin and Jessica have added much to the joy and hope of history.

J.A.S.

De Kalb, Illinois
March, 1970

CONTENTS

THE INTERREGNUM OF DESPAIR

☆ ☆ ☆ ☆ ☆

1

A VERY DIFFICULT TIME

The "New Era" described an enthusiasm that pervaded Washington during the twentieth century's third decade. Unlike the other "New" phrases that have heralded programs or governmental philosophies in our history—New Nationalism, New Freedom, etc.—this term simply characterized a ubiquitous attitude that good times had arrived and better times were on the way. Warren Harding set the mood in his inaugural address: "The forward course of the business cycle is unmistakable." Not only was this the correct thing to say in the midst of a depression, but admitting the presence of a business cycle hedged against expectations of linear improvement. The business cycle would not be abolished but its impact would be decidedly ameliorated. Material improvement, most Americans believed, was as inevitable as the occasional break in confidence that sent stock prices skidding—a "technical correction," in the euphemism of Wall Street. The quick economic recovery that followed Harding's reassurance seemed to justify his forecast. American capitalism appeared headed for a millenium in which all shared a veritable cornucopia.

The years following Harding's demise in 1923 were filled with unparalleled economic achievement. In the score of years previous to the Great War, reflected popular economist John Moody in 1928, "there never was a time in which one could fairly count on a long period of sustained prosperity in this country." Moody clearly believed that the United States had entered such a period after the war. Profits, prices, dividends, and wages were higher, jobs more plentiful, technology more creative, and public satisfaction more evident. There seemed to be no end to this expansiveness. "No one can examine the panorama of business and finance in America during the past half-dozen years without realizing that we are living in a new era," Moody wrote; America had not ended the business cycle, but its economic growth would "continue through many years to come, thus adding steadily to and maintaining a relative plethora of available capital and credit." The only qualifying note in his cheery analysis was that the latter factors required sustained public confidence: "their plentitude depends on faith."[1]

And if there should be a paucity of faith, then it became the obligation of national leaders to exhort the people, but not to intrude upon their activities. Abundance, it was reasoned, was the natural product of our economic system. Washington's role in the industrial effort during the Great War had distorted the proper relationship between government and business. "Our most dangerous tendency is to expect too much of government," Harding warned. Government should practice economy and efficiency while the rest of the nation should respond to problems with voluntarism and cooperation. According to the imagery of the age, government should be no more than a policeman and preacher for the rest of society. Yet it would be erroneous to presume that these concepts required an inert government. Policemen and preachers are always active in surveillance, organization, mediation, and exhortation. Washington would serve the people as a clearing house and a good example.

The distinction the Republican presidents of the 1920's made between the correct governmental activity and mischievous intervention often was as precise as the demarcation between the White House and Congress. While the executive performed as preacher and policeman, a good Congress for the most part limited

[1] David A. Shannon (ed.), *Progressivism and Postwar Disillusionment* (New York, 1966), pp. 315–19.

its functions to revenue and appropriation matters. An errant Congress indulged in farm relief or proposed government development of public power. Like Grover Cleveland, the Republican presidents believed that a sovereign people would support themselves and the government, expecting little or no succor from Washington. As Coolidge discovered when he gave Congress a free hand in Mississippi Valley flood relief in 1928, vote-hungry legislators seized every opportunity to indulge in pork-barrel extravagancies.[2] The lesson was evident: emergency relief was an administrative responsibility; when Congress became involved the result was a raid upon the federal treasury. And nothing disturbed business confidence as much as free-wheeling lawmakers. To maintain stability, Congress must be either disciplined or ignored.

Coolidge's relations with Congress, as a rule, were cordial as long as the president courted his party's leaders and insisted upon the integrity of their respective spheres of influence. In moments of exasperation he suggested that the nation was out of harm's way only if Congress was out of session. A Congress in session disturbed business' tranquility which the president carefully guarded. With Congress and "uncertainties removed as much as they can be," he told the press in May, 1925, business could function "without being in jeopardy of change of law or something of that kind that might change conditions in such a way that their investments would become uncertain."[3] When Herbert Hoover succeeded to the presidency after a heady electoral triumph, he had learned all these lessons well. His mistake would be in thinking that he could discipline Congress.

After its decisive triumph in the 1928 elections, the Republican party reigned with an authority that seemed impregnable for a generation to come. Its presidential nominee, Herbert Hoover,

[2] Donald R. McCoy, *Calvin Coolidge: The Quiet President* (New York, 1967), pp. 329–32.
[3] *Ibid.*, pp. 193–99, 267–81; Howard H. Quint and Robert H. Ferrell (eds.), *The Talkative President: The Off-the-Record Press Conferences of Calvin Coolidge* (Amherst, Mass., 1964), pp. 127–28.

had won 58 per cent of the major party vote, a magnificent political achievement in any year. With the initial handicap of a Democratic South, Republican candidates for the House of Representatives surprisingly captured 57.4 per cent of all the votes for a major party nationwide. From New England, where Republican nominees won 55.3 per cent of the votes, to the Pacific states, where the GOP rang up 81.2 per cent, the election had devastated the Democrats. Republican House candidates in Illinois won 56.9 per cent of the vote, 52.4 per cent in Massachusetts, 73.3 per cent in Michigan, 51.1 per cent in New York, 60.8 per cent in Ohio, and 69.4 per cent in Pennsylvania.[4] The 1928 election confirmed Republican supremacy.

Buoyed by what he confidently called a mandate, President Hoover convened a special session of Congress for April 15 to consider legislation for agricultural relief and tariff revision. Most political observers anticipated that the substantial Republican majorities in Congress—56 to 39 in the Senate, 267 to 167 in the House—would deliver the Hoover program in short order. Speaker of the House Nicholas Longworth predicted the session would last only a month or thereabouts. Longworth could not be too far wrong if the president used the momentum of his electoral popularity to secure the legislation. A few days after the special session began, Senator Peter Norbeck remarked: "The President is so immensely popular over the country that the Republicans here are on their knees and the Democrats have their hats off. They are also over-awed by the great feeling of confidence and good will for the new chief." Even Frank Kent, a skeptical columnist, grudgingly admitted that Hoover had "a better mental engine than anybody else in Washington." The capital anticipated a virtuoso performance of leadership by the new Chief Executive. "The skies appear clear blue for the Hoover administration," a New York *Times* correspondent wrote; "the indications are that harmony will be the rule."[5]

[4] American Institute of Public Opinion, *The Gallup Political Almanac for 1948* (Princeton, N.J., 1948), pp. 16, 28, 71, 111, 143, 148, 192, 205, 219.
[5] Harris Gaylord Warren, *Herbert Hoover and the Great Depression* (New

Nevertheless, the struggle for the agricultural marketing bill demonstrated that it would not be so easy to translate Hoover's prestige into legislative support. The farm bloc in the Senate earnestly sought adoption of its export debenture proposal which Hoover adamantly resisted because he deemed it an impractical device. The House proved more willing to follow Hoover but for nearly two months the Senate tangled over the issue before the administration prevailed.[6]

Again, on the tariff issue, Congress taught Hoover that November's votes were not redeemable in bills. The president demanded the power to change rates as much as 50 per cent on the recommendation of the Tariff Commission. Unfortunately for Hoover, he was not adept at the legislative horse-trading involved in writing a tariff. Several Republicans, including Speaker Longworth, proved reluctant to approve his plan. Already annoyed by some cavalier treatment from the huge GOP majority, Democrats were in no mood to give Hoover this flexible provision. The special session lumbered on through 1929 ingloriously threatening to infringe on the regular congressional term without producing a tariff bill. In late October, Senator Bronson M. Cutting of New Mexico wrote: "Every day it seems more impossible to pass a tariff bill in the special session and now that both the Republican and Democratic leaders have decided to leave us and go on a vacation, there seems no good reason why we should not follow their example."[7] The legislators talked rates for three more weeks, than adjourned for a brief rest before resuming the hassle in December.

The second session of the 71st Congress commenced in a different atmosphere. In September the stock market had received a sharp jolt as selling sent prices skidding; more setbacks hit it in the last week of October as a full-blown panic set in. By Novem-

York, 1959), pp. 87–88; Peter Norbeck to G. J. Moen, April 20, 1929, Norbeck MSS; Frank Kent to Bernard Baruch, May 13, 1929, Baruch MSS; New York *Times*, April 7, 1929.
[6] For an explanation of the Agricultural Marketing Act, see John D. Hicks, *Republican Ascendancy, 1921–1933* (New York, 1960), p. 218.
[7] Bronson M. Cutting to Edward L. Safford, October 30, 1929, Cutting MSS.

ber the market had collapsed and the effects began to be felt throughout the economy. The American people were about to enter a new decade and a fearful new period in their history; the Great Depression had begun.

Washington viewed the depression during its first year as a natural turn in the nation's economic behavior. Leaders of both parties counselled calm and confidence, stressing that recovery surely would be imminent. No need for governmental action existed, they affirmed, because the decline was a product of natural economic fluctuations; the business cycle's normal behavior would restore the equilibrium. After a deflation washed out some bad money, good money would prime the economic pump again. Meanwhile, the Republicans, already plagued by poor political leadership by the White House, suffered from their position of responsibility in a time of distress. If an upturn did not materialize as forecast, the GOP stood to lose its majority status. Republican fortunes had taken a sudden turn for the worse.

Congress, however, picked up the task of writing a tariff in December as if circumstances had not altered. The tariff battle assumed classic features; the Old Guard Republicans like James E. Watson of Indiana used every available tactic to raise rates for pet interests; free traders like Representative Cordell Hull of Tennessee assailed the tariff wall which grew in spite of their efforts to demolish it; and progressives like George Norris of Nebraska cried out for the Senate to remember the common man of the field and the mill. As the tariff debate entered its second year in the spring of 1930, Hoover did not commit himself on rates.

His major concern centered on the flexible provision and he threatened to veto any tariff bill which did not contain this power. Yet a majority of Congress stood against it. Many congressmen feared that Hoover sought, as Robert L. Doughton of North Carolina said, "to practically transfer the levying of taxes from the Legislative to the Executive Department of the Government." Sentiments like this abounded. "It is too much power to give to any President," declared Democratic financier Bernard Baruch.

Senator Key Pittman of Nevada agreed but suspected that Hoover would just as well do without a tariff act as lose his flexible provision.[8]

"Whoever controlled the Republican party during the second session of the Seventy-first Congress, it was not Herbert Hoover," a historian friendly to the president has written;[9] this was evident in the tariff bill signed by the president in June, 1930. The Hawley-Smoot tariff, conceived in prosperity, born in depression, would ever after be stigmatized as the illegitimate offspring of the Republican party. Although the tariff would be identified with the depression, it belonged more to the wonderland of the twenties than to the anguish of the thirties. Congress wrote it with indifference to Hoover's request for a flexible provision, successfully challenging the president's legislative leadership. A few years later, a New Deal Congress would give Franklin Roosevelt those powers to negotiate reciprocal trade agreements which had been denied to Hoover.

The White House committed another tactical error when it nominated John J. Parker for the Supreme Court in the spring of 1930. Parker, a North Carolina Republican, had already earned the enmity of organized labor by upholding the "yellow dog contract" in a circuit court case. But the major opposition to Senate approval of his nomination came from Negroes who recalled a slurring remark by Parker during the 1922 campaign. Led by the National Association for the Advancement of Colored People, Negroes informed the party of Lincoln that Parker's nomination was an affront to them. Republicans responded to this pressure. In early May, 1930, a few days before the Parker vote, Senator Hiram Johnson of California forecast defeat, "because our Ethiopian brethren are so aroused. . . ." On the other hand, Senator Carter Glass of Virginia bitterly complained that rejection of the nomination "would practically mean that no Southern man,

---

[8] Robert L. Doughton to A. J. L. Moritz, May 5, 1930, Doughton MSS; Baruch to Key Pittman, February 24, Pittman to Baruch, March 3, 1930, Pittman MSS.
[9] Warren, p. 92.

Democrat or Republican, could ever get on the Supreme Court bench. We would be precluded as a section from representation."[10]

The president chose to ignore the opposition. Hoover relied on southern support for Parker after seventeen Republicans, led by Majority Leader James E. Watson, petitioned the president to withdraw the nomination. Hoover replied that the Republicans were unduly alarmed by the interest groups. According to Watson, Hoover was determined to alter his weak public image, "saying that he had been charged with vacillation and lack of backbone and that he wished the Senate to know that this was not true." But Watson saw Hoover's adamant stand as "firmness at the wrong time and in the wrong way,"[11] and most of the Old Guard abandoned Hoover in this fight. Not only did the president ignore the political effect of the nomination, but he overlooked the moral significance of it. "No man is entitled to go to the Supreme Court Bench who says that 15,000,000 American citizens are not entitled to participate in their government," wrote Senator Arthur Vandenberg of Michigan.[12] On May 7 the Senate rejected the nomination, 41 to 39. Supreme Court nominations were rarely vetoed by the Senate and embarrassed Republicans were annoyed that Hoover had neither heeded warnings nor consulted with them in advance.[13]

The 71st Congress had earned a reputation for contentiousness. "The session, which actually began with the Republican party united and expressing extreme friendliness to the administration, quickly became critical of the administration," the New York

[10] Hiram Johnson to C. K. McClatchy, May 3, 1930, Johnson MSS; Carter Glass to Baruch, April 30, 1930, Glass MSS.

[11] New York *Times*, April 8, 1930; James E. Watson, *Memoirs: As I Knew Them* (Indianapolis, 1936), p. 265.

[12] "The Parker Vote," May 7, 1930, Scrapbook 2, Vandenberg MSS. About those who criticized him for his opposition to Parker, Vandenberg said: "They drive me toward liberalism. I think 'the underdog' deserves a few more friends."

[13] For a summary of the Parker case, see Richard L. Watson, Jr., "The Defeat of Judge Parker: A Study in Pressure Groups and Politics," *Mississippi Valley Historical Review*, L (September, 1963): 213–34; also Doughton to C. J. Taylor, May 8, 1930, Doughton MSS.

Times noted. "As it progressed, Republicans vehemently attacked the President because of his refusal to state his views on the tariff bill and for many months this hostility has been manifest." Some observers blamed the protracted tariff debate on Hoover's hesitancy to give a vigorous parliamentary leadership. Whether or not this is fair to Hoover, he had apparently created the impression, in the words of a contemporary political scientist, of being "as reluctant as any President to intervene publicly in behalf of particular legislation."[14] The president seemed to have squandered his prestige. A year after the convening of the 71st Congress, it appeared to Representative Robert L. Doughton, a North Carolina Democrat, that the president had lost all influence with Congress: "His administration is so unpopular that each and every Republican Member seems to be going his own way." Although Frank Kent found Hoover a more capable man than Harding or Coolidge, the events of the past year had proven that their successor was "the most left-footed President politically the world ever saw." A Washington lawyer noted that the capital was rife with tales of Republican dissension. Hoover was in political trouble. As political scientist Lawrence H. Chamberlain has written, "His decision in favor of a more passive role deprived him of an opportunity to establish his leadership at the very outset of what proved to be an unhappy administration."[15]

The depression compounded Hoover's problems but he preferred to handle it without Congress. At the first crack in the stock market, Hoover confronted the imminence of a depression. He understood American business behavior and knew that the break in stock prices foreshadowed sharply reduced employment; business would endeavor to liquidate holdings, cut production, and subsist with less capital. Believing that these practices were inimi-

14 New York *Times*, July 4, 1930; Arthur W. Macmahon, "Second Session of the Seventy-first Congress," *American Political Science Review*, XXIV (November, 1930): 930.

15 Robert L. Doughton to R. A. Doughton, May 15, 1930, Doughton MSS; Kent to Baruch, May 22, 1930, Baruch MSS; R. W. Woolley to Edward M. House, November 1, 1929, House MSS; Lawrence H. Chamberlain, *The President, Congress and Legislation* (New York, 1946), pp. 130–31.

cal to economic recovery, the president sought to persuade corporations not to slash output and payrolls. In 1922, as Secretary of Commerce and chairman of President Harding's Conference on Unemployment, Hoover had advocated the policy of an alert federal government which, instead of liquidating its own nonessential functions, would boost industry with expanded public works. Thus on November 18, 1929, Hoover recommended an expansion of the Federal Public Buildings program, a move which required only an additional appropriation, not new legislation. As Albert U. Romasco observes, Hoover sought to exclude Congress from participation in recovery: "During these early months of domestic crisis, Congress was in session but Hoover showed no inclination to enlist its aid."[16] Providing relief in 1930 would be solely an executive function utilizing the existing federal machinery.

Hoover defined Congress' role in the depression as a spectator while he and business performed the task of recovery. In conferences with business leaders he sought their assurances that there would be no liquidation. He emphasized that Washington would not interfere with private enterprise. Businessmen voluntarily cooperating with each other and the White House would restore economic vitality by holding the line on production and employment. In other words, as Romasco concludes, Hoover functioned as "an influential adviser and well-placed cheerleader." He tied presidential leadership to the willingness of businessmen to deal responsibly in the interests of the society they served. What he was doing, he said, was "organizing cooperation in the constructive forces of the community . . . and stimulating every element of initiative and self-reliance in the country." Congress could do nothing in this crisis because only the normal functioning of the economy could rectify the situation. The belief, he declaimed, that "we can legislate ourselves out of a world-wide depression,"

[16] William Starr Myers and Walter H. Newton, *The Hoover Administration: A Documented Narrative* (New York, 1936), p. 25; Albert U. Romasco, *The Poverty of Abundance: Hoover, the Nation, the Depression* (New York, 1965), p. 38.

was tantamount to thinking that "we can exorcise a Caribbean hurricane by statutory law."[17] By equating the depression with a natural disaster, he thereby justified a passive role for Congress. In times like these, he argued, men could only restrain selfish behavior, practice cooperation, and maintain faith in the system.

The act of faith needed an affirmation of confidence. Hoover declared on March 7, 1930, that an economic survey forecast "that the worst effects of the crash upon unemployment will have been passed during the next sixty days." The administration never possessed the statistics to warrant such optimism. When the expected improvement did not develop, Republicans began to fret over the possible political repercussions. "Everyone here, including the White House, realizes the 'sixty' day announcement was a mistake," GOP lawyer Edward Tracy Clark told Calvin Coolidge. Hoover had made his prognosis with the hope "that a prediction of prosperity would create it."[18]

Expressions of confidence could not mitigate the impact of growing unemployment and reduced wages. Business-minded Republicans endeavored to guard against ill-advised pronouncements which raised false hopes such as the president's "sixty day" statement. Secretary of State Henry L. Stimson, reporting to the president on his talks with pro-administration leaders in industry and finance, told Hoover that

> the consensus of opinion was that this was a cycle of depression which, of course, would surely end but that we did not know yet scientifically the causes of such depressions well enough to determine or prophecy when such a depression would end. I emphasized the importance of not making any prophecy during this campaign, how each prophecy would lose votes. With a grim smile he pulled out a speech which he was going to make on

---

[17] Romasco, pp. 36 and 24–65 *passim*; William Starr Myers (ed.), *The State Papers and Other Public Writings of Herbert Hoover* (Garden City, N.Y., 1934), I: 576, 578. Hoover most succinctly expounded on his policies in the Indianapolis speech of June 15, 1931, quoted in Myers, I: 572–83.

[18] Quoted in Arthur M. Schlesinger, Jr., *The Crisis of the Old Order, 1919–1933* (Boston, 1957), p. 165; Edward Tracy Clark to Calvin Coolidge, July 1, August 12, 1930, Clark MSS.

Thursday before the bankers at Cleveland, and read me portions of it to ask whether I thought this was a violation of the rule against prophecy.

Stimson said it was not and the interview ended.[19]

Still, what else could Hoover do? Of course, it was courting disaster if baseless prognostications did not come true; but, on the other hand, pessimism might perpetuate panic. What Hoover did was to give voice to business beliefs that depressions were endemic to capitalism. Given the ebb and flow of trade and capital, the economy alternately suffered and healed itself; prosperity always returned in greater doses following the debacle. Indeed, the economy unfailingly achieved higher levels following the salutary effect of a crash. After the first market crash, Wall Street wizard Bernard Baruch rejoiced that prices were low enough to "do business with real confidence." He forecast on October 30, 1929, that business would be bad for only sixty days, "just long enough for us to get a good investment market and a strong situation." A week later he declared that the "technical and forced liquidation [was] about completed." In a similar vein, Ohio Senator Simeon D. Fess declared in 1930 that not only was the depression inevitable, but "outside of individual losses, it has been a rather good thing for the country and in thirty days from now probably we will not know there was such a thing."[20] Americans engaged in the rhetoric of confidence, secure in the knowledge that if history taught anything about depressions, it was that recovery always followed, although not necessarily in sixty days.

The nation had been born sanguine and no depression ever dulled its euphoria. As John Kenneth Galbraith put it, "Pessimism was not openly equated with fear and trepidation." Dour pronouncements were considered bad form; Washington preferred to

[19] Diary, September 30, 1930, Stimson mss. Schlesinger, p. 506, has noted that the sixty-day forecast oddly is not included in Hoover's *State Papers* and not mentioned in the other semiofficial accounts of the Hoover administration.

[20] Baruch to George Armsby, October 30, Baruch to John Morron (telegram), November 7, 1929, Baruch mss; New York *Times*, February 9, 1930.

look ahead instead of about. Hoover himself set the tone: "Unless our country is headed for complete destruction—and no one can believe that," he told Senator Arthur Capper of Kansas a year after it began, "we will have a turn in the situation and we will recover." Hoover never invoked a moratorium on optimism; it would be part of his legacy that he "had converted the simple business ritual of reassurance into a major instrument of public policy."[21]

Washingtonians often comforted themselves by reminding friends that prosperity was just around the corner. Six months after the crash Bernard Baruch confided to his fellow Democrat, Senator Carter Glass of Virginia, that he anticipated Hoover would be "fortunate enough, before the next election, to have a rising tide and then he will be pictured as the great master mind who led the country out of its economic misery." "That we will achieve a certain prosperity again in due course is, I think, very certain," said Harlan Fiske Stone, Supreme Court justice and member of Hoover's "medicine-ball cabinet." Stone tempered his optimism by saying that another generation would pass before the country would see a boom like the one that had just ended.[22]

The Republican Old Guard, confronted by an incipient political disaster, was fervent in its anticipation of an economic revival. In the words of Pennsylvania's David A. Reed, "By the workings of natural forces and the collective good sense of the American people . . . we shall recover our economic equilibrium." "Of course it goes without saying that we will go through the depression and pass on to another plane of activity," Simeon Fess affirmed and cautiously added, "but just when . . . is a matter of considerable doubt." Even as the months turned to years and recovery seemed remote, many men never wavered in their faith. As 1932 approached, Senator Josiah W. Bailey wrote: "I would

21 John Kenneth Galbraith, *The Great Crash 1929* (Boston, 1951), pp. 75, 149; Herbert Hoover to Arthur Capper, November 8, 1930, Capper MSS.
22 Baruch to Glass, May 23, 1930, Glass MSS; Alpheus Thomas Mason, *Harlan Fiske Stone: Pillar of Law* (New York, 1956), p. 283.

very much like to be able to conclude that the depression is only an incident, not unlike other depressions."[23]

Numerous senators agreed with Hoover that Congress could do little or nothing to set natural recuperative forces in motion. Reed warned against what he characterized as "legislative quackery," insisting that "fussy government meddling" had proven the need for more individual initiative. Relief should never come from the federal government, reasoned Hiram Bingham of Connecticut: "It is not the business of Washington to look out for the general welfare of the States. It is the business of the States to look out for the general welfare of the people." The best plan was one for inaction. "The thing to do," said Fess, "is to sit steady in the boat and make the best of a bad situation." Quite a few Democrats agreed with their GOP brethren. Bernard Baruch asserted, "No government agency . . . can cure this situation." Joe T. Robinson of Arkansas repeated the "sit steady in the boat" metaphor and confided to Baruch, "I grow more and more impressed with the necessity of conservative action. . . ."[24]

This did not mean, however, that these men opted for complete inaction. When they called for government inertia, they directed their remarks against schemes for federal public works and unemployment relief. Several conservatives harbored pet plans for reconstruction. Reed Smoot of Utah, co-author of the highest tariff in U.S. history, insisted that even higher rates might be in order. Bingham's panacea for the depression was to end prohibition; "repeal is the one thing which will restore prosperity," he declared. Telling a Daughters of the American Revolution convention that he found it a pleasure to address Americans without hyphens and that he was proud that his initials, too, were D.A.R.,

[23] New York *Times*, August 21, 1931; Simeon Fess to C. S. Fess, October 27, 1931, Fess MSS; Josiah W. Bailey to George Rountree, December 11, 1931, Bailey MSS.
[24] William C. Murphy, Jr., "Senator Reed," *North American Review*, CCXXXI (May, 1931): 427; Hiram Bingham, "Is Wagner Proposal for Federal Employment Agencies Sound?" *Congressional Digest*, X (January, 1931): 12–16; Simeon Fess to C. S. Fess, October 27, 1931, Fess MSS; Baruch to Winston Churchill, July 1, Joe T. Robinson to Baruch, November 29, 1930, Baruch MSS.

the patriotic David A. Reed proposed an end to immigration for two years to solve the unemployment problem.[25]

The depression ineluctably lurked prominently in the background during the congressional campaign of 1930. Nobody knew for certain how many people were then unemployed in the United States. A haphazard count of the jobless revealed a number that exceeded three million as of late April. Yet, as Broadus Mitchell has pointed out, this figure did not include young people of working age who had never held jobs nor individuals reluctant to admit that they were unemployed.[26] Thus, the jobless toll probably was closer to five million and surpassed that by November's election. Even those individuals who had saved for these dismal times might easily be victimized by one of the 1,345 banks that failed in 1930, more than double the number of suspended banks in 1929.

Nonpresidential election years normally favor the minority party in Congress and 1930 promised to be no exception. Democrats appreciated the predicament in which the depression had placed the Republicans, and were almost grateful that the American public had not restored them to leadership in 1928. "Were the Democrats in power and conditions as they are, we could not get started on a race in this campaign," Robert Doughton declared.[27] Arthur Capper, a ranking Senate Republican, resignedly anticipated a reduced GOP vote because of independent defections. One Republican could not resist the ominous prognostication that "the Republican party is going to get the damnedest licking it has had for a long time. . . ."[28] The GOP looked in vain for indicators that the voters' revolt would not be as great as they feared. In 1928 Hoover had won North Carolina with the as-

[25] Reed Smoot, "Our Tariff and the Depression," *Current History*, XXXV (November, 1931): 173–81; Bingham, pp. 12–16; New York *Times*, November 24, 1931.
[26] Broadus Mitchell, *Depression Decade* (New York, 1947), pp. 91–92, 128.
[27] Doughton to J. F. Hurley, May 21, 1930, Doughton MSS.
[28] Capper to Charles McNary, October 8, 1930, McNary MSS; Henry P. Fletcher to William Allen White, October 29, 1930, White MSS.

sistance of Democratic Senator Furnifold Simmons; in June, 1930, the Democrats turned down Simmons' bid for renomination in the primary, a setback many interpreted as North Carolina's way of turning its back on Hoover. In September Maine performed according to tradition and a few hardy Republicans ignored the reduced majorities to proclaim that the nation would still go with the Down Easterners. It took a cheerless Columbia University social scientist to remind Republicans that the old saw, "As Maine goes, so goes the nation," did not apply to congressional elections.[29]

November 4, 1930, election day, Secretary of State Stimson set the administration mood down in his diary: "It is a dull, rainy day, and it is reported that it is raining hard up in New York State, so that Mr. Hoover's ill luck is following him, even with the weather again. This long drought is broken on the day when good weather might help him. At Cabinet Meeting the discussion was largely over the election, and was rather gloomy and depressed." Hoover admitted to Stimson that he no longer believed that the Republicans could retain the House of Representatives. The next day Stimson observed, "This was surely the day after the storm, and there was a general atmosphere of wreckage politically."[30]

Republican losses were abundant. Their Senate lead in the forthcoming 72nd Congress had been slashed to a plurality of one with a solitary Farmer-Laborite holding the potential of a deadlocked Senate. The vote of the vice-president suddenly assumed commanding proportions for the Senate GOP. Their control of the House was similarly questionable. Immediately following the election it appeared that the Republicans had emerged with a scant majority of a few representatives. Some races were still awaiting recounts and in these years prior to the 20th Amendment, it would be thirteen months before the new Congress would convene in regular session. It was not unlikely

[29] "Why North Carolina Drops Her 'Little Giant,'" *Literary Digest*, June 21, 1930, pp. 10–11; "Squabbling over Maine's Election," *ibid.*, September 20, 1930, pp. 7–8.
[30] Diary, November 4, 5, 1930, Stimson MSS.

that the Democrats would have responsibility for organizing the new House.

Nevertheless, the returns were not all disheartening to the GOP. With over nine million fewer people voting in 1930 than had balloted in 1928, the Republicans had won the popular vote with 54.1 per cent of the total cast for major party candidates for the House, a loss of 3.3 per cent from 1928. The GOP retained a majority percentage in all sections except the South although it suffered small losses everywhere over the previous two years. In a few states like Michigan, Massachusetts, and Pennsylvania, the Republicans actually widened their margin over the Democrats. But, although Mark Sullivan, newspaperman and member of the medicine-ball cabinet, asserted that the outcome was "not at all sensational" and "not abnormal" for congressional races,[31] not since 1922, in the midst of another economic slump, had the Republicans lost as heavily.

There were some very ominous portents for the GOP in the Midwest. Republican House candidates in Illinois lost five seats with 49.6 per cent of the vote as compared to 56.9 per cent in 1928. Democrat James Hamilton Lewis routed Mrs. Ruth Hanna McCormick by over 700,000 votes in their Senate race, whereas Republican Senator Hiram Johnson of California had expected the lady to win "very handily." Indiana Republicans were hit hard as their usually comfortable majority for House candidates was reduced to 47.2 per cent of the vote. Hoosier Republicans in the new House would be outnumbered by their Democratic counterparts 9 to 4, reversing their old 10-to-3 edge. GOP stalwarts from Indiana like Appropriations Committee Chairman Will Wood and Majority Whip Albert H. Vestal barely retained their House seats. Senator James E. Watson, up for re-election in 1932, worriedly summed up the feeling among Indiana Republicans when he acknowledged, "Well, we got a fine licking here."[32]

[31] American Institute of Public Opinion, pp. 16, 28, 143, 219; New York *Herald Tribune*, November 6, 7, 8, 1930.

[32] Johnson to Harold Ickes, April 19, 1930, Johnson MSS; diary, November 4, 1930, Stimson MSS.

Iowa Republicans polled better than 60 per cent of the House vote to retain all their places but this was nearly 10 per cent below the 1928 count. The Ohio plurality won by Republican House nominees fell 9.6 per cent, along with six seats; Speaker Nicholas Longworth barely squeezed through in his Cincinnati stronghold. Democrat Robert J. Bulkley upset his Republican opponent in the Ohio senatorial contest, winning 54.8 per cent of the vote. Indicative of GOP futility was the Nebraska organization's comic attempt to run a grocer from Broken Bow named George W. Norris against the namesake senator in reprisal for his 1928 apostasy. The real Norris triumphed and Charles Beard remarked, "Not since P. T. Barnum and Artemus Ward departed this life has the nation been so lacking in political talents."[33]

Two Senate races in Kansas provided unusual interest for Republicans. The venerable and often independent Arthur Capper retained his seat handily with 61.1 per cent of the vote while Henry Allen lost Vice-President Charles Curtis' old seat to a progressive Democrat. The Allen defeat achieved significance because he had sought to identify himself with Hoover during his brief stay in the Senate. Allen had voted closely along administration lines and had become a personal favorite of the president. "I am much depressed by the loss of Senator Allen," Hoover confided to Capper, and he quickly sought a State Department post which would keep Allen in Washington. Analyzing Allen's loss in Kansas, William Allen White said, "Labor and the colored people punished him for the Parker vote. The farmers . . . punished him for being a friend of the President. . . ."[34]

No election since 1922 so elated progressives as this one. Thirteen new senators were elected, eleven of them Democrats, most of whom were expected to be more friendly to progressive causes

[33] Charles A. Beard, "Conservatism Hits Bottom," *New Republic*, LVIII (August 19, 1931): 7–11.

[34] Hoover to Capper, November 8, 1930, Capper MSS; diary, November 10, 1930, Stimson MSS; White to Arthur M. Hyde, November 25, 1930, White MSS. Roy Wilkins has recalled that he campaigned against Allen in 1930 for the NAACP in "The Reminiscences of Roy Wilkins," Columbia Oral History Collection, Columbia University (hereafter cited as COHC), pp. 36–37.

than their predecessors. Whether wearing the Republican or Democratic label, it was a good year to be a progressive. William E. Borah of Idaho, George W. Norris of Nebraska, Thomas J. Walsh of Montana, and James C. Couzens of Michigan whipped challengers for their Senate seats; Cordell Hull of Tennessee, Marcus A. Coolidge of Massachusetts, George McGill of Kansas, Edward P. Costigan of Colorado, Lewis of Illinois, and Bulkley of Ohio were among the eleven new Democrats. "Wasn't it a grand election?" exulted the sage of Emporia, William Allen White; "how true the people are when they have a fair chance at a brave honest man."[35] The euphoric Felix Frankfurter hailed the 1930 results as signalling "a new creative era in politics."[36]

Although the Democrats had ended the GOP supremacy without establishing their own, greater defeats awaited the Republicans, as indicated by the startling inroads made by the Democrats in the Midwest, unless the GOP could check the course of events which had precipitated its decline. Midwestern Republicans blamed the depression for turning a troublesome congressional election into an upset. Moreover, there were some hints that Hoover's popularity had slipped and injured the Republicans. One Kansas Republican who managed to retain his House seat grumbled that falling farm prices and "the opposition to the President . . . caused my district to go Democratic. . . ."[37] Justice Stone, noting that his fellow Republicans were "pretty glum," blamed Hoover for a poor political job. Publicly, Republicans said nothing about responsibility for the debacle; privately, they condemned the president for inept leadership. "There is no question," commented Senator Capper, "President Hoover's stock at this time is very low."[38] The balloting appeared to have registered a warning to the Chief Executive and his party that they must demonstrate effective leadership in combating the depression or,

[35] White to Rodney Elwood, November 10, 1930, White MSS; White to Edward P. Costigan, November 5, 1930, Costigan MSS.
[36] Felix Frankfurter to Costigan, February 24, 1931, Costigan MSS.
[37] New York *World*, New York *Herald Tribune*, November 6, 1930; James G. Strong to White, November 5, 1930, White MSS.
[38] Capper to White, December 30, 1930, White MSS.

should the decline of the previous year not be ephemeral as they supposed, they could anticipate the complete loss of their fragmentary majorities and the White House in 1932. "It is going to be a very difficult time for the President these next two years," Stone prophesied.[39]

[39] Mason, p. 284.

WAGNER'S WAR
ON UNEMPLOYMENT

EVER SINCE he entered the Senate in 1927, Robert F. Wagner of New York had sought to focus congressional attention on the jobless before the depression made them commonplace. He had considered industrial problems as a legislator in Albany and Washington for two decades. On January 9, 1930, he introduced three bills constituting a limited program for dealing with unemployment, patiently reminding the Senate they were products of hearings by the Education and Labor Committee on cyclical and technical unemployment in 1928. Measures developed in the twenties were not expected to solve the problems of the thirties, but they constituted a beginning. In effect, they merely confronted hitherto ignored dilemmas.

The first of these bills, S. 3059, the employment stabilization bill, would create a federal board to plan public works projects to be executed, on approval by the president, when the jobless toll warranted government action. Even in such an emergency, not more than $150 million a year could be spent for temporary public works. In order to use and deploy the idle workers more properly, a second bill, S. 3060, would abolish the existing United States Employment Service in favor of a cooperative system of federal and state employment exchanges. But both of these governmental innovations would operate with as much ignorance as the present USES unless there was necessary information. Hence, S. 3061, Wagner's third measure, would direct the Secretary of Labor to gather pertinent statistics for estimating the number of employed persons every month. By discovering approximately how many were unemployed, operating informed and active agencies for securing employment, and having available a reserve of public works projects for creating jobs, Wagner hoped for an effective assault on unemployment.[1]

Amid the euphoria of Washington in the spring of 1930, Wagner needed to demonstrate conclusively that unemployment had reached proportions requiring government action. Holding a photograph of a New York City breadline, he argued at a subcommittee hearing of the Senate Commerce Committee that Congress neither knew how many needy men there were nor how to aid them. A parade of academic economists supported him, confessing ignorance of the true condition of the economy; social workers described the ultimate horrors of deprivation by idleness, and labor leaders demanded no wage cuts or worker lay-offs. With considerable sanguinity Wagner declared that enactment of his proposals intact would "practically eliminate what we call cyclical unemployment."[2]

Wagner represented the incipient political power of northern urbanism. In the opinion of one reporter, he was "the only real product of the American city in that rural and suburban body, the United States Senate. He is the only person in the Senate who has any conception of the social and industrial problems of the country." Both sentences are overstatements, but excusable because they must have seemed true in many instances. He had been brought to the United States from Germany as a boy and became as much a product of Tammany Hall as Al Smith. He had risen with Smith in the New York legislature, Smith going to the governorship, Wagner to the United States Senate. Wagner, a graduate of the City College of New York, had the education and law degree which Smith lacked, and he approached industrial problems with a greater understanding of their social manifesta-

---

[1] *Congressional Record*, 71st Cong., 2nd sess., p. 1287.
[2] U.S. Congress, Senate, *Unemployment in the United States*, Hearings before a Subcommittee on Commerce on S. 3059, S. 3060, and S. 3061, March 18, 21, April 1, 1930, 71st Cong., 2nd sess., p. 72; New York *Times*, March 19, 22, April 2, 1930.

tions. However, it is doubtful that his education figured as greatly in his social awareness as his compassion and German background.[3]

Wagner was committed to the welfare state principle. He once said, "I lived among the people of the tenements. Unless you have . . . , you cannot know the haunting sense of insecurity which hangs over the home of the worker." He freely quoted the British Fabian, Sidney Webb, on the insecurity of the American worker and added a warning of his own: "As society is organized today the destitution of any one threatens the security of all. In the last analysis there can be real security for none unless there be ample security for all." Wagner was a social reformer and not a socialist. He did not believe the entire economic system was wrong but, as he told an interviewer: ". . . I think we need greater precision and better organization in the existing system. The ingenuity which succeeded in multiplying the production of the requisites of life and comfort a thousand times is assuredly equal to the task of distributing the benefits of that production to all the people." Instead of abolishing capitalism outright, Wagner would eradicate unemployment in order to insure the government's "own stability and the continuity of the institutions under which it exists."[4] He would conserve the economic system by reform, confident that American society inherently was morally responsible. Certainly no other senator would be so identified with the aspirations of the worker in the thirties as Bob Wagner.

Wagner respected institutions and endeavored to utilize them to achieve his program. He believed in 1930 that unemployment insurance, social security for the aged, and disability compensation were imperative to improve the society. And to accomplish these objectives, he became an adroit conciliator in the Senate,

[3] The Gentleman at the Keyhole, "Big-Town Bob," *Colliers*, March 21, 1931, p. 38; Owen P. White, "When the Public Needs a Friend," *ibid.*, June 2, 1934, p. 18; Irving Bernstein, *The Lean Years* (Boston, 1960), pp. 263–67.

[4] "Wagner: 'Thorough' Senator Has Known Fear of Insecurity," *News-Week*, February 2, 1935, p. 21; Robert F. Wagner, "The Problem of 25,000,000," *New Outlook*, CLXI (October, 1932): 35–37; S. J. Woolf, "A Senator Asks Security for Workers," *New York Times Magazine*, January 11, 1931, p. 6; *Congressional Record*, 71st Cong., 2nd sess., p. 7797.

always mindful that attaining two steps may require postponing the second to secure the first. As a later commentator on senatorial behavior described a contemporary, he "unerringly set his purposes to be in harmony with the forms and spirit of the place"; indeed, Wagner recognized that a senator, in William S. White's words, "*cannot* forever refuse there to make any compromise at all and remain a good, or effective, member. The art of high negotiation is an absolutely necessary part of his Senatorial equipment."[5] Wagner became an expert promoter of legislation by "going along" with the Senate's ways.

The Wagner proposals of 1930 were intended to be education devices, cautious advances designed so as not to antagonize sympathetic conservatives. For example, the public works projects would go into operation only at the president's discretion; an unrealistically low appropriation would restrict them from accomplishing much. Funds for employment agencies would be given to states which were not able or willing to operate them. The labor statistics bill seemed most feasible, partly because of the embarrassment that in a census year nobody knew for certain how many were jobless. Wagner's colleagues seemed to ignore the bills' importance. The Senate Commerce Committee held superficial inquiries, not penetrating probes, on the jobless problem. As the committee's chairman, Hiram Johnson, admitted: "It has not been our purpose in great detail to go into the unemployment question, but only incidentally." Others wished the Senate would be bolder; testifying for a stronger federal relief scheme, Benjamin C. Marsh and John Dewey assailed the Wagner bills as "futile."[6] Thus, Wagner had to contend with advocates of planning who were impatient for action and conservatives determined to resist it.

On April 3 the committee reported the statistics and stabilization bills to the Senate while withholding the employment service

[5] William S. White, *Citadel: The Story of the U.S. Senate* (New York, 1956), p. 115.
[6] Hiram Johnson to E. P. Clarke, March 27, 1930, Johnson MSS; New York *Times*, March 27, April 7, 1930.

bill pending a legal brief to be submitted by the National Association of Manufacturers. Written by the NAM's general counsel, James A. Emery, the brief hailed the good intentions of the Wagner bills but branded the employment agency plan unconstitutional. The latter was "an invalid exercise of the power of appropriation to control the police policy of the individual States," warned the NAM; the federal government would coerce the states to engage in services they wished to avoid, such as establishing employment agencies with federal funds. The NAM raised the flag of states' rights: "No scheme is better calculated to establish a precedent to enlarge Federal power at the expense of local authority," it admonished; "no plan is more certain to hasten the vanishing rights of the States."[7] The NAM brief did not prevent S. 3060 from reaching the Senate floor, but it did create an argument for resistance.

While S. 3060 was delayed, the Senate debated its companion bills on April 28. Wagner led the drive for passage, declaring, "The ideas embodied in the proposed legislation have met very little articulate opposition. The obstacles in the way of its more rapid adoption have been rather the inertia of an old-time attitude now no longer justified—the attitude . . . that unemployment was a personal affair brought about by individual incompetence or indolence, resulting in a problem which it was for the individual working man to solve in his own way." Unemployment was not merely a personal concern but a social problem. Wagner stressed that the scope and the impact of unemployment necessitated urgent federal action in order to forestall unrest and maintain the society's equilibrium. He directed his appeal to moderates, emphasizing the conserving virtues of his bills; instead of being socialistic, they were preventives of socialism. The Senate agreed with him. Arthur Vandenberg, a Republican close to the White House, spoke favorably for the bills and the Senate passed S. 3059 and S. 3061 without dissent.[8]

[7] Senate, *Unemployment in the United States*, p. 108; New York *Times*, April 4, 10, 1930.
[8] *Congressional Record*, 71st Cong., 1st sess., p. 7797.

But the employment exchanges bill had been singled out for disapproval by Old Guard Republicans who claimed that aid to the states in setting up the exchanges would violate states' rights. The Senate debate over S. 3060 was vigorous. Because twenty-six states lacked any employment service, Hiram Bingham of Connecticut called it a "bribe" to those states which, he presumed, did not want one. Bingham used the NAM brief to argue that the bill would rob the states of their responsibilities and self-reliance; states already having an employment service would be forced to participate in the federal program or face federal competition. Virginia Democrat Carter Glass protested that the employment exchanges would require substantial appropriations and additional taxation; in effect, it would extract money from the states and then "dole" it back to them. Nevertheless, the Senate passed the bill, 34 to 27, the bulk of the support coming from Wagner's fellow Democrats and progressive Republicans.[9]

The three bills now underwent House scrutiny. Only the labor statistics bill, which would provide figures published monthly on employment, wages paid, and hours worked, received uncontested approval. On July 1 the House passed it with but one negative voice, a Wisconsin man who called the labor statistics bureau an excuse for "red tape and bureaucracy."[10] Six days later the president signed S. 3061 into law.

The House gave the employment stabilization bill a mixed reception. Unaccountably it came under the jurisdiction of the House Judiciary Committee chaired by Philadelphia Republican George S. Graham, a 79-year-old corporation lawyer; the statistics bill had been considered by the Labor Committee. The hearings did not turn up any new opponents of the measure. Hundreds of leading clergymen, economists, sociologists, social workers, statisticians, personnel administrators, and others connected

---

[9] Bernstein, p. 269; *Congressional Record*, 71st Cong., 2nd sess., pp. 8742, 8745, 7806–7, 8749. The party division was twenty-one Democrats, twelve Republicans, and one Farmer-Laborite for and three Democrats and twenty-four Republicans against S. 3060.
[10] New York *Times*, July 2, 1930.

professionally with unemployment petitioned the committee to adopt the Wagner bill in its author's form.[11]

Of the three bills, Wagner deemed this one the most important because it committed the federal government to a prominent role in regulating the nation's economy. Section 10 declared that the measure's purpose was "to arrange the construction of public works, so far as practicable, in such a manner as will assist in the stabilization of industry and employment through the proper timing of such construction, and that to further this object there shall be advance planning of public works."[12] This landmark measure assumed that the federal government could influence the business cycle by accelerating its building programs at opportune moments.

The Republicans were set against the bill. Under Graham's leadership, the Judiciary Committee extracted major provisions of the bill, including Section 10. The committee report called it "unnecessary" although Senator Wagner valued it as the heart of the bill. Emanuel Celler and Fiorello La Guardia, New Yorkers of opposing parties, dissented from the report, La Guardia insisting that it left the government unprepared for future emergencies without the concept of advance planning; the bill without Section 10 was like the American Revolution without the Declaration of Independence. Others in the House New York City delegation strongly defended Wagner's bill. Thomas R. Cullen denounced the committee's version as a "skillful job of surgery" which left "only a mere gesture" of the author's intent. It was "a skeleton bill" and "utterly ridiculous," John J. Boylan declared. Wagner himself, arguing that the bill was consistent with Hoover's oft-stated public works philosophy, accused the president of opposing it "for petty political reasons."[13] Hoping to reinstate Section 10 in a House-Senate conference, Wagner's House

[11] *Ibid.*, June 9, 1930.
[12] Quoted in Bernstein, p. 271.
[13] *Congressional Record*, 71st Cong., 2nd sess., pp. 12239-41, 12245; New York *Times*, June 20, July 2, 1930. For more discussion on public works theories in the twenties, see Chapter 6.

supporters reluctantly voted to approve the amended version; however, the conference deadlocked and the employment stabilization bill went over to the next session of Congress.

The House Republicans were determined to pigeonhole the employment exchanges bill as well. Again Graham led the opposition, invoking the NAM's arguments that the exchanges unconstitutionally infringed on states' rights. Professor Paul Douglas reported that the NAM feared that the employment services would foster unionism. The private employment agencies entered the debate to complain of unfair government competition with free enterprise. As Graham maneuvered to kill the measure, its backers thwarted him by meeting certain objections with conciliation. But Graham's tactics delayed the bill and it did not leave the Judiciary Committee until the end of June, too late for the House to debate S. 3060 in that session.[14]

When Congress adjourned in July, Wagner's most significant accomplishment had been pedagogical. The bill for employment statistics had become law but with weak financial support; Arthur Woods, chairman of the President's Emergency Committee for Employment, pleaded with Hoover for "urgently needed" funds.[15] The public works bill had passed both houses in different versions that awaited harmonizing, and the agency bill faced a very uncertain future in the lame-duck session commencing in December. Nevertheless, Congress had never been so aware of unemployment as it was in July, 1930. Even the sole House opponent of the statistics bill, William H. Stafford of Milwaukee, acknowledged that "there is no problem of greater moment before the American people than that of unemployment."[16] Although some lawmakers still characterized all jobless individuals as lazy, others confronted the tragic irony which beset the nation. As James M. Mead of Buffalo put it,

[14] *Congressional Record*, 71st Cong., 2nd sess., p. 12243; New York *Times*, June 29, 1930; Bernstein, pp. 276–77.
[15] Arthur Woods to Herbert Hoover, November 26, 1930, Container 1-E/273, Hoover MSS; also see entry for December 2, 1930, Colonel Arthur Woods Diary, Woods MSS.
[16] *Congressional Record*, 71st Cong., 2nd sess., pp. 12257–62, 12246, 12249.

What a strange situation confronts us today. Will not our grandchildren regard it as quite incomprehensible that in 1930 millions of Americans went hungry because they had produced too much food; that millions of men, women and children were cold because they produced too much clothing, that they suffered from the chilly blasts of winter because they produced too much coal? I am not speaking in parables. This is the literal truth. To-day we are suffering want in the midst of unprecedented plenty. Our workers are without wages because they have learned to work too well. . . . We cannot regard unemployment as inevitable and poverty as incurable, especially in a land where, as President Hoover recently stated, the warehouses are bursting with a surplus of supplies, and still people are denied them.[17]

This, then, was what the Wagner bills had helped accomplish: a willingness to investigate the causes of unemployment, its extent, and how to remedy the problem. Wagner and deteriorating economic conditions compelled more congressmen to consider unemployment as a crisis which required their attention rather than their patience. Before Congress adjourned it unanimously adopted a concurrent resolution expressing the hope that federal public works in progress would be fully expedited "to the end that the unemployment prevailing throughout the country may be relieved."[18] Certainly nobody could wish otherwise.

During the summer Hoover requested the various executive departments to furnish him with a list of building projects which could be accelerated with available appropriations. On October 17 he announced the formation of an Emergency Committee for Employment to work with state governors and voluntary organizations in coordinating federal public works projects with state needs. He appointed as its chairman Colonel Arthur Woods, who had organized unemployment relief in 1921. Hoover presented no specific program to deal with unemployment but spoke only of cooperating with industry and reviewing government con-

[17] *Ibid.*, p. 12262.
[18] New York *Times*, July 4, 1930.

struction plans while investigating the situation. He applauded state and local efforts to aid "those of our people who are in honest difficulties." After the 1930 election, the White House declared that Congress would be asked to increase the appropriations for public works projects "as would normally have taken place a year or two hence." Conspicuously absent from the president's two messages was a call for new legislation to deal with unemployment, as sought by Wagner. Hoover still defined relief as the immediate concern of state and local governments in cooperation with business and the administration; in such a scheme he excluded Congress from any dynamic role.[19]

Fresh from renewed contact with their constituents, many congressmen returned in December anxious to take an active part in restoring prosperity. They demonstrated their concern with the year-old depression by filling the hoppers with a wide assortment of remedial proposals. There were bills for public works, distribution of wheat to relief organizations, immigration restriction, an embargo on all imports from the Soviet Union, surplus oats for horses (but no bread for children), and distribution of army and navy surplus to the needy. Their anxiety was heightened by photographs of breadlines and soup kitchens which appeared in newspapers with increasing frequency. Evidence that the depression was worsening accumulated rapidly. Colonel Woods reported that there were at least a million unemployed in the automobile and construction industries alone and that state and local governments were creating only temporary jobs. A high-ranking Republican senator, Charles L. McNary of Oregon, argued for emergency relief funds to alleviate the suffering: "We have plenty of precedents in relief extended so generously to foreign nations and to people in various States who have suffered from droughts and unreasonable conditions." Senator Arthur Capper of Kansas, another GOP farm belt leader, wrote that

[19] Hoover to Andrew Mellon, July 7, 1931, Container 1-I/80, Hoover MSS; William Starr Myers (ed.), *The State Papers and Other Public Writings of Herbert Hoover* (Garden City, N.Y., 1934), I: 401–2, 411; William Starr Myers and Walter H. Newton, *The Hoover Administration: A Documented Narrative* (New York, 1936), pp. 40, 44, 52–54.

32

"the situation calls for action, not philosophizing" and unemployment would have to be first on Congress' agenda. "This depression with its attendant unemployment has reached a state where the safety of the republic is threatened," Fiorello La Guardia declaimed in a manner calculated to send shivers down conservative spines.[20]

However, the potpourri of panaceas only demonstrated that Congress sorely lacked leadership. Obviously many congressmen believed that President Hoover's acceleration of public works was inadequate but they had no program to supplement his. Progressive Republicans and a few Democrats had just begun to exchange their disparate ideas in an effort to formulate a sound approach to the problem. Senator Bronson Cutting feared that the lame-duck Congress would adjourn in March after three months of inaction. "The great trouble here," Hiram Johnson declared, "is that there is utter confusion as to remedial legislation, and the little that can be done will, I presume, be wholly ephemeral, and of small consequence."[21]

Federal relief advocates found that conservatives in both parties preferred an inert Congress. Seven national Democratic leaders offered the Hoover administration a pledge of cooperation following their party's gains, but congressional Democrats rebelled against giving carte blanche approval to White House policies.[22] Within two weeks after reconvening, Congress passed the appropriations legislation for the employment statistics bill which the Republicans had delayed the previous June. Senator Robert M. La Follette, Jr., of Wisconsin pronounced the president's program of guided voluntarism a failure; he declared, "The time has come for Congress to assert its leadership."[23] As 1931

[20] New York *Times*, December 4, November 11, 12, 1930; *Capper's Weekly*, November 8, December 27, 1930, in scrapbooks, Capper MSS.

[21] Bronson M. Cutting to mother, November 20, 1930, Cutting MSS; Johnson to C. K. McClatchy, December 7, 1930, Johnson MSS.

[22] The seven were Democratic presidential nominees James M. Cox, John W. Davis, and Alfred E. Smith, John J. Raskob and Jouett Shouse of the Democratic National Committee, and the ranking congressional Democrats, Senator Joseph T. Robinson and Representative John Nance Garner.

[23] New York *Times*, January 12, 23, 1931; *Congressional Record*, 71st Cong., 3rd sess., pp. 1662–68.

dawned, congressional activists seized the initiative and forwarded the Wagner program to enactment.

Hoover nonetheless continued to limit the role of Congress in the crisis to its appropriation function. The president served notice in his State of the Union message that he would ask Congress for an additional allotment of $100 to $150 million, suggesting but not specifying that the money would go for public works. Near the conclusion of the address Hoover began to project himself to a time when the depression would be past and he could "consider a number of other questions as to what action may be taken by the Government to remove possible governmental influences which make for instability and to better organize mitigation of the effect of the depression. It is as yet too soon to constructively formulate such measures."[24] The president's nebulous prose implied that long-range planning to prevent unemployment belonged to a period of stability and not to the immediate depression, suggesting that the administration would propose nothing new in behalf of recovery in 1931.

The relief advocates responded angrily. Senator Wagner called the president's statement "astounding." Another Democrat, Senator David I. Walsh, denounced Hoover's proposals as niggardly. "There are worse misfortunes than heavy taxes," the Massachusetts man said. "One is unrest, discontent and the spread of bolshevism. One infinitely worse misfortune is the failure of the government to show an interest in removing the spectre of starvation and misery and idleness and unrest which looms on our horizon. . . . It is hypocritical to talk about doing anything for the relief of unemployment in this country unless we understand and appreciate that such relief will necessitate increased expenses to the government and increased income taxes upon the rich."[25]

The hail of relief proposals and the Democratic barbs stung Hoover and on December 10, 1930, he lashed out. Ever attuned to cost figures, he predicted that if every panacea became law, they would cost the government four and a half billion dollars.

[24] Myers, I: 421.
[25] New York *Times*, December 9, 1930.

"Prosperity cannot be restored by raids upon the public treasury," Hoover proclaimed. He praised the party leaders for their cooperation, but labelled some of the suggested measures "ill considered" and their proponents "enthusiasts"; "some represent the desire of individuals to show that they are more generous than even the leaders of their own parties. They are playing politics at the expense of human misery." The last sentence enraged Democrats. For two days Democratic senators berated the president for his indifference to misery while only a couple of Republicans rose to his defense. Senator Wagner wondered aloud what had become of the Hoover who once advocated advance planning of public works to relieve unemployment.[26]

While a few senators sought a more effective relief program, Congress turned back to the Wagner employment bills outstanding from the previous session. In late November Colonel Woods had recommended administration approval, with amendments, of both bills. This influential support might have been decisive in rendering the employment stabilization bill to a condition satisfactory to its author and ramming it through the Senate and House over scant opposition. On February 10, 1931, President Hoover signed it into law and claimed substantial credit for the administration and the Republicans: "Senator Wagner and Representative Graham have worked out an admirable measure in which they adopted the constructive suggestions of the various government departments." Under the law, the president and the Federal Employment Stabilization Board would attempt to regulate the ebb and flow of jobs by promoting construction.[27]

Despite the fact that President Hoover ignored it then and subsequently, the Federal Employment Stabilization Act of 1931 may have been the most noteworthy law passed during his administration. Never before had the United States government committed itself to control the business cycle. Fifteen years later,

[26] *Ibid.*, December 10, 11, 12, 14, 1930; Myers, I: 459–60.
[27] Woods to Hoover, November 26, 1930, Container 1–E/273, Hoover MSS; "Congress Adopts Public Works Planning," *American Labor Legislative Review*, XXI (March, 1931): 95–96; New York *Times*, February 11, 1931; Bernstein, pp. 272–73.

the Senate, again led by Wagner of New York, passed a bill which irrevocably obligated Washington to use all its powers to prevent an economic collapse similar to that of the thirties. As Stephen Kemp Bailey has noted, S. 3059 "was probably the most significant legislative precedent underlying the Full Employment Bill of 1945."[28] In effect, the Employment Act of 1946 pledged the government to seek the highest possible level of employment, a vow which Hoover in 1930 hoped to extract voluntarily from industry. Wagner reminded the Senate several times that Hoover had advocated advance planning to forestall unemployment in the twenties. Hoover viewed such action as a preventive to be employed in good times; on the other hand, Wagner sought to take advantage of economic adversity to set a precedent for government intervention in the business cycle. After opposing this principle, Hoover and the GOP accepted Wagner's bill knowing that it was inoperable without executive action.

With two-thirds of Wagner's program acted upon, there remained only the employment service bill, which had been detained by the formidable opposition of the National Association of Manufacturers. While the bill awaited House action, Colonel Woods recommended that Hoover endorse the Wagner bill, with a few minor alterations, in his State of the Union address. Even within the cabinet there was counsel for the Wagner bill. Back in March, 1930, Secretary of Labor James J. Davis had endorsed S. 3060. Since then "Puddler Jim" Davis had been elected to the Senate and William N. Doak had replaced him in December. Doak, in his former capacities as legislative representative for the Brotherhood of Railroad Trainmen and a vice-president of the American Association for Labor Legislation, already had supported the employment service bill.[29]

But the White House did not want it. With the realization that the NAM arguments alone were not enough to defeat the bill,

---

[28] Stephen Kemp Bailey, *Congress Makes a Law* (New York, 1964), p. 80.
[29] Woods to Hoover, November 26, 1930, Container 1–E/273, Hoover MSS; Bernstein, pp. 272–78; New York *Times*, March 5, 1930; *Congressional Record,* 71st Cong., 3rd sess., p. 5755.

Hoover "built a fire against it," as his press secretary later described the maneuver. Doak drafted a new bill and sent it to the House Judiciary Committee, although the committee already had reported the Wagner bill. The Doak bill did little to change the existing arrangement under the United States Employment Service except to make the head of the agency an Assistant Secretary of Labor at a salary of $9,000 annually. When Doak asked Wagner to back the new bill, the senator tartly replied: "Very frankly I am convinced that your proposal does not change my bill, but destroys it. I cannot find, even after the closest scrutiny, anything in the new proposal which materially changes the existing unsatisfactory situation. That alone is sufficient evidence that it is not a desirable piece of legislation. . . ." Wagner insisted that his bill strengthened local responsibility in employment with federal cooperation whereas the Doak bill weakened local jurisdiction by putting the burden of placement on Washington. "The new proposal," Wagner charged, "mentions the word cooperation, but it provides neither the means nor the incentives to its attainment."[30] Implicit in his answer was the accusation that the administration had offered its bill only in order to sidetrack his own.

The White House persevered in its ambition to derail the Wagner bill. The House Judiciary Committee, under Graham's direction, voted 13 to 6 to substitute the Doak bill for the measure it had already reported out. Fiorello La Guardia fought hard on the House floor to restore the Wagner bill's precedence, reminding the body that organized labor backed the original version. He quoted a 1921 statement by Hoover that agreed in principle with Wagner's bill and conflicted with Doak's. Calling the new bill "the Grundy substitute" and Doak its "alleged father," La Guardia accused the NAM of masterminding the substitute in order to keep wages down. Graham responded that Wagner's uncompromising attitude had forced the substitute proposal; furthermore, the Wagner aid to the states constituted a "dole."

---

[30] Theodore G. Joslin, *Hoover Off the Record* (Garden City, N.Y., 1935), p. 75; Bernstein, pp. 278–79; Robert F. Wagner to W. N. Doak, February 16, 1931, Wagner MSS.

But the House rejected the Doak bill, 182 to 84, and rapidly approved the Wagner measure. The next move had to come from the White House.[31]

"Don't blame me," Doak once told John B. Andrews, "if the bill is vetoed."[32] All indications pointed to a presidential rejection of S. 3060, but its proponents mounted pressure to head it off. One hundred and twenty-eight economists, industrialists, labor leaders, social workers, and personnel administrators petitioned Hoover to approve the bill; they said it would be a "tragedy" if the White House vetoed it. Signers included Paul Douglas, Frances Perkins, Broadus Mitchell, Irving Fisher, H. V. Kaltenborn, and Sidney Hillman.[33] Many academicians and industrialists wrote pleading letters for the bill and the deluge of letters and telegrams upon the White House bolstered Wagner's hope that Hoover would bow to the clamor. Republican Congressman William A. Pittenger reminded the White House that three Minnesota cities were vitally interested in the bill. On March 7 Wagner wired the president: "I appeal to you with all the earnestness at my command to give it your approval . . . and thus bring a gleam of hope to the millions of our citizens who are in need of encouragement."[34] Later that day the White House announced the pocket veto of S. 3060.

In his veto message, Hoover explained that he had rejected the Wagner employment agency bill in order to "prevent a serious blow to labor." Although favoring an extension of such services, he feared that it "abolishes the whole of the present well-developed Federal Employment Service" to "substitute for it 48 practically independent agencies" supported by the federal gov-

[31] New York *Times*, February 20, 21, 22, 24, 25, 1931; *Congressional Record*, 71st Cong., 3rd sess., pp. 5240–41, 5752–76.

[32] Quoted in Bernstein, p. 278.

[33] Some others were Paul U. Kellogg, Lillian Wald, Father John A. Ryan, F. W. Taussig, Bruce Bliven, Mary Dewson, Josephine Goldmark, Corliss Lamont, Ordway Tead, and Rabbi Stephen S. Wise. New York *Times*, February 16, 1931.

[34] William A. Pittenger to Walter H. Newton, March 5, 1931, Container 1–E/276, Hoover mss; Wagner to Dr. Harold G. Moulton, March 4, to Hoover, March 7, 1931, Wagner mss.

ernment. Besides, it would not be effective for a long time to come: "It is not only changing horses while crossing a stream but the other horse would not arrive for many months." For the present, Hoover said, "there is . . . ample time to consider the whole of the questions involved." He appended to his veto message a letter from Attorney General William D. Mitchell which elaborated upon Hoover's arguments without posing any legal questions. Characteristically, Hoover sought to fortify his case with expert opinions; by employing the Justice Department's testimony in support of his veto, the president cast doubt upon the constitutionality of the bill.[35]

Reactions to Hoover's statement varied but many people doubted its candor. Political scientist Arthur W. Macmahon wrote: "It is questionable whether there could be found a more disingenuous document among recent state documents." Economists Sumner Slichter and D. D. Lescohier labelled it "dishonest." New York social workers like Mary Van Kleeck of the Russell Sage Foundation and State Industrial Commissioner Frances Perkins were enraged by what they considered to be a message filled with non sequiturs.[36]

Naturally Wagner also denounced the veto. He categorically denied that the existing Federal Employment Service was effective, that labor preferred the Doak bill to his own, or that there would be a suspension in operation during the transition from the present set-up to the new one. "The theme of Mr. Hoover's veto," Wagner observed, "is to be found in his words 'there is therefore

[35] Myers, I: 530–32. In his *Memoirs: The Great Depression, 1929–1941* (New York, 1952), p. 47, Hoover claimed that the veto withheld power from the "political machines, such as Tammany in New York, or the Hague gang of Jersey City." The bill, however, applied only to state governments and New Jersey's statehouse was in Republican hands. Also, Hoover's account of events distorts the sequence so as to make Wagner's bill appear in response to Hoover's expansion of the Federal Employment Service (which he later reorganized) and the proposed Doak bill.
[36] Arthur W. Macmahon, "Third Session of the Seventy-first Congress," *American Political Science Review*, XXV (November, 1931): 946; Bernstein, p. 282. Doak and Slichter exchanged accusations a month after the veto. See Slichter to Hoover, April 6, and Doak to Slichter, April 10, 1931, Container 1–E/276, Hoover MSS.

ample time' to reconsider the question. These words are becoming characteristic of the administration's policy of persistent postponement and procrastination." Hoover, Wagner charged, "has failed every man who is out pounding pavements in search of work." From unexpected quarters came a belated cheer for Wagner. "Effective" was how the Republican New York *Herald Tribune* described Wagner's answer to Hoover's veto; the bill had "met an obviously pressing demand and in lieu of a bitter message deserved his signature."[37]

Why did Hoover veto the Wagner bill? Irving Bernstein closely examined the president's reasoning and concludes, "Beyond Hoover's assertion that he had given the matter 'earnest study,' there is nothing true in the message." Instead, Bernstein suggests that "the motive most consistent with Hoover's character and outlook that inspired him to reject S. 3060 was the desire to avoid an increase in federal expenditures." If Bernstein is correct, why did Hoover bring in so many extraneous arguments? Why did Hoover ignore the pleas of his employment committee chairman, Woods, who would soon resign? The increased expenditures argument certainly would apply to other Hoover vetoes during February and early March, but Hoover himself did not give it much emphasis in the Wagner bill veto. His correspondence indicates concern over "the intrusion of the federal government into the operation of local unemployment offices," but the Wagner bill would have strengthened local autonomy. There was something enigmatic in the veto as there was in his personality. "He is a queer bird," William Allen White ruefully noted; "I don't make him out."[38]

Hoover seemed afraid to lose the political initiative to Congress. In the lame-duck session, he vetoed twelve bills, including a veterans' bonus and Norris' Muscle Shoals development bill, the former veto being overridden. Partisan New York Democrats her-

---

[37] New York *Times*, New York *Herald Tribune*, March 9, 1931.
[38] Bernstein, pp. 282–84; Julius Klein to Hoover, March 5, 1931, Container 1–E/273, Hoover MSS; William Allen White to Paul U. Kellogg, March 10, 1931, White MSS.

alded Wagner's assertiveness as embarrassing to the do-nothing president. "Hoover is afraid of Wagner," Representative Emanuel Celler charged; "Wagner has achieved too much distinction." Washington gossip alleged that White House confidants knew Hoover had vetoed the Wagner bill because of "his personal prejudice against Wagner."[39] This, perhaps, overdramatized Wagner's importance; however, it did mark the beginning of a "credit war" between the administration and the Democrats. It began when Hoover, failing to get credit via the Doak substitute, vetoed Wagner's employment service bill. Stung by election setbacks, the flood of congressional relief proposals, and several legislative defeats which suggested an absence of effective leadership, Hoover had decided to show that opposition to congressional enthusiasts was courageous and correct.[40] This thinking would influence the remainder of his presidency.

Hoover knew that he had not seen the last of Wagner's unemployment bills. In December, 1930, the New Yorker had introduced a bill for unemployment insurance. Fiorello La Guardia, too, had filed a plan for unemployment insurance, but Wagner's took precedence. Wagner defined the purpose of his plan simply: "To supply income to the wage earner during the period of unemployment." He declared this an inevitable step if purchasing power was to be expanded. He proposed that, pending further study, Congress create a temporary system of insurance in which expenses would be shared by the federal government and the states, the latter contributing double the amount of the former.[41]

Opposition to unemployment insurance had been anticipated by its congressional boosters. For several months John Andrews of the American Association for Labor Legislation had urged Wagner to include it in his original program, but Wagner hesitated, fearing its inclusion would increase accusations of imminent

---

[39] New York *Times*, March 9, 1931; [Robert S. Allen and Drew Pearson], *More Washington Merry-Go-Round* (New York, 1932), p. 40.

[40] This interpretation is developed in Chapter 3.

[41] New York *Times*, December 7, 17, 28, 1930, January 10, 1931. For a history of this welfare movement, see Daniel Nelson, *Unemployment Insurance: The American Experience, 1915–1935* (Madison, Wis., 1969).

socialism, thereby defeating the other three bills with it. Wagner believed it "inadvisable," in May, 1930, "to frighten away possible support by the introduction of other legislation which they are not ready to follow." He changed his mind after the election and hit back at NAM charges that his plan would constitute a dole.

Ironically, the American Federation of Labor sided with the NAM against federal unemployment insurance, although their reasons shared nothing in common. The A.F. of L. opposition was traditional; in 1930, for the eighth time in the last quarter century, the organization's resolutions committee had rejected the concept of government unemployment insurance in favor of voluntary insurance. The federation's Abraham, Samuel Gompers, had declared in 1918: "No one will bring insurance against unemployment of an effective character but the working people themselves." Federal insurance, said Gompers, would make labor "subject to the regulation, the discipline, and the decision of government." Gompers' successor, William Green, informed Wagner that the A.F. of L. had not changed. Green conceded that Wagner's scheme "on the surface appears to be practical and workable" for labor, but it would ultimately "rob it of economic freedom."[42]

With so little enthusiasm for it, Wagner's jobless insurance bill never got out of committee in 1931. However, the Senate on February 28 created a special committee to study existing unemployment insurance plans. It was anticipated that Wagner, as sponsor of the resolution, would head the investigatory group. But two Republican regulars, Felix Hebert of Rhode Island and Otis F. Glenn of Illinois, were chosen to share the assignment with Wagner, and Vice-President Curtis appointed Hebert to chair the committee. Wagner and his friends were upset because the job of investigating government unemployment insurance plans had been given to detractors (Hebert was on the board of an insurance corporation). They accused the White House of rig-

[42] Bernstein, p. 490; *New York Times Magazine*, January 11, 1931, p. 6; *New York Times*, October 14, 1930; William Green to Wagner, January 19, 1931, Wagner MSS.

ging Hebert's selection as chairman; nobody contradicted them (Curtis often attended cabinet meetings). That spring Hoover told Secretary Stimson that unemployment insurance would be an "overshadowing issue" in the next Congress and outlined a program he was considering; not too surprisingly, it relied on industry to assume leadership.[43]

The Wagner bills had developed a genuine dialogue on the problem of relief. Wagner had asserted that it was a federal matter which required Washington's leadership and financing. Only new legislation could deal effectively with the unemployment situation. This directly contradicted Hoover's faith in local, state, and voluntary agencies providing relief under the coordination of executive committees. He would brook no congressional interference with his cooperative program. Not only would he thwart relief bills pushed by federal activists like Wagner, he also would see to it that Congress received little encouragement to debate unemployment. The easiest way to accomplish that was to keep it out of session until the Constitution required it to meet.

The 71st Congress ended with bitterness, and most commentators blamed it for the political turmoil in Washington. Calvin Coolidge believed that Hoover "ought to be most grateful" for the ineptitude of the Senate Democratic leadership. The Philadelphia *Public Ledger*, noting a "war" between Congress and the president, condemned the "continuously contentious Congress." Wagner, La Follette, and their fellow activists appraised it as a Congress that did too little; conservatives wished it gone because it endeavored to do too much. The Louisville *Courier-Journal* summed it up for the latter: "Congress has provided farm relief, unemployment relief, drought relief, veterans' relief and its adjournment will provide general relief."[44]

But the third session of the 71st Congress had shown a greater

[43] [Robert S. Allen and Drew Pearson], *Washington Merry-Go-Round* (New York, 1931), p. 69; Bernstein, pp. 502–3; New York *Times*, March 9, 1931; diary, April 10, 1931, Stimson MSS. Also see Colonel Arthur Woods Diary, April 10, 1931, Woods MSS.
[44] Calvin Coolidge to Edward Tracy Clark, January 21, 1931, Clark MSS; quoted in Washington *Post*, March 5, 6, 1931.

awareness and willingness to confront the issue of unemployment than had been exhibited heretofore in the Capitol. "Those who hope for a permanency in our institutions can and must face the solution of the unemployment problem," Representative Pittenger had declared in behalf of Wagner's employment service bill; "unless it is solved, the destruction of society and government will become inevitable." In discussing the confrontation of the unemployment crisis by the lame-duck Congress, Arthur W. Macmahon observed: "No one can say that Congressional debate during the session was lacking in concrete realization of problems."[45] Yet, the farrago of remedies required leadership and coordination, which is what Wagner had attempted to give Congress with his three bills. Wagner's program, however modest, had encouraged the recognition that this storm needed more than weathering it out.

Congress adjourned with an artificial festivity that belied the times. The Marine Band accompanied the Interstate Commerce Commission chorus in the House chamber while several congressmen contributed musical talents that "would have done credit to a first-class vaudeville circuit." But Herbert Hoover hit the true note when he told Arthur Vandenberg, "When you come back we will need all the resolution and courage we can summon for the next session."[46] Demanding days lay ahead.

[45] *Congressional Record*, 71st Cong., 3rd sess., p. 4726; Macmahon, pp. 937–38.
[46] New York *Herald Tribune*, March 5, 1931; Hoover to Arthur H. Vandenberg, March 7, 1931, Scrapbook 3, Vandenberg mss.

☆ ☆ ☆ ☆ ☆

3

STRATEGY AND
STRATEGISTS OF 1931

FEW PRESIDENTS have come to the White House with such an imposing reputation for executive talent as Herbert Hoover. "As an administrator and executive," Ogden Mills wrote more than a year before Hoover's inauguration, "he has few equals"; he would be a great president "if intellectual vigor, knowledge, experience, judgment and training are controlling factors."[1] Apparently these qualities alone do not make great leaders. Significantly, Mills did not credit Hoover with political aptitude or charismatic qualities. Hoover had been esteemed in the twenties because he rose above the crass politics of the Versailles Treaty, Teapot Dome, and tariff-writing. He rationalized the national interest and seemed to restore politics to the Rooseveltian principles of character and integrity in public life.

Hoover belonged to the GOP in name only and this never ceased to rankle many congressional Republicans. He was almost a party unto himself, a fourth faction added to the minimum of three which already existed in Congress. First came the Old Guard, several of whom had had their political baptism in the days of Nelson Aldrich, "Uncle Joe" Cannon, and Boies Penrose, none of whom had foresworn the corporation politics of the nineties. A second kind of Republicanism eschewed the policies of the first, espousing the needs of farmers and the nonindustrial regions of the nation. They were not as tory as the Old Guard, but neither did they bolt party lines with the regularity of the progressives.

[1] Ogden L. Mills to Ogden M. Reid, October 21, 1927, Mills MSS.

The latter were populistic insurgents without numbers, cohesiveness, or a program, hopelessly functioning as individualistic party pariahs.[2]

Most of the Old Guard never forgave Hoover for not rising to prominence through the party ranks. The Hoover-Republican alliance was purely a marriage of convenience: he needed a party vehicle and they valued the prestige of his war service record. Some GOP solons doubted his Republicanism because his introduction to public life came under a Democratic president, Woodrow Wilson. When he returned to his homeland with enviable accomplishments as a businessman and as war relief administrator, politicians in both parties considered him an attractive political figure. Franklin Roosevelt wanted to make him president in 1920.[3] Hoover had endorsed Wilson's plea for a Democratic Congress in 1918 and supported American participation in the League of Nations. Few people knew for certain which party he identified himself with until he declared his Republican affiliation. Some Republicans suspected that Hoover was an opportunist joining in the reaction against Wilson. In fact, however, his family had been registered Republicans in Iowa although Herbert had voted the Bull Moose ticket in 1912. A few zealous GOP supporters put his name in nomination at their 1920 convention but the Old Guard treated him as an interloper; Alice Roosevelt Longworth believed that he was the only candidate mentioned whom the Senate politicos would absolutely veto.[4]

Although Hoover never endeared himself to the Old Guard, he forced them to confront his prestige. Appointed by President Harding as Secretary of Commerce, he built a minor department into the most representative federal agency of the 1920's. Hoover's influence ranged from Mississippi River Valley flood relief to agricultural policy to foreign relations; by 1928 only Andrew Mellon in the Treasury rivaled his dominance of the

[2] See Appendix.
[3] Arthur M. Schlesinger, Jr., *The Crisis of the Old Order, 1919–1933* (Boston, 1957), p. 82.
[4] Alice Roosevelt Longworth, *Crowded Hours* (New York, 1935), p. 306.

cabinet. When Calvin Coolidge's "I do not choose to run" was construed as a negative decision, the press and Republicans outside of Congress celebrated Hoover as the likeliest successor, even though he had never held an elective public office. James E. Watson, Charles Curtis, and other senators coveted the nomination but were surprised to find themselves outmaneuvered by a political neophyte. An eleventh-hour "stop Hoover" drive fell short; the "smoke-filled rooms" of 1920 proved ineffective in 1928. This defeat irked the Senate politicos who earnestly believed that only one of their kind could handle Congress.[5] If they wanted to prove this in the next four years, they could threaten the success of Hoover's presidency.

A major area of conflict between Hoover and the Old Guard was foreign relations. Their isolationism piqued him as much as his internationalist perspective annoyed them. He had vigorously protested the reservationist opposition to the League of Nations, joining the GOP, he said later, even though he disliked such Republican league opponents as Senators Penrose, Watson, Knox, Lodge, and their followers. They returned his antipathy. Ohio's Simeon Fess had opposed permitting postwar relief funds to be administered by Hoover and his inclusion in Harding's cabinet on the grounds of doubtful Republican loyalty. Hoover's many years spent abroad bothered Republican nationalists; prior to the 1928 convention, Fess had forecast that the Republicans would not accept as their standard-bearer an internationalist "whose Americanism is . . . in question and whose political views are . . . a matter for speculation." To a xenophobic progressive like Hiram Johnson, Hoover was "the Englishman in the White House."[6]

In the White House Hoover rarely attempted to win the Old Guard over. His supporters looked askance at the Senate and maintained the highly personalized organization which had characterized his campaign for the White House. In his previous posi-

---

[5] *Ibid.*, p. 327; James E. Watson, *Memoirs: As I Knew Them* (Indianapolis, 1936), pp. 259–60.

[6] Herbert Hoover, *Memoirs: The Cabinet and the Presidency* (New York, 1952), p. 34; Ray T. Tucker, "Faithful Fess," *Outlook*, CLXI (September 10, 1930): 75; Hiram Johnson to Charles K. McClatchy, March 5, 1931, Johnson MSS.

tions, Hoover always had demanded and received the devotion of his subordinates. Maximum loyalty to him appeared to be the first criterion for staff members and some cabinet members. Henry Stimson, a Wall Street Bull Moose Republican, became his Secretary of State and like others in the cabinet, with the exception of Postmaster General Walter F. Brown of Ohio, had never held a high elective office. Andrew Mellon was carried over in the Treasury Department. In general, Hoover selected a very apolitical cabinet, men who, Stimson remarked, "apparently had no humanity for anything except business." Interest groups seemed to be ignored by Hoover when he chose Arthur M. Hyde, a Missouri automobile dealer, to be Secretary of Agriculture; neither farm organizations nor Hyde himself understood the logic of his appointment.[7] Ray Lyman Wilbur, Secretary of the Interior, enjoyed antagonizing conservation-minded senators and representatives concerned with departmental appropriations.[8] Hoover's White House staff, ably led by Walter Newton and Lawrence Richey, displayed more concern for political protocol. For good relations with the Washington press corps, Hoover depended upon the well-liked press secretary George Akerson; when Akerson departed in 1931, he was succeeded by Theodore Joslin of the arch-conservative Boston *Transcript*, a reporter so intensely disliked by fellow members of the fourth estate that one is alleged to have gibed that the appointment marked "the first known instance of a rat joining a sinking ship."[9]

There is a legion of tales on Hoover's political ineptitude. The great administrator seemed a different man in the presidency. Like many who had known him as food administrator during the war, Harvey H. Bundy, an Assistant Secretary of State, recalled that the same man in the White House provided "one of the most extraordinary contrasts I've ever known." "The President seems

[7] Diary, November 1, 1930, Stimson MSS; "The Reminiscences of M. L. Wilson," COHC, pp. 233–35. Also see Harris G. Warren, *Herbert Hoover and the Great Depression* (New York, 1959), p. 55.

[8] "The Reminiscences of Horace M. Albright," COHC, pp. 294–99.

[9] Warren, p. 57; Edward Tracy Clark to Calvin Coolidge, March 28, 1931, Clark MSS.

to get off on the wrong foot when he tackles any political problem," remarked Justice Harlan Fiske Stone, a member of Hoover's medicine-ball cabinet.[10] Some Republican senators relished Hoover's political fumblings if only because he distinguished their mastery of the science. "If the engineer who was successful in Africa had more political acumen," Charles McNary disdainfully commented, "mole hills would not be viewed as mountains and tempests would take place at sea rather than in the teapot."[11] Hoover partisans in the Senate often offered the president advice and then suffered quietly when he disregarded it with unfortunate consequences.[12]

Early in his administration Hoover and the Senate GOP leadership did little to conceal their contempt for each other. Majority Leader James E. Watson was, in Hoover's words, a man of "spasmodic loyalties and abilities" but the president failed to convince the Old Guard that Watson should be replaced by the younger David A. Reed. Watson swaggered around the Capitol gloating over Hoover's inconsistencies: "How can a man follow the President unless he has St. Vitus' dance?" he cracked. The Hoosier enjoyed outmaneuvering the president, as when he forced rates considerably higher than Hoover considered desirable in the Hawley-Smoot tariff. "I don't talk *to* the President," Watson bragged to cronies, "I talk *at* him."[13] Hoover anticipated conflict with the Democratic opposition and GOP insurgents, but, as columnist J. F. Essary noted, "That loyalty which most Presidents receive from their party associates in Congress was lacking. Many of the Old Guardsmen secretly enjoyed the hectoring of Mr. Hoover at the hands of insurging members."[14]

[10] "The Reminiscences of Harvey H. Bundy," COHC, pp. 112–13; Alpheus T. Mason, *Harlan Fiske Stone: Pillar of Law* (New York, 1956), p. 283.
[11] Charles L. McNary to John H. McNary, December 17, 1931, McNary MSS.
[12] "Just One More of Those Little Hoover Mistakes," November 2, 1930, Scrapbook 3, Vandenberg MSS.
[13] Herbert Hoover, *Memoirs: The Great Depression* (New York, 1952), p. 103; Watson, pp. 259–60; Gentleman at the Keyhole, " 'A Real Republican,' " *Colliers*, October 10, 1931, p. 28; Thomas L. Stokes, *Chip Off My Shoulder* (Princeton, N.J., 1940), p. 267; Gentleman at the Keyhole, "The Oregon Trader," *Colliers*, February 21, 1931, p. 53.
[14] Baltimore *Evening Sun*, March 1, 1931.

Frustrated by the lack of automatic deference and support from Republicans for their titular party head, Hoover reacted with bitterness and bewilderment. Democrats often assailed the president with impunity as Senate GOP leaders hid in the cloakrooms, unwilling, as Hoover put it, to "exert themselves energetically in their traditional duty to counter-attack and expose misrepresentations."[15] On one occasion when Democratic denunciations hit a vituperative high in the Senate and no Republican returned the fire, Hoover called Watson on the carpet to complain about the Old Guard's "supine attitude." Clearly most of the Senate leadership did not desire to be identified with Hoover.[16] "This job," Hoover once growled, "is nothing but a twenty-ring circus—with a whole lot of bad actors"; he left little doubt who the bad actors were.[17]

As the depression worsened, Hoover's political problems multiplied. His personality had few heroic traits which might have rallied men to him in moments of adversity. He seemed to shrink from a fight and when he delivered combative rhetoric, it seemed almost out of character for him. There was, British socialist Harold J. Laski observed prior to Hoover's inauguration, "an unpleasant dourness about him" which made one uneasy. Indeed, Hoover tended toward morbid pessimism, an unhappy trait for a period which, he so well knew, required cheerful optimism. Nor could he hide his moodiness. ". . . He took an unnecessarily dark view of situations," Bernard Baruch recalled. All who knew Hoover admired him for the intensity with which he worked, but Henry Stimson believed that this diligence drained his spirit. Sometimes, the Secretary of State noted, "It was like sitting in a bath of ink to sit in his room. . . ." Stimson believed that Hoover frequently took affairs of state personally and irrationally. An "ever present feeling of gloom . . . pervades everything connected with the Administration," Stimson told his diary; "I really never knew such unenlivened occasions as our Cabinet meetings."

---

[15] Hoover, *The Cabinet and the Presidency*, p. 220.
[16] Clark to Coolidge, December 15, 1930, Clark MSS.
[17] Theodore Joslin, *Hoover Off the Record* (Garden City, N.Y., 1935), p. 163.

When Stimson wished Hoover a good New Year for 1931, the president "smiled one of his rather rare but sweet smiles and said, 'Well, it couldn't be any worse than this one anyhow.' "[18]

Perhaps it was because of his limited experience in national politics that Hoover tended to overdramatize party machinations. Several times he expressed nearly paranoiac fears that certain elements in the GOP were conspiring to destroy him politically or destroy the party because of him. Soon after the 1930 elections he claimed that Borah of Idaho was plotting with certain unnamed progressives and Democrats to create a third party because Borah harbored grudges against him. Experienced observers knew that Borah was incapable of any effective political collaboration. Another time Hoover insisted that "the Norris group" sought an alliance of agriculture, public power, and prohibition advocates in order to "destroy the Republican Party and to erect a new party on its ruins." Undoubtedly Senator George Norris would have liked this, but he recognized the impossibility of such an enterprise even if Hoover took it seriously. Not too long after the New York *Herald Tribune* ridiculed his veto of the Wagner employment bill, Hoover confided to Stimson that he suspected the newspaper of leading a group of Republicans who sought to deprive him of renomination by building Calvin Coolidge up as an alternative.[19] To an extent, although hardly worrisome to a seasoned politician, these latter suspicions were more realistic.

Nothing better illustrated his isolation from the Senate GOP than Hoover's decision to formulate strategy for the 72nd Con-

---

[18] Mark DeWolfe Howe, *Holmes-Laski Letters*, abridged by Alger Hiss (New York, 1963), II: 241; Bernard Baruch, *The Public Years* (New York, 1960), p. 88; diary, June 18, 1931, July 22, 1932, November 1, 1931, December 28, 1930, Stimson MSS.

It should be noted that Stimson, like the rest of the cabinet, was devoted to Hoover. Hoover's pensive moods exasperated Stimson. He once wrote, "How I wish I could cheer up the poor old President and make him feel the importance of a little brightness and recreation in his own work. But after all I suppose he would reply and say that he gets his recreation in his own way and that my way would not suit him at all." November 1, 1931.

[19] Diary, November 25, December 28, 1930, April 28, 1931, Stimson MSS. For an assessment of progressive activities, see Jordan A. Schwarz, "The Politics of Fear: Congress and the Depression during the Hoover Administration," Ph.D. dissertation, Columbia University, 1967, Chapter IV.

gress independently of its Republican leadership. He reasoned that under no circumstances could he control legislating in the new Congress and that the voters had repudiated the congressional GOP, not the White House leadership. Therefore, he hoped to impose his plans on the discredited politicos.

First, however, Hoover wanted no part of the new Congress any earlier than necessary. He flatly rejected all suggestions for a special session of the 72nd Congress because he would brook no legislative interference with his remedial plans. From March 4 to December 7, 1931, he would be able to deal with the depression in his own way without legislative second-guessing. He told a Gridiron Club dinner on December 13, 1930, "It is an extraordinary thing . . . that the whole nation should shudder with apprehension and fear of an extra session of its great legislative body." He approved of an Iowa insurance executive's declaration that "no greater injury . . . could happen to business than an extra session of Congress." The U.S. Chamber of Commerce announced that business organizations were overwhelmingly opposed to an additional session. John E. Edgerton of the NAM applauded Hoover's resistance to "dangerous expedients of legislative compulsion."[20] On May 22 Hoover gave the press a pithy four-sentence statement: "I do not propose to call an extra session of Congress. I know of nothing that would so disturb the healing process now undoubtedly going on in the economic situation. We cannot legislate ourselves out of a world economic depression; we can and will work ourselves out. A poll of the members of Congress would show that a large majority agree with me in opposing an extra session."[21] He ignored arguments and pleas for the special session and continued to foster support for his antilegislative stand in the fall of 1931. When GOP Senator Arthur Vandenberg of Michigan suggested that the banking situation required legislative suc-

[20] William Starr Myers (ed.), *The State Papers and Other Public Writings of Herbert Hoover* (Garden City, N.Y., 1934), I: 468; William C. MacArthur to Herbert Hoover, February 6, 1931, press release of Chamber of Commerce of the United States, John E. Edgerton to Hoover (telegram), August 20, February 5, 1931, Container 1–E/104, Hoover MSS.

[21] Myers, *State Papers*, I: 565.

cor, Hoover loftily replied that the country should "pull itself together and check its phantasmagoria. It is worth taking the risk."[22]

When Congress finally did convene, Hoover planned to have the Republicans permit the Democrats to organize both houses of Congress. Neither party had an effective majority in either house; the House would probably be barely Democratic by December, 1931, while the Senate would be Republican by one vote. In both houses the GOP would have to deal with about a dozen insurgent progressives in their ranks. Therefore, Hoover wanted the Republicans to relinquish control of the upper chamber to give Democrats the sole burden for legislating. "I could deal more constructively with the Democratic leaders if they held full responsibility in both houses," he explained, "than with an opposition in the Senate conspiring in the cloakrooms to use every proposal of mine for demagoguery."[23] In this way the legislative record of the 72nd Congress automatically would have become Democratic property.

Hoover planned to resist anticipated Democratic "raids" on the Treasury which upset the budget and business confidence. White House advisers believed that the president had to exhibit "courage" by defending the government's fiscal integrity against the expediency of federal spending for relief. Recalling the public acclaim for Coolidge's veto of a veterans' bonus bill in 1924, and believing that public works and other spending bills were inevitable in the new Congress, Hoover would spare the GOP political embarrassment if Congress was clearly Democratic. Given the mood and make-up of Congress, Hoover's use of the veto seemed inevitable. (Two of Hoover's vetoes were overridden during the Republican 71st's lame-duck session.) Indeed, the administration believed that such resistance could yield political profits. William Starr Myers, an academic friend and occasional guest at Hoover's

---

[22] Hoover to Arthur H. Vandenberg, October 8, 1931, Container 1-1/310, Hoover MSS. For more correspondence, pro and con, on the extra session, see Container 1-E/104.

[23] Hoover, *The Great Depression*, p. 101.

vacation retreat, summed up the administration's expectations: "While very irritating and wearing upon him, any struggle with that body will be apt to add to his popularity and political strength. . . . The voters will not be indifferent to any struggle waged or victory gained by the President. Such events also would serve to dramatize his work and his administration of national affairs."[24]

The Senate Republican leadership, however, did not concur on all this strategy. They viewed abdication from organizing the Senate as one more colossal political blunder. The shrewd Ted Clark,[25] knowing that congressional party leaders valued the committee chairmanships and other rewards for a majority party, attempted to dissuade Hoover from personally proposing the scheme. "It never occurs to him," Clark lamented, "that these chairmanships are the very pinnacle of the political careers of men in the House and the Senate, that they, at least theoretically, are vitally important in influencing the type and character of legislation." Of course Hoover believed that he could determine legislation by wielding his executive veto, but this only signified to the GOP leadership that Hoover did not comprehend how Congress functioned. No chance existed for GOP cooperation. As the amused Senator Borah put it, "I wish I were as sure of the Kingdom of Heaven as I am that the Republicans will never give up their Senate Chairmanships while they have the vote to retain them." Yet Hoover believed that his plan involved higher strategy as against the Senate leaders' pettiness. When Watson flatly rejected it, Hoover interpreted this as meaning that Watson "liked the extra importance of being majority leader, and the Republi-

[24] Joslin, p. 119; Clark to Coolidge, November 29, 1930, November 17, 1931, Clark MSS; William Starr Myers, "Looking toward 1932," *American Political Science Review*, XXV (November, 1931): 929–30.

[25] Clark had been secretary to President Coolidge and had been offered a similar post by President Hoover, declining it in favor of operating as a Washington lobbyist. During the Hoover years Clark maintained his Republican connections in Congress and the White House while serving as a political listening post for Coolidge who had retired to Northampton, Mass. Hoover often tried to employ Clark's political savvy and Clark assumed some White House duties briefly while others vacationed in August, 1932.

cans liked to hold committee chairmanships and the nicer offices in the capitol."[26]

Hoover correctly gauged the limited vision of certain Republican Senate leaders. Genial Jim Watson, for example, symbolized the nadir of Republicanism in Congress. To one reporter, it was "preposterous that he should be leader." Washington rated Watson as an adroit politician given to flamboyant orations and an amiability which, for all its disingenuousness, fended off personality clashes. His supporters had buttressed his abortive presidential ambitions of Al Smith; the rural, dry, southern and western better than anybody else. His ingratiating personality served as his greatest asset. This "lovable old humbug," as his friends called him, was uninterested in books, bored by details, and studied issues only to an extent which enabled him to deliver robust speeches. Politics alone held his sustained attention.[27]

Watson was a gilded-age Republican whose career spanned from Harrison to Hoover. He had served for twelve years in the House and had been in the Senate since 1917. In the twenties he courted the support of such groups as the American Manufacturers Association and the Ku Klux Klan while building a reputation for protectionism and isolationism. During the Hawley-Smoot tariff debates on sugar, Watson exchanged a blank note for sugar stock and proceeded to fight for higher schedules on sugar. One correspondent labelled him "the most scandal-smeared member of the United States Senate—and yet the most beloved." He never attached his name to any notable piece of legislation, but he always made certain that Indiana got what it wanted.[28]

Like Watson, George H. Moses of New Hampshire excelled

[26] Clark to Coolidge, August 17, 1931, Clark MSS; Marian C. McKenna, *Borah* (Ann Arbor, Mich., 1961), p. 268; Hoover, *The Great Depression*, p. 101.
[27] Gentleman at the Keyhole, "Put Your Best Foot Forward," *Colliers*, January 19, 1929, p. 47; Arthur W. Macmahon, "First Session of the Seventy-first Congress," *American Political Science Review*, XXIV (February, 1930): 41; Frank R. Kent, "Senator James E. Watson: The Professional Public Servant," *Atlantic Monthly*, CXLIX (February, 1932): 184–90; Burton K. Wheeler with Paul E. Healy, *Yankee from the West* (Garden City, N.Y., 1962), p. 270.
[28] Gentleman, "Put Your Best Foot Forward"; Kent; Schlesinger, p. 164; Clark to Coolidge, November 11, 1931, Clark MSS.

in oratory rather than in legislating. The proud possessor of an acerbic tongue and wit, it was said that Republicans had elected him Senate president pro tempore in honor of the abuse which he heaped upon Democrats. But Moses did not save his scorn for Democrats alone. He had assured himself of a place in American political lexicography the day he branded Republican insurgents as "Sons of the Wild Jackass." He assailed the farm bloc as "an awful affliction" whose purpose was to "farm the farmers" and transform the United States "from the land of the free to the region of the regulated." They were the radicals responsible for the income tax, "only a modern legislative adaptation of the Communistic doctrine of Karl Marx."[29]

Watson and Moses were paradigms of the Old Guard senator. Their concerns rarely ranged beyond those of their constituents and their goals rarely surpassed the pursuit of power or its retention. In such an environment, only a man who gave fealty to the party could expect its rewards. Individual success became inextricably tied to the party's and deviations from regularity were deplored as apostasy. In a moment of appreciation of the fact that the party's welfare and the success of his administration were one, Hoover installed Senator Simeon Fess of Ohio as chairman of the Republican National Committee in August, 1930.

It appeared that the job had found the man, for "Faithful Fess" was a party man in every political commitment. A former professor of American history at Ohio Northern University and president of Antioch College, Fess boasted that he "always held to constructive statement in all my political history," which meant that Republicans committed no wrongs. Warren Harding remained without a blemish in Fess's hagiography of Republicans; Hoover, reviled as late as 1928, now wrote inspiring pages into the party record. With a high nasal voice and a humorless pedantic manner, Fess would lecture his Senate audiences on the recti-

---

[29] Ray T. Tucker, "The Senate's Bad Boy," *Outlook*, CLVI (October 22, 1930): 294–96; George H. Moses, "Speaking of the Senate," *Saturday Evening Post*, July 25, 1931, pp. 8–9; Moses, "Death—and Taxes," *ibid.*, June 27, 1931, p. 97; Merrill A. Symonds, "George Higgins Moses of New Hampshire—The Man and the Era," Ph.D. dissertation, Clark University, 1955.

tude of the party. Others might deride Fess, but Republicans appreciated his consistency.[30]

For other Republicans, however, when party loyalty ran counter to constituent interests, the latter prevailed. Regular Republicans from midwestern and Pacific states, where agriculture and public power were articles of faith, often deviated from GOP preachments on government noninvolvement in the economy. Although inherently conservative advocates who never questioned the free enterprise system, they nevertheless sought federal aid for poverty-stricken farmers and federal development of hydro-electric power in the Pacific Northwest. To achieve these ends, they worked within the GOP political hierarchy where men like Wesley L. Jones and Charles L. McNary were accorded party recognition.

Jones of Washington state had spent over twenty years in the Senate to gain his position as assistant Republican leader and chairman of the Appropriations Committee. He valued the latter most of all because it enabled him to influence river, harbor, reclamation, and power legislation. Jones in the twenties had been a prime advocate of nationwide public power development and other works projects in order to gain the support of all regions for the development of the Columbia River Basin. Although this issue allied him with the progressives, few would have thought to label Jones as one.[31]

Like Hoover, McNary had been born in 1874, grew up in Salem, Oregon, and attended Leland Stanford Junior University. Unlike Hoover, McNary was a lawyer and political conciliator. Despite his sponsorship of one of the most controversial legislative measures in the 1920's, the McNary-Haugen farm bill, McNary after twelve years in the Senate had won enough respect from colleagues to become majority whip in 1931, second in rank among Senate Republicans. He shrewdly avoided identification

[30] Warren, p. 124; Simeon Fess to Sumner Fess, September 20, 1932, Fess MSS; Ray T. Tucker, "Faithful Fess," *Outlook*, CLXI (September 10, 1930): 43–45; Gentleman at the Keyhole, "Simeon Pure," *Colliers*, September 27, 1930, p. 55.
[31] William S. Forth, "Wesley L. Jones: A Political Biography," Ph.D. dissertation, University of Washington, 1962, pp. iii–iv, Chapter XII, 759–60.

with either the Old Guard or progressives and cultivated the role of mediator. He was, a reporter observed, "amenity itself." Two Coolidge vetoes of the McNary-Haugen bill and conflict over public power never ruptured the Oregonian's relations with that president. McNary skillfully applied what he described as "the science of politics." Congressman Marvin Jones, a Democrat who shared his concern for agriculture, recalled that "the Senate had great confidence in McNary," which enabled him to become "a great manager" of legislation.[32]

The shrewdness with which the Old Guard ruled the upper chamber was missing in the House Republican leadership. The Speaker of the House when Hoover became president was Nicholas Longworth, husband of Theodore Roosevelt's daughter Alice. A Cincinnati GOP stalwart, Longworth had opposed his father-in-law's insurgent presidential candidacy in 1912, preferring his neighbor, William Howard Taft. Longworth appeared incongruous as the leader of a bunch of tough, poker-playing politicians because his society manners and dapper appearance gave him the air of a diplomat (spats, cane, splendidly groomed mustache, hairless pate). But Longworth was a genial politician who made few enemies and cultivated powerful friends like House Democratic leader John Nance Garner. His poker-playing camaraderie made Longworth a popular Speaker of whom it was said he "ruled as a crony rather than a czar." Together with Majority Leader John Q. Tilson and Rules Committee Chairman Bertrand Snell, Longworth led a formidable triumvirate which dominated the House in such a fashion as to remind old-timers of the heyday of "Uncle Joe" Cannon.[33] With such an ally Hoover had few problems in the House. But Longworth died suddenly at 61 in April, 1931.

[32] Gentleman at the Keyhole, "Anti-Knock Charlie," *Colliers*, January 25, 1930, p. 40; Douglas Gilbert in the New York *World-Telegram*, February 2, 1932; Charles L. McNary to John H. McNary, March 6, 1929, McNary MSS; "The Reminiscences of Marvin Jones," COHC, pp. 259–60. For a favorable progressive view of McNary, see George W. Norris, *Fighting Liberal* (New York, 1961), p. 308.
[33] "Nicholas Longworth," *Nation*, XXXII (April 22, 1931): 441; A.F.C., "Backstage in Washington," *Outlook and Independent*, May 14, 1930, p. 60.

Assaying the congressional situation, Mark Sullivan found that Longworth's death brought "further confusion to a situation already acutely confused." Both Tilson and Snell lacked the tact, political skill, and popularity of the deceased Speaker.[34] Tilson of New Haven, Connccticut, was a lawyer with a bland personality whose greatest attributes were organizational ability and steadfastness. Snell was a plodding businessman from the Adirondacks region of New York who impressed Hoover as "sturdy, honest and devoted," one way of saying that Snell was little more than a party hack.[35] For almost eight months through 1931 the two rivals for Longworth's mantle hustled between Wisconsin progressives and Pennsylvania tories in an effort to round up enough votes to win the GOP leadership. Tilson claimed to be the stauncher supporter of Hoover, solemnly depicting the president as "the steady hand at the helm [who] kept the recent depression from being as bad as other depressions." But Snell gave western Republicans concessions on liberalizing House rules and, after eight ballots on November 30, captured the party's leadership.[36]

With a slim Democratic House majority, however, the Speakership would go to Garner if the Democrats chose to organize the House. The Democrats in 1931 "seemed more hopeful than bold," a political scientist wrote; "events seemed to be going their way; they had no wish to incur premature responsibility." The obligation of presenting a remedial program belonged to the incumbent party; with the White House and the Senate in GOP hands, Democratic rule of the House, in the words of Carter Glass, would "give the Republicans an opportunity to charge us with obstructing the wise policies of their administration." Besides, it was doubtful that the Democrats could unite behind one program. "With the bigoted and prejudiced attitudes that many people

[34] "Party Perplexity after Longworth," *Literary Digest*, April 25, 1931, p. 11; A.F.C., "Backstage in Washington," *Outlook and Independent*, April 22, 1931, p. 555.
[35] Hoover, *The Great Depression*, p. 103; Warren, p. 153.
[36] New York *Times*, April 14, 18, May 13, November 16, 28, December 1, 2, 1931.

take upon different questions," Bernard Baruch commented, "I fear we should make an exhibition of inability to get together."[37]

Indeed, the strongest unifying factor among Democrats was their lust for victory. Not since 1916 had the Democrats won a majority in Congress. Since 1894 the Democrats had been a national minority party. In the 1920's they "were like poor relations at a family reunion," wrote Marquis Childs, "grateful to be there but a little resentful at being made to wait always for the second table."[38] Prohibition and sectional and urban-rural conflicts preoccupied Jefferson's party. Clearly there were two Democratic parties in the 1920's: the wet, eastern, urban group with its main strength in Massachusetts and New York promoted the presidential ambitions of Al Smith; the rural, dry, southern and western coalition ruled in the Congress.[39] The nature and personnel of the congressional Democratic leadership had changed little since the Wilsonian ascendancy. In fact, many of them were veterans of the New Freedom. They were the same rural people who had pushed for the Federal Reserve Act, the income tax, and tariff reform. Not until the New Deal would New York City and Chicago Democrats accumulate enough seniority to gain chairmanships on a few key committees. Meanwhile they were captained by men whose economics was tinged with populism and whose oratory atavistically paid respect to Jefferson. As Senator Key Pittman correctly observed, "Our party is still a local, free trade, southern party as far as the administration of party policies is concerned in Congress."[40]

Throughout the Hoover years, the Smith men in the Democratic National Committee enjoyed the New Yorker's nominal hold on the party's executive. Smith's appointees, former General

[37] Arthur W. Macmahon, "Second Session of the Seventy-first Congress," *American Political Science Review,* XXIV (November, 1930): 936–37; Carter Glass to Bernard Baruch, October 1, 1931, Box 280, Glass MSS; Baruch to Thomas J. Walsh, October 10, 1931, T. J. Walsh MSS.

[38] Marquis W. Childs, *I Write from Washington* (New York, 1942), p. 88.

[39] For an excellent discussion of this see David Burner, *The Politics of Parochialism: The Democratic Party in Transition, 1918–1932* (New York, 1967).

[40] Key Pittman to Baruch, March 3, 1930, Pittman MSS.

Motors head John J. Raskob and Kentucky politician Jouett Shouse, sought to line up the National Committee in 1931 behind a resolution declaring prohibition a matter for the individual states without federal enforcement. Shouse called a committee meeting for March 4 and 5, after Congress adjourned, because "there would not be the danger of having extended speeches made on the floors of each House of Congress upon the controversial question. . . ."[41] The meeting posed a challenge to dry Democrats in Congress whom the Smith people considered treasonous to the 1928 nominee. On behalf of his southern congressional friends, Bernard Baruch, although hostile to prohibition, pleaded with Raskob not to incite any more party squabbles by raising sensitive issues. Raskob brusquely replied that he hoped Baruch's message was "not the beginning of an organized attempt to dictate to the National Committee. . . ."[42] Democratic harmony rarely was achieved through amiable conciliation.

The Smith people were economic conservatives who feared that prohibition had become secondary to the depression as an issue, thereby opening the way for congressional remedial proposals. They did not dissent from the Hoover recovery policies, a fact which made promotion of the prohibition issue appear to be a smokescreen to distract Democrats from bread-and-butter concerns. Democratic senators like Alben Barkley suspected that the National Committee was "trying to merge . . . with the Republican party on everything except Prohibition." William G. McAdoo warned that if the Smith forces succeeded, the result would be "suicidal" to the party. Like many Democrats in the House, William A. Ayres of Kansas insisted that the party concern itself only with the depression. Even Senator David I. Walsh, a loyal Smith partisan from Massachusetts, denounced Raskob's economic views as too conservative and advised the party to be wary

[41] Jouett Shouse to John J. Raskob, December 1, 1930, to John W. Davis, February 28, 1932, Shouse MSS.
[42] Telegrams, Baruch to Raskob, Raskob to Baruch, February 16, 1931, Baruch MSS.

of the prohibition issue.[43] Nevertheless, the Smith camp continued its efforts to substitute liquor for unemployment as the 1932 issue. The Democratic leadership in 1931 tended to avoid the substantive matters of relief and recovery. Under the guise of bipartisanship, Democratic leaders planned to abstain from initiating remedial measures while permitting the Republicans to make or break themselves in the depression crucible. Abhorring a potential congressional rampage against the Hoover administration, Democratic leaders in Congress and out sought to bind the legislators to nonpartisan activities. Instead of emergency legislation, Democrats should offer only urgent cooperation. Promising they would not rock the boat, the opposition chieftains committed themselves to confirming Hoover's plans.[44] They also agreed that there should not be a special session of the 72nd Congress, Robinson and Garner giving public assurances that they would not seek one. Doubting the wisdom of an early meeting of the new Congress, the persuasive Democratic financier, Bernard Baruch, clinically observed, "The country is in a highly excited condition. What it needs is rest, not any more changes."[45]

Arguing that the only Democratic obligation was to keep Republicans on the defensive, conservatives cautioned against advocating alternatives to GOP policies. "The Party in power must defend its record," counseled Senator Josiah W. Bailey of North Carolina; "the opposition party has the duty of keeping it on the defensive, and in 1932 this may be done without committing our party to a definite program. The issue in the election is Hoover. Why take any step calculated to divert attention from that issue[?]" Democrats wanted it to remain a Republican depression. "Let us be careful not to get in a position where the Republicans will be able to unload this onus on us," Bernard Baruch advised

---

[43] Alben W. Barkley to William G. McAdoo, April 7, 1931, McAdoo to Barkley, March 23, 1931, Barkley MSS; New York *Times*, March 17, 1931; Boston *Post*, March 8, 1931, in scrapbooks, D. I. Walsh MSS. For more on the Democratic National Committee meeting of March 4 and 5, 1931, see Chapter 7.

[44] New York *Times*, November 8, 1930.

[45] Walter H. Newton to J. T. Robinson (telegram), November 15, 1930, Container 1-E/104, Hoover MSS; Robinson to Josephus Daniels, February 9, 1931, Daniels MSS; Baruch to M. M. Neely, November 10, 1930, Baruch MSS.

Senate Democrats; "let us not try to rectify too many things by laws now." Democrats should give Hoover whatever legislation he wanted, confident that the tide of events would carry them to victory in spite of the president's efforts. "We don't have to follow him as the source of all wisdom," Baruch pontificated, "but we should be careful not to tie him up. His own people will do that."[46]

Several Senate Democrats disagreed with that strategy. The cooperation statement by the seven Democratic leaders drew considerable dissent from Democrats around the nation. Accustomed to an opposition party's role, these Democrats disapproved of the leaders' efforts to demonstrate "statesmanship" by rubber-stamping inoffensive administration proposals. Such behavior was "acquiescence" to the venerable Senator Thomas J. Walsh. Josephus Daniels criticized the leaders for timidity and defensiveness. Other Democrats accused them of being apologetic for their victories and argued that their 1930 successes were public mandates to develop alternatives to the administration's program for economic recovery. "Conciliation must not degenerate into surrender of principle," admonished Senator-elect Edward P. Costigan; ". . . no immediate hopes may now be indulged of any permanent union of the Administration and other progressive opposition." Some Senate Democrats were angered because the leaders had not consulted with them prior to the statement's release. Reporters euphemistically characterized the acrimony heard on the Senate floor and in the cloakrooms as "rumblings of dissatisfaction." A few Democratic senators publicly warned Joe Robinson that they might vote independently of his legislative command.[47]

The self-styled progressive Democrats of the Senate feared that the lack of an independent program might be construed by the public as Democratic drift. That impression would destroy any

[46] Josiah W. Bailey to Robinson, November 4, 1931, Bailey MSS; Baruch to Pittman, November 11, 1930, Baruch MSS; Baruch to Glass, September 28, 1931, Box 280, Glass MSS. Also see Daniel Roper to Shouse, November 5, Shouse to Roper, November 15, 1930, Shouse MSS.

[47] New York *Times*, November 9, December 5, 7, 1930; Edward P. Costigan, "A National Political Armistice?" *Atlantic Monthly*, CXLVII (February, 1931): 260.

hopes for victory in 1932. "Only the Democratic party by its failure to function can save the republican party and its Hoover administration from overwhelming defeat in 1932," wrote Senator Cordell Hull of Tennessee. It followed that Democrats should not sit by quietly and leave the initiative to the GOP, but should work out their own legislative proposals. Together with Tom Walsh, Costigan, and others, Hull in 1931 developed the outline of a positive legislative agenda so that, Walsh declared, "the party might be said to have a real constructive program and not be merely a party of negation."[48] By November, 1931, the Democratic progressives presented their leadership with a seven-point program calling for unemployment relief via public works financed by bond sales, passage of the Wagner bills for employment services and unemployment insurance, increased revenue from higher income, inheritance, gift, and luxury taxes, lower tariff rates, new stock exchange regulations, expanded credit facilities for farmers, homeowners, and businessmen, and farm relief. This ambitious program could not be wholly enacted by the 72nd Congress, but they believed that a start had to be made.[49]

From the activist perspective, Democratic control of the House was essential. Not only would it permit Democrats to enjoy the fruits of House patronage, it would also permit them to enact laws which would contrast with the administration's inertia. With some candor Tom Walsh declared: "I think the organization of the House by us will be a step toward success in 1932."[50] Surprisingly, a few Democrats viewed their organization of the House the way Hoover viewed GOP control of the Senate—as

[48] Cordell Hull to W. E. Norvell, Jr., April 31, 1931, Hull MSS; Walsh to Baruch, October 16, 1931, T. J. Walsh MSS.
[49] Walsh to Robinson, November 7, 1931, T. J. Walsh MSS.
[50] Walsh to Baruch, October 6, 1931, T. J. Walsh MSS.
Governor Franklin D. Roosevelt of New York, already the favorite of many Democratic senators for the 1932 presidential nomination, agreed on the necessity of organizing the House to establish a party record. When requested to appoint Representative Emanuel Celler of Brooklyn to a county judgeship, he refused lest he "reduce the Democratic [House] total by even one vote. . . ." Franklin D. Roosevelt to Glass, December 22, 1931, Box 6, Glass MSS.

responsibility undesirable at that time. In the end, the question was academic. As Baruch said, "If we have a majority in the House, then, of course, we cannot avoid organizing it."[51] The November, 1931, make-up elections resolved the issue.

Of course everyone knew that Democratic strategy in the House or Senate would be determined by its leadership irrespective of the program developed by a few activists. And the leaders were decidedly cautious. Going into the thirties they had been "at best a listless opposition, driven only rarely to oratorical revolts."[52] They were accustomed to enhancing their power by collaboration with the majority. Their dissent tended to be perfunctory. To become a majority party, the Democrats needed a crisis like the depression. But when it came, they were immobilized by doubts as to what constituted the correct response.

The man who led the House Democrats, John Nance Garner of Texas, typified their confusion. The wealthiest man in the prairie town of Uvalde, Garner had been in Congress since 1903. He had fostered a populist image of himself in earlier days as a leading Wilsonian advocate of the Federal Reserve System and the income tax and as an arch-enemy of the regressive Mellon tax policies of the twenties. With Garner in command, the Democrats seemed clothed in homespun. He drank more than his share and prefaced each drink with the antiprohibition cry, "Strike a blow for liberty!" When other words failed him, he exploded with homely expressions like "Hell's bells and cockle shells!" There was no better man to lead the party of Jefferson and Jackson in the lower chamber; Garner symbolized, a reporter wrote, "the demand of the common man for a larger portion of the profits of his toil."

This veneer belied a sophisticated politician. "Cactus Jack" Garner had earned the Speakership; he had mastered the House's operation and commanded the respect of his colleagues. "He had an uncanny way of guessing what the House would do," Marvin

[51] Baruch to Walsh, October 10, 1931, T. J. Walsh MSS.
[52] Childs, p. 88.

65

Jones recalled. He was a practical man who "made no pretense of being engaged on vast undertakings for the salvation of mankind."[53] Some Washingtonians wondered if Garner had too close a friendship with his opposite number, Nicholas Longworth; they were, cracked Edward T. Folliard of the Washington *Post*, "the Damon and Pythias of Capitol Hill." Having been dependent upon the Republicans for favors, Garner might have been reluctant to utilize his Speakership to oppose the White House. Herbert Hoover considered Garner "a man of real statesmanship when he took off his political pistols," but some Democrats feared that the "Texas Tiger" had hung up his guns. Nonetheless, conservative Democrats like Newton Baker, emphasizing party unity above any program, were pleased that Garner appeared to be "building the Democratic representation into a coherent and effective Party organization."[54]

Henry T. Rainey of Illinois succeeded Garner as Democratic floor leader. Seventy-one in 1931, white-haired, handsome, constantly wearing a black Windsor tie, Rainey looked like a caricature of a congressman. He had always idolized William Jennings Bryan and never outgrew a disposition for agrarian radicalism or liberal causes; he had enthusiastically endorsed New Freedom legislation, government ownership of Muscle Shoals, McNary-Haugenism, and recognition of the Soviet Union. Hoover disliked him intensely, calling Rainey a demagogue and "an ardent collectivist of a muddled variety."[55] Still, for all his belief in governmental activism, Rainey was above all a regular Demo-

[53] Ray T. Tucker, "Tiger from Texas," *Outlook and Independent*, CLVI (November 26, 1930): 492–94; New York *World-Telegram*, January 25, 1932; "The Reminiscences of Marvin Jones," COHC, p. 564; Cordell Hull, *Memoirs* (New York, 1948), p. 133; "The Reminiscences of Henry Bruere," COHC, pp. 162–63.

[54] Washington *Post*, November 6, 1930; Hoover, *The Great Depression*, p. 101; Newton D. Baker to James M. Cox, May 9, 1930, Baker MSS. For more on Garner see Bascom N. Timmons, *Garner of Texas* (New York, 1948), and Chapter 7 of this book.

[55] Robert A. Waller, "Congressman Henry T. Rainey of Illinois: His Rise to the Speakership, 1903–1934," Ph.D. dissertation, University of Illinois, 1963; New York *World-Telegram*, February 1, 1932; [Robert S. Allen and Drew Pearson], *Washington Merry-Go-Round* (New York, 1931), pp. 245–46; Timmons, p. 136; Hoover, *The Great Depression*, p. 102.

crat and in 1931 he went along with the thinking that the party should wait upon Hoover's leadership.[56]

Outside of Rainey, the House Democratic leadership was all southern. John McDuffie of Alabama, with only twelve years in the House, served as party whip. McDuffie, a close friend of Garner, was ambitious for the Speakership and a staunch ally of big corporations. Sam Rayburn of Texas had eighteen years' tenure and was known as Garner's protégé. The leading committees like Rules, Appropriations, and Ways and Means were chaired by William B. Bankhead of Alabama, Joseph W. Byrns of Tennessee, and William Collier of Mississippi. The northern Democrats needed a sustained reign like the Republican twenties to rival the South's hold on the top House positions.

The story was pretty much the same in the Senate. Westerners filled a few of the leadership posts, but their interests were primarily as agrarian as the Southerners'. Joe T. Robinson of Arkansas had led the Senate Democrats since 1923. He was a tough political veteran who had never lost in five tries for the House, one for the governorship, and three for the Senate; his only losing race was in 1928, for vice-president with Al Smith. He was an ambitious man who hankered for the presidency or a seat on the Supreme Court. On the Senate floor, the large Arkansan cut an impressive figure and his powerful voice often dominated debate.[57]

Robinson was a southern Bourbon. Raymond Clapper deftly identified him as "a statesman of the old school, conservative in outlook, sympathetic with the established order. . . ." The White House recognized him as a man with whom it could deal; the president consulted him on pending legislation with a regularity that might have made Jim Watson envious. Hoover later remembered Robinson as "a man of considerable statesmanship" and volunteered the fact that "at times he gave me cooperation," high

[56] For more on Rainey's role, see Chapter 5.
[57] Elliot Thurston, "Senator Joseph T. Robinson," *Forum*, LXXXVI (October, 1931): 254–56; Charles Morrow Wilson, "Mighty Like a Giant," *Outlook*, CLX (January 6, 1932): 11–12; "Bad Parliamentary Manners," Scrapbook 4, Vandenberg MSS. Also see Nevin E. Neal, "A Biography of Joseph T. Robinson," Ph.D. dissertation, University of Oklahoma, 1958.

praise for a Democrat. Indeed, in Hoover's judgment, "had he not been under the constant influence of malign politics, he would have gone down in history as a distinguished senator. He, however, was a senior of the old school of southern opposition."[58] Progressive Democrats sometimes wondered if only geography made Robinson a member of the opposition. His participation in the cooperation statement damaged his standing among Senate Democrats but no movement existed to deprive him of his leadership.

Key Pittman of Nevada was the Democratic whip. Although a Westerner by adoption, Pittman was southern-born and educated and still reflected attitudes of his native region. Since coming to the Senate in 1913, Pittman had distinguished himself chiefly as a follower, first of Wilson, then Robinson. Pittman, wrote the acerbic Senator Moses, had "no continuity of interest in anything which cannot be turned to his personal advantage. . . ." His principal concern was the economic advancement of Nevada, which meant silver mining and coinage or federal reclamation and irrigation projects. As the ranking Democrat on the Senate Foreign Relations Committee, Pittman's sole interest in foreign affairs was the international price of silver. At international conferences he tended to drink in excess which made him, according to Secretary of State Stimson, "a very troublesome man."[59]

If the activities of senators like Robinson, Pittman, and Mississippi's Pat Harrison, ranking Democrat on the Senate Finance Committee, are to be fully understood, then the influence of financier Bernard Baruch must be appreciated. Baruch in later years had the popular reputation as an adviser to presidents from Wilson to Eisenhower; but in the twenties and thirties he was a more powerful influence on senators. After accumulating a fortune as a Wall Street speculator, he had entered government ser-

[58] Raymond Clapper, "Senate Leaders and Orators," *Review of Reviews*, LXXXIX (February, 1934): 29–30; Hoover, *The Great Depression*, p. 102.

[59] George H. Moses to W. H. Brevoort, March 30, 1934, Moses mss; Fred L. Israel, *Nevada's Key Pittman* (Lincoln, Nebr., 1963); "The Reminiscences of Henry L. Stimson," COHC, p. 213.

vice in the Wilson years and served as head of the War Industries Board and an adviser on the Treaty of Paris. When asked how he made his money in the stock market, Baruch would reply that he bought when others sold; in the twenties, when others politically sold out on the Democrats, Baruch invested heavily. He gave generously to losing Democratic presidential campaigns and sustained an unknown number of Democratic political careers that were considered poor risks. In the 1930 campaign, as in previous ones, Baruch donated $38,800 to the Senate Democratic Campaign Committee for fourteen candidates of his choosing; the recipients, to be sure, were informed of their benefactor's identity.[60] He tended to favor conservative Southerners although any Democrat in good standing could expect some contribution to his war chest. Rarely did the cagey Baruch express a presidential preference prior to the party's nomination, lest he alienate the winner. (He had made an exception in 1924 with fellow Wilsonian William G. McAdoo.) "You jump a lot of fences between campaigns," teased columnist Frank Kent, "but when the bell rings for the horses to go to the post, you are up in front, check book in one big paw and fountain pen in the other."[61]

It would be simplistic, however, to suggest that Baruch built his influence on contributions alone. For in a society that often measures economic knowledge by the accumulation of wealth, Baruch's credentials as a seer were impressive. Any man who invested so wisely surely understood a great deal about American capitalism; little wonder he had been offered the post of Secretary of the Treasury by President Wilson. And when the Senate Finance Committee held hearings on causes and remedies for the depression, Baruch led off the testimony and sat longer than any who followed him while senators from both parties listened with a respect that bordered upon awe. Nor did it hurt his reputation that he apparently thrived in the depression when other moguls

---

[60] E. A. Halsey to Baruch, September 18, October 11, 29, Millard Tydings to Baruch, September 16, November 8, 1930, Baruch MSS. For Baruch on his role in the twenties, see Baruch, *The Public Years*, Chapter XII.

[61] Frank Kent to Baruch, May 28, 1930, Baruch MSS.

floundered.[62] He persuaded Joe Robinson so easily that Frank Kent could not distinguish a Robinson proposal free from the financier's sway. Sometimes during a congressional session, Baruch invited Robinson, Pittman, and Harrison for a hunt at Hobcaw, his South Carolina plantation retreat; it seems safe to say that politics entered the discussion over quail. When Baruch came to Washington, "Joe, Key and Pat" could be found in his hotel suite that evening. No other outsider wielded such power in the Senate.[63]

But not all senators extended Baruch the reverence which conservatives gave him. In 1931, when Baruch called for a balanced budget through government retrenchment, Assistant Floor Leader Thomas J. Walsh disagreed vigorously. Walsh, a beneficiary of Baruch's campaign largesse, listened to Baruch cite Macaulay on the virtues of government inaction and then informed him that such notions were increasingly antiquated.[64] Instead, Walsh collaborated with progressives who sought to demonstrate that Democrats had a positive response to the crisis. Walsh had always been an independent man in politics and had won enduring fame as the dogged prosecutor of the Teapot Dome scandal. Never did his independence approach the insurgency of his junior colleague from Montana, Burton K. Wheeler, who had bolted the party to run for vice-president with "Battle Bob" La Follette on the 1924 Progressive ticket. A lean man at 72, Walsh wore a broad mustache which gave him an unmistakable western air. His progressivism, party regularity, and judicial demeanor had earned the respect of his Senate associates.

Walsh had the distinction in 1931 of being the sole senator in the leadership of both parties seeking legislative initiative against the depression. Most of the activist Democrats were back-benchers

---

[62] For example, see one congressman's reply to Baruch advice (". . . Am impressed by your opinions by reason of your superior knowledge of business matters . . .") in telegrams, Baruch to J. J. McSwain, McSwain to Baruch, March 28, 1932, McSwain MSS.

[63] Kent to Baruch, May 13, Baruch to Kent, May 15, 1929, Baruch to Robinson, Robinson to Baruch (telegrams), January 11, June 16, 1932, Baruch MSS.

[64] Baruch to Walsh, October 10, Walsh to Baruch, October 16, 1931, T. J. Walsh MSS.

like Cordell Hull, who had been elected to the Senate after many outstanding years in the lower chamber, Edward P. Costigan, another freshman in the Senate, and Robert F. Wagner, whose New York liberalism could not be comprehended by the southern leadership. Political expediency and impatience with the depression were on the side of the activists. Governor Franklin D. Roosevelt of New York, an oft-mentioned potential candidate for the presidency, expressed in 1931 his deep concern "lest our Party be misled along conservative or reactionary paths by those who fatuously compete with our Republican friends for the support of certain interests." Roosevelt suggested that Democrats should act more independently of the GOP. "I believe the country is ready for a more progressive policy," he declared.[65] But was Congress? Were the Democrats?

For the time being, the Democrats were unwilling to tamper with a Republican mess. Ted Clark noted the Democratic caution in late 1931 when he doubted that Hoover would "get many dangerously radical bills which he can bravely veto in times like these. . . ." He predicted that the Democratic leadership would "hesitate about doing anything which seems to forfeit the confidence of the business world."[66] After two years of depression a conservative consensus prevailed in Washington. Little had changed since the Coolidge years.

[65] Franklin D. Roosevelt to Royal Copeland, February 23, 1931, Copeland MSS.
[66] Clark to Coolidge, November 11, 1931, Clark MSS.

☆ ☆ ☆ ☆ ☆

4

THE KISSING BEE

MUCH OF THE POLITICAL HISTORY of the Hoover administration has been written by members of the cabinet, friends, or the president himself. Soon after leaving the White House, Herbert Hoover sought to document the story of his four years. He sponsored the publishing of William Starr Myers' two-volume edition of his *State Papers* and his financial adviser, Edgar Rickard, saw to it that libraries received copies.[1] Myers also collaborated with White House political strategist Walter H. Newton on a documented narrative of the Hoover years. Cabinet members Ray Lyman Wilbur and Arthur M. Hyde contributed another record of *The Hoover Policies* and by 1937 the administration had tirelessly stated its defense. It only remained for the president to publish his memoirs in 1952 for the Hoover case to be complete. Adulatory biographers have written in abundance about the Quaker president. There are only two attempts by academic historians to draw a complete picture of the Hoover presidency and one of them relies on these published materials and is sympathetic to the man in the White House.[2]

The standard theme in the history of the president's relationship with Congress is one of conflict. Congress, it is said, was "hostile," "antagonistic," and "obstructionist" toward Hoover.[3] When, ac-

[1] See Hoover correspondence in Myers MSS.
[2] Harris G. Warren, *Herbert Hoover and the Great Depression* (New York, 1959). A more balanced history is Albert U. Romasco, *The Poverty of Abundance: Hoover, the Nation, the Depression* (New York, 1965).
[3] Let these examples suffice for the rest. For the conflict thesis, see Arthur

cording to this version, Congress panicked and attempted to institute a potpourri of programs, the president, fearing governmental tampering with the economy would hinder recovery, preferred voluntary succor to the unemployed to federal "doles." The 72nd Congress is seen as a donnybrook: the Democrats were forced to accept much of the Hoover program—the debt moratorium, the Reconstruction Finance Corporation, and the Glass-Steagall act—because they had no program of their own. But during most of the 72nd Congress, it is claimed, the Democrats played politics, killing the manufacturers' sales tax which would have balanced the budget, pushing unwanted tariff revision, and sending Hoover a gigantic pork barrel bill he was compelled to veto. The Democrats have been charged with attempting to capitalize politically on hard times; and it has been suggested that they deliberately shook business confidence at a time when the economy was going through a resurgence because recovery would impair their chances in 1932.

This interpretation of Hoover's relation to Congress has some merits but omits much of what really happened. The fact is that Hoover had the cooperation of an acquiescent Congress, especially of its Democratic leaders, for over a hundred days after the beginning of the 72nd Congress. From December, 1931, to March, 1932, with the support of the Democratic leadership, the administration rode roughshod over wispy opposition, securing passage of its entire program. Not until mid-March did the House Democratic membership revolt over the sales tax. And even with House Democrats demonstrating their independence, the president manipulated legislation to his satisfaction with the assistance of Democratic leaders. To condemn the 72nd Congress as hostile, destructive, and uncooperative does a disservice to those who helped to establish the Hoover legislative record.

To Hoover's good fortune, almost one-fourth of the membership of the 72nd Congress were novices; lacking prior congressional experience, they were willing followers. "I knew very few

S. Link, *American Epoch: A History of the United States Since 1890* (New York, 1967), pp. 379, 381; Paul Conkin, *The New Deal* (New York, 1967), pp. 25–26.

of the Congressmen," commented Henry Stimson after meeting a group; "they are almost entirely a new lot." The turnover in Congress made it difficult to ascertain the mood of the membership or predict its response to events. Nevertheless, a veteran solon like David Walsh forecast that "the next Congress will be conservative. . . . It is now apparent that the depression is longer than anyone dared to predict and that recovery will be slow and certain but not precipitate. In view of these conditions a spirit of caution and conservatism has become noticeable among the public men of the country."[4] Inexperience and apprehension were on the side of Hoover's legislative leadership.

With the onset of the third winter of the depression, few people dared to suggest that the long-awaited corner would be turned soon. The impact of the depression on the public was difficult to gauge. Obviously the president had suffered politically; Chief Justice Charles Evans Hughes speculated that if Coolidge had run again in 1928 and Hoover had remained as Secretary of Commerce, the people and the Republicans would look upon Hoover as a potential deliverer from suffering.[5] The American people seemed lethargic. "Beyond the Potomac there is silence," Anne O'Hare McCormick wrote. "The politician in power is left in a vacuum; no life-giving breath of popular enthusiasm or popular indignation, no current of that famous energy that propels the American dynamo, refreshes the devitalized atmosphere of government." Mrs. McCormick seemed to speak the question in the minds of many people: "Is America growing old?"

> Have we—the young adventurers, the Innocents Abroad, the
> pioneers, the buccaneers, the racketeers—slumped into that sad
> maturity which submits to events, accepts the universe? . . . The
> Great American nation is to be discovered in an attitude as elder-
> ly and unenterprising as that of Mr. Micawber. Our inertia, if
> it is that, is no more physical than his; never were we more in
> motion, but aimlessly, going around in circles.

[4] Diary, January 26, 1932, Stimson MSS; Boston *Post*, May 6, 1931, in scrapbooks, D. I. Walsh MSS.
[5] Diary, December 20, 1931, Stimson MSS

It is not even mental; we think in circles, too, grow wrinkles trying to figure out the lost quantity in equations that yesterday seemed so simple. The lull is suspense. Un-American as it sounds, we are all waiting for something to turn up. We look a little like that fat comedian in the movies who sits in heavy contemplation after he gets tangled in his own gear.

She concluded that Americans were becoming timid because they were losing an assertiveness which sprang from brash optimism. "Faith in the American formula of prosperity is wavering," she said.[6]

Walter Lippmann agreed with Mrs. McCormick that theirs was a nation in sustained anticipation. "This belief in the automatic restoration of prosperity has made us for the time being a nation of fatalists," he said.

> We have told ourselves in a thousand public statements that if winter comes spring cannot be far behind. . . . The chief effect of all this prophesying and waiting for a turn has been to divert the mind of the American people from honest consideration of their problems, and to substitute for the stern business of facing the facts the wholly frivolous business of fortune-telling. Ineluctably this fatalism affected legislators who waited for leadership rather than providing it. The mood for Congress to follow the President has been set.

Lippman believed that Americans had become demoralized, "so demoralized that we look upon the assembling of the next Congress not as an opportunity for collective action, but as a nightmare."[7]

Indeed, congressmen were awaiting and dreading the 72nd Congress with all the unpleasantness and aimlessness which it promised. "I do not anticipate the work of the session with any degree of pleasure," Senator John B. Kendrick of Wyoming wrote; ". . . there are strong indications that it will be a good session for the Irish, that is, one in which a man can have any kind

[6] Anne O'Hare McCormick, *The World at Home* (New York, 1956), pp. 72–76, 82.
[7] Walter Lippmann, *Interpretations, 1931–1932* (New York, 1933), p. 6.

of a fight he wants and is looking for." William E. Borah agreed: "We are going to have a hard-working session this winter and also, I suppose, a harassing session."[8] Several points of contention were expected at the outset. The House anticipated a drive by progressives and Democrats to liberalize the rules on extracting bills from committees; in the Senate, progressives threatened to block the re-election of George Moses as president pro tempore. Communist-led "hunger marchers" picketed the Capitol as Congress convened on December 7 and talk of dissension and threats of conflict were heard in the cloakrooms.

In the Democratically controlled House, Garner's election as Speaker went off without a hitch. But in the Republican Senate, progressives bolted over Moses' candidacy for Senate president pro tem. The insurgents had been smoldering ever since Moses' "Sons of the Wild Jackass" remark and some held Moses responsible for the "Grocer Norris" incident of 1930. Moses, with his usual lack of tact, raised their ire by threatening to vote for Democratic organization of the Senate in order to thwart GOP progressives from chairmanships of committees.[9] Without agreeing on one candidate, progressives hindered the Senate from obtaining a majority for president pro tem. The progressives split their votes between candidates not endorsed by either party and switched from day to day.[10] All other business had to be suspended since it required unanimous consent to bypass this organizational vote. Every day until the Christmas recess the Senate voted for its president pro tem; progressives permitted no other business save the moratorium debate. Finally, on January 6, 1932, after twenty-five ballots, Moses agreed to continue in his post

[8] John B. Kendrick to C. P. Arnold, December 4, 1931, Kendrick MSS; William E. Borah to Arthur Capper, September 21, 1931, Capper MSS.

[9] Progressives holding committee chairmanships were Borah of Foreign Relations, Norris of Judiciary, Couzens of Interstate Commerce, Howell of Claims, Johnson of Commerce, Frazier of Indian Affairs, La Follette of Manufactures, and Nye of Public Lands.

[10] New York *Times*, November 22, 25, December 4, 1931. McNary observed that the Moses candidacy had generated "a lot of bad feeling" in the Senate, but Tom Walsh expected the rebellion "to come to naught." Charles L. McNary to John H. McNary, December 15, 1931, McNary MSS; Thomas J. Walsh to J. T. Carroll, December 1, 1931, T. J. Walsh MSS.

under an 1890 resolution which permitted the president pro tem to serve until his successor was chosen.[11]

Vituperative partisanship also erupted on the House floor on December 10. Led by Frank Oliver of New York City, Democrats taunted Republicans for a variety of political misfortunes. He taunted Hoover and branded Republican congressional leaders as hypocritical in their support of Hoover while his fellow Democrats egged him on. His abusive address sounded like a declaration of war; "our enmity is open and above board," he needlessly added. Amid the turmoil Fiorello La Guardia dramatically rose to admonish the House for its "poor start"; he begged lawmakers "to cut out politics now, get down to business, and do something for the millions of unemployed people."[12] Yet it was all rhetoric which made good newspaper copy and meant little. Lest the GOP forget that this session preceded a national election and the Democrats were the opposition party, the latter felt compelled to periodically hector the administration. In no way did the Democratic attacks bode a session filled with actual party strife. These outbursts were only public reminders that, although the Democrats seconded Republican legislation, they reserved the right to carp at the administration.

The savage oratory acted as a catharsis for the politicians. "The air of truculent self-righteousness with which so many of the Congressmen are expressing themselves can perhaps be explained as an eruption of accumulated discontent," said Walter Lippmann. Later Hoover would ascribe the parliamentary assault to a determined malevolence to destroy his program. Lippmann, however, did not explain it in such simplistic terms nor did he fault the legislators: "Congress has not been allowed to meet for nine months. The Administration has kept it in idleness brooding impotently upon the hard times and upon all manner of reasons to

---

11 New York *Times*, December 11, 13, 14, 16, 17, 18, 20, 21, 1931, January 5, 7, 1932; see Key Pittman to John W. Davis, December 17, 1931, Pittman MSS, and Fred L. Israel, *Nevada's Key Pittman* (Lincoln, Nebr., 1963), p. 72, for a Democratic view of the fight.

12 *Congressional Record*, 72nd Cong., 1st sess., pp. 340–43; New York *Times*, December 11, 1931.

explain them. The safety valve of popular government has been fastened down, and now that it is released the pent-up angers are exploding. The effect is disconcerting. It works cruelly upon the President. It is greatly damaging to the good name of the country. It is destructive to the already weakened fabric of faith and credit among the peoples."[13] Thus, in December the beginning of a New Congress pulled the cork on a fermenting brew; it remained to be seen whether the exploding cork would be more memorable than any nectar in the bottle.

Notwithstanding the partisan din, the two-party leadership had made it amply clear that this would, for various reasons, be a productive session. Indeed, Congress had been chafing to get at an issue which Hoover had raised back at the beginning of the summer—a moratorium on debts owed the United States by the European powers from the world war. "The purpose of this action," Hoover declared on June 20, 1931, "is to give the forthcoming year to economic recovery and to help free the recuperative forces already in motion in the United States from retarding influences from abroad."[14] The postponement of debt payments for the fiscal year beginning July 1 was designed to relieve the economic burdens of both the United States and her European debtors, particularly Germany. Americans, the president reasoned, could glean some confidence from their ability to grant the extension of time; also, Europeans would have more money with which to purchase our goods. Hoover preferred this trade stimulant to government assistance to the economy.

The moratorium also served as a psychological stimulant for the nation. Stimson described the administration mood at the beginning of June as "pure indigo," but the moratorium had an exhilarating effect on Washington. At the time it seemed to be the ingenious move that everybody had expected from Hoover to reverse the downward spiral. "It looks as if the corner all of us have been seeking, is being turned," declared Arthur Capper; "al-

[13] Lippmann, p. 159.
[14] William Starr Myers (ed.), *The State Papers and Other Public Writings of Herbert Hoover* (Garden City, N.Y., 1934), I: 592.

ready the immediate effects, the encouragement, the saner outlook ahead, coming as a direct result of the moratorium, are
apparent." "We can look for a better condition," affirmed
sanguine Simeon Fess. The moratorium won ardent bipartisan
backing. Mississippi's Pat Harrison hailed it as a "proper and constructive move" and lavishly praised Hoover for having the "highest motives." Even some progressives like La Follette were
generous with their encomiums for the moratorium.[15]

The press sensed a turning point in the hitherto bleak history
of the Hoover administration. Saluting the move as a "brave
and admirable beginning," the *Nation*, rarely a friend of Hoover,
estimated that "it probably constitutes the most far-reaching and
the most praiseworthy step taken by an American President since
the treaty of peace." Many newspapers acclaimed the moratorium
as a brilliant political move. The Memphis *Commercial-Appeal*
believed that the Democrats had been dealt a setback; both the
Richmond *Times-Dispatch* and the Norfolk *Virginian-Pilot* suspected that Hoover had strengthened himself considerably and
would be "a marvelously rehabilitated candidate" in 1932. Arthur
Sears Henning in the Chicago *Tribune* detected Republican
leaders "fairly bursting with elation." Another pundit, Frank R.
Kent of the Democratic Baltimore *Sun*, admitted that Hoover
critics like himself were "for the time being in a condition of
suspended animation"; the president had made "the picture of a
cowering, dismayed and bewildered Hoover which the extremists
have been so busily painting seem more or less ridiculous."[16]

Because Hoover was constitutionally obligated to seek Congress' approval of the moratorium, in June he took the unusual
step of informally polling all congressmen by telegram to secure
their temporary assent. By June 20 he had the assured support of
thirty-nine ranking senators and representatives with more cer-

[15] Diary, June 2, 1931, Stimson MSS; "A Moratorium Is Not Cancellation,"
Capper's Farmer, undated, in scrapbook, Capper MSS; Simeon Fess to Charles
Sumner Fess, June 25, 1931, Fess MSS; New York *Times*, June 21, 24, 27, 1931.
[16] "President Hoover's Great Action," *Nation*, CXXXIII (July 1, 1931): 4;
"Political Effects of the Hoover Adventure," *Literary Digest*, August 1, 1931,
pp. 5–6.

tain to follow. The moratorium would take effect on July 1, the next payment was due on December 15, and Congress would not officially act on the postponement until December. Although Hoover had secured Congress' unofficial endorsement, the president discovered two dismaying facts: first, the Democrats gave their approval more readily than his own party and second, the moratorium had touched off a wave of demands for a special session of Congress.

When Hoover first decided to go ahead with the moratorium, he began by sounding out those senators still in the capital in June. Tom Walsh surprised the administration by agreeing with Hoover's view of the national interest. But Jim Watson was unhappy over the idea and flabbergasted Hoover. "It would be pretty hard for me to approach the Democrats, if I cannot get control of my own party," said the glum Chief Executive. Nevertheless, the White House continued to send out feelers. The president called Bernard Baruch who, while not expressing any fervor for the plan, promised to use his influence with Democratic leaders in Congress. Baruch wanted Hoover to have a free hand so that Democrats could not be accused of obstruction. Pat Harrison, ranking Democrat on the Senate Finance Committee, received the next call and gave his almost zealous approval. Only Joe Robinson and John Garner were noncommittal at first, but both assented after talking with Baruch. Thus, by July, Hoover had assurances of Democratic backing and even Simeon Fess was gratified by their attitude.[17]

But several congressmen wanted Hoover to convene Congress early. During White House conferences on the moratorium, Hoover brushed aside certain Democratic suggestions for a special session of Congress. Some Democrats like Harrison merely recommended that Congress meet fifteen to thirty days prior to its original date. Progressives like La Follette were eager to have Congress return at once. Even a Brahmin Republican like Rep-

[17] Diary, June 15, 18, 19, 20, Stimson mss; Bernard M. Baruch to Walsh, September 29, 1931, T. J. Walsh mss; Bernard M. Baruch, *The Public Years* (New York, 1960), p. 233; New York *Times*, July 11, 1931.

resentative Allen Treadway of the Bay State urged the president to summon Congress early; he argued that Congress would have only seven working days before the December 15 due date for the debt payments and most of that time would be spent organizing the national legislature.[18] Reporters quoted another unnamed Republican as saying that Congress should be called by November 15. Treadway's argument hit its mark and even Reed Smoot admitted that it might take Congress six weeks to dispose of the debt plan, well past the due date for payments which the administration wanted to suspend. However, in the words of a New York *Times* correspondent, "the whole desire of the administration appears to be to delay the 'evil day' as long as possible"; thus, Hoover would not allow Congress to meet before the Constitution required it.[19]

The Old Guard heartily endorsed Hoover's adamant stand against an early meeting of the 72nd Congress. No necessity existed for a special session, Jim Watson said; "the Senate is organized now as much as it ever has been." Republicans were afraid to face the inevitable barrage of relief legislation. House Appropriations Committee Chairman Will R. Wood explained: "You can't convene an extra session to consider one specific thing. Other issues would be bound to enter the picture." "To call Congress into session now," said David Reed of Pennsylvania, "would only encourage the sort of legislative quackery that always makes its appearance at times like the present."[20]

The delay in approval, however, served to build opposition to the moratorium. The aura of good will surrounding the proposal eroded in the intervening five months while isolationists and xenophobes began to articulate opposition sentiments. Hiram Johnson accused international bankers of plotting the wholesale cancellation of the debts; Johnson's old friend, C. K. McClatchy of the Sacramento *Bee*, was thankful that "there are still some Johnsons to stand like the Rock of Gibralter against such a betrayal of the

18 New York *Times*, June 21, 24, July 24, 1931.
19 *Ibid.*, June 26, September 17, June 21, 1931.
20 *Ibid.*, June 26, August 21, 1931.

people." A Hearst columnist blamed Hoover for having "thrust this Republic deep into the mire of European politics, and thus for the first time since the Revolutionary War executed a right about face on our foreign policy." Brookhart of Iowa branded it "a very fine Wall Street party" and McKellar of Tennessee saw the hand of Lombard Street in the postponement. James Couzens of Michigan attacked it as "another example of America's dumb diplomacy." John Rankin of Mississippi detected a plot to unload the debts on the American people "and thereby enable those international financiers to more easily collect their private loans abroad." Alabama's Hugo Black believed that Americans were the forgotten people in the administration's schemes. In October, when the initial enthusiasm for the moratorium had worn down, Congressman Byrns correctly observed: "There is a 'show me' attitude on the moratorium."[21]

The administration had to confront the suspicions of many congressmen who saw the moratorium as a Trojan horse for cancellation of the debts. Senators like John Blaine of Wisconsin approved of the moratorium but feared that it would be an opening wedge for cancellation. "On the face of it, I do not find fault with what is proposed," George Norris explained, "but I cannot help but be suspicious that it is a fore-runner for the cancellation of the balance—or at least a major portion of the balance—due us from foreign governments." Norris, in this rare instance, spoke for a widely held sentiment in Congress. Even conservatives like Hiram Bingham and George Moses opposed cancelling the debts and "saddling them on the taxpayers of this country." The respected Will Wood, ranking Republican on the House Appropriations Committee, vowed, "I will never vote for a dollar of cancellation or reduction."[22]

---

[21] "Political Effects of the Hoover Adventure," pp. 5–6; New York *Times*, August 23, October 8, July 8, 26, 29, November 21, June 21, 1931; *Congressional Record*, 72nd Cong., 1st sess., p. 333.

[22] John J. Blaine to Herbert Hoover, June 24, 1931, Blaine MSS; George Norris to J. M. Maher, June 23, to Val J. Peter, June 26, 1931, Norris MSS; New York *Times*, June 9, 1931; Washington *Post*, December 11, 1931.

French Premier Pierre Laval's visit to Washington in late October heightened trepidations that a nullification of obligations was in the works. As the lawmakers girded to prevent any cancellation or reduction, for a brief while it seemed as if even the moratorium had been placed in jeopardy. "The words, moratoriums, reductions, and cancellation all mean the same thing," John Rankin charged. The administration had to watch its step. The GOP tetrarch in the Senate, Jim Watson, warned that "opposition may arise to any program devised to extend the moratorium after next June." Leaders counted eight Democratic senators against the moratorium, although one of them, C. C. Dill, showed a willingness to support it with a provision prohibiting cancellation.[23]

The more Congress debated the moratorium, the more it accused the administration of ulterior motives. Some congressmen scathingly indicted Hoover for not calling Congress earlier if the matter rated their urgent attention. Rankin of Mississippi, who led the assault for the Democrats, tied the issue to unemployment:

> If the President wanted this question taken up, he should have called Congress into session in June. . . . If he had, we might have done something toward relieving unemployment. . . . We are not going to be rushed hastily into action either, and you are not going to get it passed by the fifteenth of December, if you get it passed at all, which I seriously doubt. . . . I am not in favor of a dole. But I am not willing to see men, women, and children starve. You are about to be asked to vote for a dole. Are you willing to give a dole to these international bankers?

From across the aisle Republicans Daniel Reed of New York and James Strong of Kansas shouted "NO!"[24] Had the president sought to deceive Congress? Senator Josiah W. Bailey of North Carolina thought that "the President has not come clean with the Members of Congress. . . . I am here intending to support the Moratorium, and I think, as a matter of honor, I may yet have to

---

[23] New York *Times*, October 27, November 21, December 11, 1931; *Congressional Record*, 72nd Cong., 1st sess., p. 333.
[24] *Congressional Record*, 72nd Cong., 1st sess., p. 334.

do so, but I cannot avoid the suspicion that Mr. Hoover was buncoed, to put the matter lightly, and that he then sand-bagged the Members of Congress."[25]

Hoover began to wonder if the pledges of June would be redeemed in December. When the administration proposed notifying the European powers that failure to meet their payments on the fifteenth of December would not constitute default, congressional leaders rebuffed it; the following day Hoover backtracked and dropped the proposal. With his support apparently dwindling against more vocal opposition, Hoover panicked and threatened to release the names of those congressmen who had committed themselves to the moratorium during the summer. But Henry Stimson and Ogden Mills, afraid that Congress would interpret it as blackmail, talked the president out of this questionable maneuver.[26]

Many isolationists, their memories of the pre-world war arms race fresh, strongly doubted that Europe intended to use money that would have gone for the debt payments for trade with the United States. "It is unthinkable," Jim Watson declared, "that the American people should shoulder Europe's debts to enable those nations to build navies and equip armies for future warfare, literally using our money for that purpose." Both sides of the House cheered when Republican Hamilton Fish declared that Europe wanted the United States to pay for the war. "Reduction of armaments in Europe," David Reed declared, "ought to precede . . . reducing the war debts." William E. Borah advised the Europeans that disarmament would aid recovery sooner than a moratorium. George Norris thought that the Europeans behaved "with poor grace" by expecting suspension of debt payments while they proceeded with their armaments.[27] Thus, the isolationists not only feared conspiracies by foreign powers and American bankers, but

[25] Josiah W. Bailey to Josephus Daniels, December 17, 19, 1931, Daniels MSS.
[26] New York *Times*, December 13, 14, 1931; diary, December 13, 1931, Stimson MSS.
[27] New York *Times*, December 12, October 11, June 21, 1931; Norris to Maher, June 23, to Alex M. Geist, December 31, 1931, Norris MSS. See also Kenneth McKellar to Frederic William Wile, January 13, 1932, McKellar MSS.

they also suspected that the moratorium would encourage the growth of European militarism.

The bipartisan opposition climaxed its attack on Hoover's moratorium on December 15 when Representative Louis T. McFadden of Pennsylvania denounced Hoover as an "Oriental potentate drunk with power" and the moratorium as an "infamous proposal." The House tensed as McFadden, a Republican and rural banker, branded the president an "agent of Germany" and of such international bankers as the Warburgs, and Kuhn, Loeb and Co. The day before John Rankin had dubbed the plan "one of the boldest schemes of financial buccaneering ever attempted," but that attack mellowed before the fury of McFadden's. An Illinois Republican, Burnett M. Chiperfield, challenged McFadden to bring in articles of impeachment against the president, if he believed his own charges, or go marked as the "foul traducer of the character of an honest man." "Shame! Shame!" cried Florence Kahn, a California Republican, shaking her finger at McFadden. However, defenders of the president's honor were scarce in the House and Tammany's John J. O'Connor insisted that Republicans protect the president's name or he would do it himself.[28]

The House spent the next day berating McFadden as Republicans showed a bit more willingness to rise in defense of their party's chief. GOP leaders threatened to cut off the patronage of the errant McFadden. Democrats like William Bankhead of Alabama and Emanuel Celler of Brooklyn denied any sympathy for McFadden, who sat listening to denunciations red-faced and half-smiling.[29]

McFadden, without meaning to do so, had outraged the House and unified it behind the moratorium. Despite the oratory, there had been little doubt that the lower chamber would approve the proposal, but after the McFadden attack the House appeared

[28] Washington *Post*, December 15, 16, 1931; New York *Times*, December 16, 1931. McFadden had a history of advocating radical financial schemes and assailing Treasury officials who disagreed with him.
[29] New York *Times*, December 17, 18, 1931.

anxious to expedite the debt suspension. Ogden Mills helped out by reminding the Ways and Means Committee, without mentioning names, that 276 representatives and sixty-eight senators had pledged themselves to the moratorium; the administration expected those pledges to be fulfilled.[30]

The Ways and Means Committee was prepared to approve the moratorium but Democrats had a surprise for the administration. By an almost straight party vote of 16 to 9, the Committee's Democrats amended the moratorium resolution with a declaration against cancellation or reduction of Europe's debts to the United States. The committee approved the gross resolution, 21 to 4.[31] The amendment was motivated in part by genuine fears that this was a step toward cancellation, in part by resentment at Republican boasting that Hoover's move had saved the western world from economic collapse.[32]

The House wound up its debate on December 18 with administration followers accepting the no-cancellation amendment. In the evening the House voted 318 to 100 for the moratorium, the opposition coming from southern and border state Democrats. The 120 Democrats who voted for the moratorium attested to its bipartisan support.[33] Undoubtedly the Democratic amendment was a mild rebuke to Hoover; the Democrats had challenged the inferred cancellation, not the moratorium.

The Senate, anxious to go home and under administration pressure to act before the Christmas holidays, wasted little time in dealing with the resolution. The Finance Committee took ten minutes to approve the House version, Thomas Gore of Okla-

---

[30] *Ibid.*, December 16, 1931.

[31] The four holdouts against the moratorium were Morgan Sanders of Texas, Clement Dickinson of Missouri, Edward Eslick of Tennessee, and Fred Vinson of Kentucky. The one Republican who voted for the amendment was Frank Crowther of New York. *Ibid.*, December 18, 1931.

[32] *Ibid.*, December 18, 19, 1931; Bascom N. Timmons, *Garner of Texas* (New York, 1948), p. 138.

[33] The lineup was: against, ninety-five Democrats, five Republicans; for, 120 Democrats, 196 Republicans, one Farmer-Laborite. New York *Times*, December 19, 1931.

homa and Tom Connally of Texas casting the only votes against it. The Senate debate repeated most of the arguments heard in the House: Walsh of Massachusetts scolded the White House for not calling a special session and "Puddler Jim" Davis warned the chamber to think more of America's needs. "Uncle Sam is the world's greatest Santa Claus," Davis declared. Hiram Johnson protested what he called "legislation by telegrams." Progressives stretched debate out to three days with verbal assaults on the administration before the Senate ratified the resolution late in the evening of December 22, 69 to 12; thanks to the prohibition on cancellation inserted by the House, the opposition received fewer votes than the fifteen or twenty that the administration had expected it to muster. As the Senate prepared to recess for the holiday, Borah and others pleaded with the solons to convene again on December 28 to consider proposals for depression relief, but the Senate rejected the motion, 39 to 33, and voted to take its customary two-week vacation.[34]

Although Hoover had secured the moratorium, the no-cancellation amendment made it appear a Pyrrhic victory for the administration. "I had a glorious fight here on the moratorium," Hiram Johnson boasted to Harold Ickes, "one of those losing fights which is won." Congress had given the president what he wanted but had effectively demonstrated its displeasure with the manner in which it was handled. Walter Lippmann observed, "The moratorium which was so popular in June had become so unpopular in December." Lippmann blamed the change on the continued deterioration of economic conditions: "Had pledges not been obtained last June the moratorium would almost certainly have been defeated in December. . . . For Americans . . . there is no longer any magic in moratoria."[35] Had Hoover sought approval in June from a special session, much of the bitterness

[34] *Ibid.*, December 20, 21, 22, 23, 1931; Washington *Post*, December 23, 1931. Of the twelve votes against the debt resolution, six came from farm bloc Republicans, the rest from Democrats.
[35] Hiram Johnson to Harold Ickes, December 28, 1931, Johnson MSS; Lippmann, pp. 167–68.

might have been avoided. Still, in two weeks, Congress had organized and complied with Hoover's request.

Hoover emerged from his qualified moratorium success determined to secure congressional approval of his program for broadening credit facilities. He first publicly broached his plan for creating a Reconstruction Finance Corporation in his State of the Union address on December 8 when he expressed concern for "the continuing credit paralysis." Four days later he issued a twelve-point program of recovery which contained an urgent appeal for bipartisan support. The seventh point called for the RFC. Quite obviously the president deemed it a cornerstone for building economic recovery.[36]

Hoover was a very reluctant proponent of the RFC. Gerald D. Nash claims that "for four months during the fall of 1931 he successfully opposed the establishment of a governmental institution such as the RFC, and assented only when he was no longer able to withstand the pressures for such an agency." Nash's argument is keyed to Hoover's initial rejection of Eugene Meyer's proposal for RFC. Meyer, its first promoter, modelled it on the War Finance Corporation, the government-spawned organization designed to finance industrial expansion in the war effort which he had directed from its inception in 1918. Revived in 1919, WFC sustained American capital through the economic difficulties of the early twenties. On September 21, 1931, Meyer urged Hoover to call a special session of Congress to revive the WFC with expanded powers. Hoover preferred creating a private credit pool with funds voluntarily subscribed by bankers and insurance men.[37]

Hoover endeavored to have bankers voluntarily loosen credit to permit the expansion of the economy but he quickly learned that, as he told Senator Capper, "it is difficult to secure cooperation from the financial institutions of the country who have lit-

[36] Myers, II: 46–47, 50.
[37] Gerald D. Nash, "Herbert Hoover and the Origins of the Reconstruction Finance Corporation," *Mississippi Valley Historical Review*, XLVI (December, 1959): 455, 461–64; Hoover to Eugene Meyer, September 8, 1931, Box 17, Richey MSS.

tle cohesion and little leadership." On October 4, 1931, Hoover met with leading New York bankers at the home of Andrew Mellon; present were Charles E. Mitchell, chairman of the board of the National City Bank, Thomas W. Lamont, senior partner of J. P. Morgan and Company, and William C. Potter, president of the Guaranty Trust Company. President Hoover requested the financiers to create a national credit institution capitalized at $500 million which Hoover deemed essential to public confidence. The bankers and the president struck a bargain: they would create the credit pool as Hoover requested and he would ask Congress for a new WFC, an extension of rediscount eligibility in the Federal Reserve System, and a strengthened Federal Farm Loan Bank System.[38] The agreement marked a defeat for Hoover's principles of voluntary cooperation. He had excluded the federal government from relief and now resignedly had capitulated to the bankers' demands for federal aid. The realization that capital did not share his convictions on the virtues of voluntarism discouraged the president.

Even within his own cabinet Hoover could not extract cooperation from bankers. In September, hearing that three or four million dollars had been raised by private sources to save the Bank of Pittsburgh, Hoover asked Andrew Mellon, himself a Pittsburgh banker, to contribute a million dollars to the emergency fund. Mellon refused, bitterly angering the president. He could hardly expect voluntarism by other bankers if his own Secretary of the Treasury failed him.[39] By October, all alternatives to federal aid to capital had been exhausted.

Although Hoover based his opposition to a new WFC on the principle of voluntarism, he also emphasized the private credit pool because it would not require congressional action. Hoover had been able to get moratorium approval without a special session of Congress, but he could not ignore the appropriation function

[38] Hoover to Capper, October 14, 1931, Capper MSS; diary, October 5, 6, 1931, Stimson MSS; George Harrison to Hoover, October 7, 1931, G. L. Harrison MSS; Hoover to Harrison, October 5, 1931, Container 1–E/146, Hoover MSS.
[39] Diary, September 22, 1931, Stimson MSS.

of Congress in reviving the WFC. Stimson in September noted
that Hoover had decided upon an activist role for government in
finance and had plans for lending capital to banks and insurance
corporations. But when the president broached the idea of a new
WFC to congressional leaders in early October, his worst fears
materialized; although they approved it, they insisted Hoover call
Congress into special session. Only with Congress scheduled to
convene in December did Hoover feel the moment was ripe to
advance the RFC idea which Meyer had promoted for months.[40]

After months of delay, Hoover suddenly moved with great
alacrity. On December 16 he told six House Republican leaders
that he wanted quick approval of the RFC. Meanwhile, Senate
hearings proceeded rapidly in spite of minor and technical opposition which retarded the bill's progress. Notwithstanding administration pronouncements underlining the urgent and bipartisan
nature of the RFC bill, the Senate Banking and Currency Committee did not approve it by Christmas. The president, unhappy
over the two-week holiday recess, sent Congress a message early
in January asking prompt passage.[41] But Congress had waited
thirteen months for the opportunity to deliberate and would not
be rushed into precipitate action now.

Some senators feared that the RFC was a plot to use public
money to correct the mistakes of the bankers. Smith Brookhart
of Iowa shouted at Eugene Meyer, "The further you seem to go
with your plans the further we get in the depression." When the
bill emerged from committee on January 5, it contained several
amendments, most of which were the handiwork of Democrats
Carter Glass of Virginia and Robert J. Bulkley of Ohio and Re-

40 Nash, pp. 464–66; diary, September 29, 1931, Stimson MSS. Furthermore,
Nash declares, "It was not until December 4 . . . that the President was reported
to have made the decision to ask for a revival of the WFC," but on October 6,
the day after his meeting with Meyer, he gave out a press statement which included a vow to recommend a new WFC. Nash's statement that "a Democratic
Congress . . . had to overcome the opposition of a Republican President to secure
. . . the re-establishment of the WFC" is without substantiation. Nash, pp. 466,
468; Myers, II: 6.

41 New York *Times*, December 17, 20, 21, 1931; Myers, II: 102–4; Lawrence
H. Chamberlain, *The President, Congress and Legislation* (New York, 1946),
pp. 289–90.

The Kissing Bee

publican James Couzens of Michigan. When the Senate leadership requested unanimous consent to place the bill at the top of the Senate calendar, John Blaine of Wisconsin temporarily objected to the sudden hurry after months of inactivity; besides, the bill would not help those who needed help most—the unemployed. Only the bankers would be helped, Blaine declared, "the very men who have to a large extent brought on the present depression...."[42]

Despite this visible hostility, the debate was uninspiring except for an urban challenge. New York's Royal Copeland proposed that RFC loan powers be broadened to include loans to municipal governments. New York City's mayor, Jimmy Walker, had asked for the amendment after being unable to secure a loan from bankers to cover the city's relief program. Frederic Walcott of Connecticut, Hoover's good friend managing the RFC bill in the Senate, opposed the amendment because, he said, it would require four or five times the amount of capital then provided for the corporation. C. C. Dill of Washington, Wagner of New York, and Lewis of Illinois joined Copeland in supporting the amendment, but it went down to defeat, 45 to 28, Democrats and progressives voting for it.[43] On January 11 the Senate approved the RFC overwhelmingly, 63 to 8, five Democrats and three progressives opposing it.[44]

The House debate was livelier but still unimaginative. La Guardia dubbed the RFC a "millionaire's dole" and McFadden declared that the RFC was being created for the "purpose of helping a gang of financial looters to cover up their tracks." Thirty-three amendments were proposed in the House but only three passed,

[42] New York *Times*, December 9, 19, 1931, January 6, 7, 1932; Chamberlain, pp. 290–91; *Congressional Record*, 72nd Cong., 1st sess., p. 1350.
[43] The only senator from the urban East to vote for the amendment besides the New Yorkers was Marcus Coolidge of Massachusetts. Surprisingly, Walsh of the Bay State voted against it. Southerners and Westerners made up the bulk of the pro-urban vote.
[44] New York *Times*, January 10, 11, 12, 1932; *Congressional Record*, 72nd Cong., 1st sess., p. 1583. The eight "nays" came from progressives Blaine, Brookhart, and Norris and Democrats Sam Bratton of New Mexico, William Bulow of South Dakota, Tom Connally of Texas, George McGill of Kansas, and Elmer Thomas of Oklahoma.

none of them of prime importance. Among the amendments beaten was a renewed effort to permit the RFC to give loans to the cities, as proposed by Adolph Sabath of Chicago. On January 15 the House voted cloture despite scattered protests of "gag rule"; by 335 to 55 the House approved the RFC, the small minority being comprised of Southerners and Midwesterners, Democrats and progressives. House and Senate versions differed, requiring some compromises by both bodies as well as concessions by the administration. However, by January 22 both houses accepted a common bill with unprecedented speed; there was "hardly a ripple of opposition," a New York *Times* correspondent noted.[45] Congress had given the RFC $500 million for loans in relief of banks, insurance companies, and railroads and permitted it to borrow up to $1 billion.

Although there was little discussion of the implications of the RFC, occasionally during the debate somebody demonstrated an awareness that this departure made the federal government a source of capital for private enterprise in peacetime. George Norris, who confessed that he was "dazed" by what was taking place, chided the administration: "I have been called a socialist, a bolshevik, a communist, and a lot of other terms of a similar nature, but in the wildest flights of my imagination I never thought of such a thing as putting the Government into business as far as this bill would put it in." The extent of the introduction of government influence over such a vital area of capitalism worried many people. "State capitalism in Russia is held to be reprehensible," said the St. Louis *Post-Dispatch;* "is the United States to engage in the same practice itself?" Representative Homer C. Parker of Georgia branded the RFC "the most decided step toward communism any civilized government has even taken with the possible exception of Russia."[46] Yet Parker and others overlooked Wall Street's desire for this "communism"; indeed, the RFC could

---

[45] New York *Times*, January 12, 13, 14, 16, 23, 1932.
[46] *Congressional Record*, 72nd Cong., 1st sess., p. 1703; "Borrowing Billions to Turn the Tide," *Literary Digest*, January 30, 1932, pp. 7–8; New York *Times*, January 22, 1932.

as easily have represented a turn to the right as well as the left, a turn to Italy as well as Russia.

Of course, the RFC was inspired by no political philosophy, only expediency. Defenders justified the RFC by pointing to the extraordinary conditions which had necessitated it. The circumstances required expediency, said Henry B. Steagall, the House banking expert from Alabama: "In such a situation we instinctively seize upon and utilize whatever method is most available and offers assurance of speediest success." At a time when banks were failing at an alarming rate, Steagall considered the RFC a "quasi-guarantee for depositors" because it would restore capital and confidence in banks.[47]

Any criticism of the RFC acted as a counterpoint to the speed and unanimity with which Congress had created the corporation. Many congressmen put aside doubts and annoyances to approve a measure that basically offended them. Progressives and urban Democrats were bothered that the unemployed would receive no relief except for what trickled down from big business. Farm bloc representatives such as Senator Peter Norbeck resented the fact that banks and railroads, opponents of federal aid to agriculture because it "put the government in business," now clamored for government relief for themselves. Several Democrats like Josiah Bailey voted for it simply because their leaders had committed themselves to it and they wished to avoid the obstructionist tag for Democrats. If some were uneasy because they suspected that businessmen would use it to bolster stock prices, they were probably correct in many instances. (Roy Chapin, president of Hudson Motors, hoped the RFC would improve the market value of his bonds.)[48]

Stated plainly, the RFC was intended to give credit to credit-giving facilities. However, as Hoover knew beforehand, this would not automatically free the flow of capital. He had sought

---

[47] New York *Times*, January 24, 1932.
[48] Gilbert C. Fite, "Peter Norbeck: Prairie Statesman," *University of Missouri Studies*, XXII (1948): 172; John R. Moore, "Josiah W. Bailey of North Carolina and the New Deal, 1931–1941," Ph.D. dissertation, Duke University, 1962, p. 64; Roy Chapin to George W. Tiedeman, February 2, 1932, Chapin MSS.

a provision in the RFC for the Federal Reserve Board to liberal-ize rediscount rates on RFC bonds, but the House-Senate con-ferees dropped it. Money had become increasingly tight since the British left the gold standard in 1931 and precipitated a run on gold in New York. The White House rejected the counsel that it should follow the British lead and leave the gold standard; Hoover would not inflate the dollar but he would inflate credit by lowering the Federal Reserve's rediscount rate. The result was the Glass-Steagall bill of February, 1932.

To a degree, Arthur Vandenberg claimed to have performed for the Glass-Steagall bill what Eugene Meyer did for the RFC; he pursued the idea with Hoover. The Republican senator from Michigan fancied himself a leader of a GOP faction whose pol-itics lay somewhere between the Old Guard and the progressives and whose loyalty belonged to Hoover. They sought, Vanden-berg claimed, to "move regular Republicanism a little to 'the left' " and put "pep in regularity." Reporters humorously dubbed them "The Young Turks." The regulars scorned Vandenberg; to tory David Reed, Vandenberg had an uncontrollable itch for publicity. On the other hand, progressive Hiram Johnson con-sidered him a Hoover sycophant, "one of the inner circle of A. K. Inc." Both may have been correct.[49]

According to Vandenberg, he first suggested lowering the Federal Reserve's rediscount rate to Hoover during a three-day stay at the president's Rapidan retreat in July, 1931. At that time, Henry M. Robinson, Los Angeles banker and good friend of Hoover's, strongly disagreed with Vandenberg, but Hoover lis-tened quietly. The Michigan senator developed his plan during August and found bankers generally hostile, with the solitary ex-ception of Roy A. Young, a governor of the Reserve Board in

[49] Thomas L. Stokes, *Chip Off My Shoulder* (Princeton, N.J., 1940), pp. 294–95; "Chronology of the 'Young Turk' Movement," Scrapbook 2, Vanden-berg MSS; diary, December 13, 1931, Stimson MSS; Johnson to C. K. McClatchy, April 24, to Ickes, December 7, 1932, Johnson MSS. It should be noted that Van-denberg's loyalty to Hoover was not uncritical and unswerving. For example, see "The Parker Vote," May 7, 1930, Scrapbook 2, and "Just One More of Those Little Hoover Mistakes," November 28, 1930, Scrapbook 3, Vanden-berg MSS.

Boston, whom Hoover respected as "able, courageous and cooperative." Young had opposed increasing the rediscount rate in 1929, and in 1931 he agreed with Vandenberg on lowering it; Young's encouragement probably was a turning point for Vandenberg. Vandenberg discussed his idea with anyone who would listen, whether it was Eugene Meyer or a Michigan realtors' convention. The only mistake Vandenberg made was recommending to Hoover that he call a special session of Congress in September to consider the proposal. If Hoover would not do this for the moratorium or the RFC, he certainly would not for Vandenberg's scheme. Nevertheless, Vandenberg talked with Hoover on October 6 and left feeling that the president had come over part way to his viewpoint. In fact, although Vandenberg may not have wielded the greatest influence, Hoover's press release that day committed him to asking Congress for additional "liquidity to the assets of the banks" by the Federal Reserve.[50]

Apparently Hoover gave priority to ratification of the moratorium and the creation of the RFC; although Vandenberg received little encouragement from Hoover in December, the president could not ignore the need to give failing banks additional liquidity and thereby stimulate construction and other enterprises. On December 9 Vandenberg introduced two bills designed to accomplish his ends and carried on fruitless discussions with the Banking and Currency Committee for the rest of the month. Senators Glass, Couzens, and others displayed distinct antipathy to the idea. When Congress did not liberalize reserve rates in the RFC bill, Hoover sent for Vandenberg and urged him to push his bills. Vandenberg conferred on January 30 with Ogden Mills, Eugene Meyer, Charles Dawes, and George Harrison on administration strategy. Meanwhile, Hoover lined up Jim Watson behind his banking proposals.

Securing the cooperation of Carter Glass proved more difficult.

[50] "Chronology of Banking Bill," Scrapbook 3, Vandenberg MSS; Hoover, *The Great Depression*, pp. 16–18; Myers, II: 6; Vandenberg to Hoover, September 10, 23, October 7, Hoover to Vandenberg, September 15, 25, October 8, 1931, Container 1–L/310, Hoover MSS; "Carter Glass" folder, Box 14, Richey MSS.

The Virginian enjoyed the title of "Father of the Federal Reserve," for his part in the authorship of the Federal Reserve Act of 1913 while a member of the House Finance Committee. Appointed to be Secretary of the Treasury in late 1918 and elected to the Senate in 1920, Glass, with the aid of economist H. Parker Willis, built the somewhat inflated reputation of a man who had more knowledge of the intricacies of banking than any other American politician.[51] He was an unabashed nineteenth-century conservative. The small, frail-looking septuagenarian deplored "mobocracy . . . the disgrace of this era."[52] Hoover found Glass, like most Democratic conservatives, "a cooperative man" except when partisan politics interfered. Knowing that Glass had the confidence of all conservatives irrespective of party and that few dared to challenge his command of banking, the White House shrewdly desired to make him a sponsor of the proposed measure.[53]

Besides, the chairman of the Senate's Banking and Currency Committee, Peter Norbeck, was weak on the subject. The South Dakotan had little technical knowledge of banking and owed his position to seniority. He acknowledged his deficiencies but kept the chairmanship as an honor to his state which he could not properly refuse. He had made his fortune drilling oil and gas wells and drew his knowledge of big finance from Louis Brandeis' *Other People's Money*. "I really begin to think I am fortunate that part of the stuff goes over my head," Norbeck once wrote; "I do not understand it at all. If I did, maybe I wouldn't sleep." He deferred to Glass's judgment on major banking matters, as indeed most of Congress did.[54]

Glass had been attempting to reform banking practices, but he opposed liberalizing credit when he thought too much credit

[51] Don Wharton, "Give 'Em Hell, Carter," *Outlook*, CLX (April, 1932): 219–20; Gentleman at the Keyhole, "Glass Edges," *Colliers*, April 18, 1931, p. 38.
[52] Undated U.S. Senate memo, "Carter Glass Diary" folder, Box 3, Glass MSS.
[53] Herbert Hoover, *Memoirs: The Cabinet and the Presidency* (New York, 1952), pp. 121–22; Wharton, pp. 219–20. Also, on Glass, see Rixey Smith and Norman Beasley, *Carter Glass: A Biography* (New York, 1939).
[54] Fite, pp. 160, 169–71.

already existed. Hoover continued to bring pressure on Glass, who could not make headway with his own banking bill over the opposition of the bankers, and the senator finally agreed to substitute the administration bill for his own. The White House also persuaded Henry Steagall of Alabama to introduce the bill and guide it through the House. Thus, the Glass-Steagall bill became the property of Democrats, although few people doubted its GOP inspiration.[55]

The press expected quick passage of the Glass-Steagall bill if only because of the widespread ignorance of banking in Congress.[56] Moreover, with scores of banks failing around the nation, the administration had fear on its side. Anything which might save the banks would be welcome. This combination of an administration-promoted bill with a Democratic label, amidst an atmosphere of urgency, helped secure passage of the Glass-Steagall bill in two weeks.

In an urgent mood comparable to wartime, Congress put everything aside for the Glass-Steagall bill. Two days after it was introduced, banking committees in both chambers reported it to the floor. Suspending the rules on February 15, the House debated the bill for several hours and then passed it by a whopping 350 to 15. The enormous majority masked some considerable anger over the secretive manner in which the bill was promoted. "I am tired of listening to a lot of conferees saying, 'If you only knew what I know,'" Joe Shannon of Missouri declared. "Well, why in the devil should not we know it and everybody else in America know it." Tom Amlie of Wisconsin voted against the Glass-Steagall bill because "we are simply told that the facts are so dangerous that we may not hear them, but we must take the word of the committee membership for it." As Newton Baker correctly observed, Congress "responded as the result of terror

[55] "Chronology of Banking Bill," Scrapbook 3, Vandenberg MSS; "Carter Glass" folder, Box 14, Richey MSS; William Starr Myers and Walter H. Newton, *The Hoover Administration: A Documented Narrative* (New York, 1936), pp. 165, 171–72; Hoover, *The Great Depression*, pp. 116–17; New York *Times*, February 11, 1932.
[56] New York *Times*, February 11, 12, 1932.

rather than conviction." Many lawmakers were unhappy over what they characterized as a "gag rule" on debate in an atmosphere of impending disaster.[57]

Bipartisanship became the watchword in Congress. The Senate passed a slightly different version on February 19, 46 to 18, and on February 27, both houses approved the Glass-Steagall bill without opposition. Although it had been dubbed "the administration bill," Republican leaders congratulated themselves for parliamentary discipline. Joe Robinson insisted that it had been a true bipartisan effort and resented GOP claims. His colleagues wondered if they had fallen into a trap where the Republicans captured all the credit for bipartisanship and any sincere objections by Democrats were attributed to political motivation.[58]

The president signed the bill on February 27 and in a prepared statement congratulated Congress for its expeditious "fine spirit of patriotic nonpartisanship." The next day Roy Young called on Vandenberg to compliment him on his role and, as he put it, "to chuckle with the Senator" over the outcome. Herbert Bayard Swope, Bernard Baruch's friend, credited Vandenberg with "zealously and unselfishly" accomplishing its enactment.[59]

At the end of February, opposition to the administration in Congress seemed more vocal than real. Congressmen had put partisanship aside except for occasional and inconsequential outbursts. In the first three months of the 72nd Congress, every important administration measure voted upon passed by a lopsided margin. The president, however, in his memoirs, tells a different story. From the State of the Union address onward, "we were in constant battle against Democratic tactics of sabotage and delay," Hoover wrote; "the country as a whole supported the administration, but the Democratic leaders were set in their determination

---

[57] *Congressional Record*, 72nd Cong., 1st sess., pp. 3983, 3991; Thomas Amlie to W. L. Smith, February 18, 1932, Amlie MSS; New York *Times*, February 15, 1932; Newton Baker to John H. Clarke, February 22, 1932, Baker MSS.

[58] *Congressional Record*, 72nd Cong., 1st sess., pp. 4223–24; New York *Times*, February 19, 20, 1932.

[59] Myers, II: 128; "Chronology of Banking Bill," Scrapbook 3, Herbert Bayard Swope to Vandenberg, February 16, 1932, Vandenberg MSS.

to delay recovery."[60] But an examination of major legislation, such as the ratification of the debt moratorium and the Reconstruction Finance Corporation and Glass-Steagall acts, reveals that the Democrats gave Hoover their fearful assistance, not sabotage and delay.[61]

No matter what rancor occurred on or off the floors of both houses, an "era of cooperation" had taken place in the Capitol.[62] On January 4, Hoover had given Congress eight proposals for prompt action; the RFC and Glass-Steagall acts fulfilled two. Congress added another by expanding the capital of the federal land banks and Hoover signed the bill on January 23. Although Congress did not pass the Home Loan Bank bill until July, its passage completed the first half of the Hoover program. Congress was dilatory in approaching the latter four because they were vague propositions, dealing with safeguarding bank deposits, strengthening railroad bonds, and maintaining economy in government.[63] Where Hoover had proposed specific legislation, Congress dispatched it with varying alacrity.

Hoover's memory of this period seems to be marred by the conflict over taxation which broke out in March. Nevertheless, in February Hoover was, said Henry Stimson, "in great form." The usually dour Chief Executive radiated greater confidence than had been seen since the opening months of his administration. On February 21 Stimson noted that Hoover "has been feeling much

[60] Hoover, *The Great Depression*, pp. 105–6, 140.
[61] Mr. Hoover had wanted a revenue bill quickly acted upon but Garner obdurately pushed for consideration of lower tariff rates, ahead of everything else. This should not have surprised Hoover although he used it to illustrate deliberate delay by the Democratic leaders. To the Democrats, it was the fulfillment of a campaign pledge. See Chapter 5 for an account of the writing of the revenue bill.
[62] Carl Degler has noted that "surprising as it may seem today . . . as late as February, 1932, the country [and Congress] was still following Hoover's view of relief. . . ." Degler elaborates upon this by pointing to the defeat of the La Follette–Costigan relief bill in the Senate, 48 to 35, in February; the administration strongly opposed it and close to half of the votes against it came from Democrats. Carl N. Degler, "The Ordeal of Herbert Hoover," *Yale Review*, LII (June, 1963): 570. See Chapter 6 for a description of the fight for the La Follette–Costigan bill.
[63] Myers, II: 102–3, 107.

better since his measures for internal relief have been going so well as they have been lately. . . . It is very evident that he was feeling much relieved and in better spirits since his financial program has been meeting with such success. . . ." A year later, columnist Anne O'Hare McCormick recalled that Hoover in the spring of 1932 "was cheerful. He was genial, for the first time at home in office. . . . [He was] putting through his emergency measures with practically no political interference." House Republicans, unaccustomed to their minority status, welcomed good relations with the Democratic majority. Bert Snell, GOP House leader, boasted to Ted Clark that he had a secret arrangement affecting revenue legislation with Speaker Garner. As late as June, a newsletter published by the Republican National Committee could say, "The truth is that there has been less partisanship, in the ordinary sense of that term, exhibited in Congress than is ordinarily the case." The *Congressional Digest* also noted that "this fairly harmonious condition lasted through December, January, and February. Of course there were clashes here and there, but in the main the legislative machinery functioned with reasonable smoothness."[64]

The Democrats were proud of their nonpolitical behavior. House Majority Leader Rainey bragged that Democrats "have shown that they are capable of rising above partisanship by the manner in which they have cooperated with the President. . . ." The Democrats "made the most of the political situation, but they cooperated in most of the measures that were proposed," recalled Marvin Jones of Texas. Jones, a ranking Democrat on the Agriculture Committee and a poker-playing buddy of John Garner, later insisted that Democrats gave Hoover maximum cooperation: "The Democrats didn't block anything. There wasn't any disposition to block anything. As a matter of fact, I talked to

[64] Diary, February 21, 1932, Stimson MSS; Anne O'Hare McCormick, "Hoover Looks Back—and Ahead," *New York Times Magazine*, February 5, 1933, p. 1; Edward Tracy Clark to Calvin Coolidge, January 27, 1932, Clark MSS; "The Matter with Congress," *The Republican*, June 11, 1932, found in "General Congressional Material 1932" folder, Reed MSS; "The Month in Congress," *Congressional Digest*, XI (June, 1932): 182.

The Kissing Bee

Garner repeatedly about that and Garner said, 'We're going to go along with anything that the President has to offer that will save this country during this period. The situation is getting desperate.' " The Democratic flock followed Garner behind the president. "When Congress convened," said Ralph Lozier of Missouri, "I forgot politics, and have voted for practically every proposal submitted by the President. . . ."[65]

Progressives who had been looking forward to combining with Democrats on liberal alternatives to the Hoover program were dismayed by the unusual political consensus. Instead of placing the Republicans on the defensive, "the Democrats in this Congress have been content to be meek and lowly followers of the Republicans and to adopt at the instance of Wall Street the exact measures which Wall Street has compelled the Republicans to pass," Hiram Johnson charged. (Johnson found one bit of irony in the situation: "The skunks of high finance have attributed that credit to the Administration. . . .") Tom Amlie asserted that Democratic House leaders "have no program other than to out-Herod Herod." As a sample of this accord, Amlie noted that the Democratic tax proposals seemed deliberately to second the GOP's. The Democratic party, Hiram Johnson concluded, is "a weak and timid echo of the Republican Party in this Congress. . . ." "This isn't a session of Congress," grumbled Fiorello La Guardia, "this is a kissing bee!"[66]

The press took note of the political transformation. "The Democrats in the House are a sorry lot these days," a periodical commented: "instead of bringing forth their own economic program, as Mr. Garner promised before the session opened, they are simply waiting upon proposals from the White House." Under Democratic leadership, newsmen wrote, Congress had "become a mere

[65] New York *Times*, February 1, 1932; "The Reminiscences of Marvin Jones," COHC, pp. 581–85; Ralph F. Lozier to H. H. Rasmussen, May 25, 1932, Lozier MSS.

[66] Johnson to McClatchy, February 29, 1932, Johnson MSS; Amlie to Elizabeth Brandeis, April 12, to Val. W. Dittman, January 26, 1932, Amlie MSS; George Milburn, "The Statesmanship of Mr. Garner," *Harper's*, CLXV (November, 1932): 669–82.

annex to the White House." With obvious hyperbole Robert S. Allen declared, "For the first time during his administration, Hoover has a working majority in Congress—made up of Democrats."

> Amiably but firmly, Garner is providing the Republican President with a type of effective cooperation such as he has never enjoyed in Congress. . . . Garner, ruling the Democrats with a steady hand, has crushed opposition and has the House "cooperating" in a way that must amaze and delight the irresolute and fumbling Mr. Hoover. The Republican House leaders look on admiringly and sit by with folded hands. They have nothing to do. The President confers with them rarely, for when he wants something done, he goes to Garner.

On the other hand, a Republican newspaper editor relished the sight of Democrats who "had an opportunity to do little, except to approve projects sent to Congress from the White House." Walter Lippmann blamed this on the Democrats' need for a program and reliance on Republican failures for future electoral success; "their chief asset at the moment is a popular desire for change," he said.[67]

Such characterizations disturbed Democrats outside of Congress although they acknowledged some validity in them. "The Democratic Party seems to be following somewhat blindly the Hoover policies without advancing any original thoughts or ideas," William Gibbs McAdoo remarked. "Truly progressive policies" were needed to make the distinction between the parties visible to the layman, Josephus Daniels argued. Daniels asked Garner what the future held for the Democrats: "The record Congress is making in helping Mr. Hoover is generous and is actuated of course by a desire to help secure better conditions, and this is above politics, but next fall when we go out and criticize Mr. Hoover everybody is going to ask what did the Democratic Congress do to prevent

[67] A.F.C., "Backstage in Washington," *Outlook and Independent*, CLX (March, 1932): 170; Robert S. Allen, "Texas Jack," *New Republic*, LXX (March 16, 1932): 119–21; Washington *Post*, February 23, 1932; Lippmann, p. 264.

a return of old conditions, what great policies have they put into effect in the House?" The Democrats were faced with the choice of presenting alternatives to Hoover's program and being called obstructionists, or endorsing the administration and being called lambs. Newton Baker succinctly summarized the party's dilemma: "The newspapers have been disposed to chide us Democrats for being inarticulate at the moment but if any of us became really articulate and said what we think, we would be charged with frustrating the Administration's present reconstruction measures and seeking to prevent a restoration of that confidence without which rehabilitation is impossible."[68]

The Democratic majority in the House had been rendered impotent. John Nance Garner had serious political problems which prevented him from becoming an aggressive leader. First, as Hoover was quick to capitalize on, Garner had no policies of his own to offer. The depression dumbfounded him: "What can we do to bring about relief and prevent a recurrence of the present condition?" he inquired of Daniels. Second, there was the institutional factor: lacking patronage and other political weapons, the Speaker could not hold his flimsy majority intact. He admitted that the appearance of party cohesiveness was a pose: the president could " 'trade in' and 'pick off' a member which gives us great difficulty in holding House Democrats together." Third, the Democratic party was a coalition of conservatives and progressives, urban and rural forces representing every section of the nation. "It is difficult, if not impossible to reconcile the different ideas predominant among Democrats. . . . It cannot be done in the House," the Speaker said.[69] Finally, there was the president's veto power which Hoover held ready to put down any Democratic insurrection.

The captive Democrats were frustrated and ripe for an eruption of protest. Open to criticism from both sides, the Speaker

[68] William G. McAdoo to W. E. Woodward, January 20, 1932, McAdoo MSS; Daniels to Cordell Hull, February 8, 13, to John N. Garner, February 8, 1932, Daniels MSS; Baker to Clarke, February 22, 1932, Baker MSS.
[69] Garner to Daniels, February 29, May 25, 1932, Daniels MSS.

verged on an outburst when cabinet members and high Republican officials began calling the emergency legislation GOP-made. Garner was furious at this breach of nonpartisanship. "It is well enough to talk of a political truce. But let me tell you that the kind of truce we intend is not that the administration shall continue the hostilities while we abstain from them," he told Arthur Krock; "we, too, have our ideas as to how to affect improvements. . . . Nobody can dictate to the Democratic group in Congress." Republican boasting and Democratic restlessness necessitated Garner's tough talk. Correspondent Ray Tucker noted that "a vocal rebellion against Mr. Garner's leadership is under way." Democrats had the feeling that blandishments for cooperation trapped them.[70]

"The 'era of cooperation' on Capitol Hill," a reporter proclaimed in February, "is about over." Hiram Johnson noted that "politics are [*sic*] beginning to creep much more into our sessions than formerly. The Democrats, I think, with some humiliations, and a very great deal of irritation, realize what asses they have made of themselves."[71]

But Hoover vigorously denied that the period of nonpartisanship ever existed. When the White House press secretary, Ted Joslin, remarked to him, "The honeymoon is over," the president erupted and challenged, "Why use that word?" Hoover's eyes snapped as he lectured Joslin:

> There has been no honeymoon. You know that perfectly well. You know that the Democrats have taken my program because they had none of their own and because the attitude of the country compelled them to take the one I put forward. They would murder our plans in a moment if they dared. The truth is that they do not dare. So they resort to pin pricking whenever they can—and they are introducing bills designed to destroy

[70] Timmons, p. 139; New York *Times*, February 22, 1932; New York *World-Telegram*, February 16, 1932.
[71] Washington *Post*, February 19, 23, 1932; Johnson to McClatchy, March 6, 1932, Johnson MSS.

all public confidence. My chance will come yet and when it does—.[72]

There were only a few months before the 1932 party conventions and thus far the Hoover administration had pushed across, with Democratic help, a conservative emergency relief program with major financial institutions as the primary beneficiaries. Under such circumstances, Democratic uneasiness and resentment was sure to grow. Then, on March 5, during a fight over an economy bill, the House dramatically reversed itself and adopted, 160 to 155, an amendment restoring salary increases for government workers. The amendment had been opposed by Garner and the Democratic leadership, but most of the support for it came from Democratic ranks as both parties split sharply. The New York *Times* called it the "worst defeat the Democratic leaders have suffered at this session."[73] For supporters of bipartisan cooperation, this relatively minor incident loomed as an ominous harbinger of congressional strife.

[72] Theodore G. Joslin, *Hoover Off the Record* (Garden City, N.Y., 1935), p. 191.
[73] New York *Times*, March 6, 1932.

☆ ☆ ☆ ☆ ☆

5

THE SALES TAX
REBELLION

ON MARCH 7, 1932, the House Ways and Means Committee, composed of fifteen Democrats and ten Republicans, reported out a revenue bill with only one dissenter, North Carolina's Robert L. Doughton. The near-unanimity was surprising, considering that in an election year, half of the projected income would come from a new 2¼ per cent manufacturers' sales tax and the remainder from increased income, corporate, estate, and miscellaneous excises. Democratic leaders, recalling the outcry when they abruptly shut off debate on the Glass-Steagall and RFC bills, promised unlimited discussion of the revenue bill on the House floor. With no organized opposition in sight, Speaker Garner confidently predicted passage within two weeks.[1]

The sales tax's insertion into the revenue bill of 1932 capped a campaign of more than a decade by businessmen's groups. During the winter of 1920–21, the National Association of Manufacturers, the New York Board of Trade, the Tax League of America, and various retail associations had deluged Congress with propaganda in order to secure a general sales tax in the revenue bill of 1921. Since 1916 these businessmen had chafed against the excess profits tax, corporation income tax, and high surtaxes Congress had burdened them with in order to meet the extraordinary costs of war and inflation. On the other hand, farm groups, labor unions, and some merchant organizations like the U.S. Chamber

[1] New York *Times*, March 8, 1932.

of Commerce assailed the proposal, effectively preventing substitution of the sales tax. For the rest of the twenties, industrialists and bankers, aided by sympathetic Republican administrations and Secretary of the Treasury Andrew Mellon, continued their fire on the remaining high tax rates. Progressives and Democrats delayed significant tax reductions until 1926 when Mellon finally won lower rates from a large GOP majority in Congress. By 1929 Congress gave "the greatest Secretary of the Treasury since Alexander Hamilton" exactly what he ordered.[2]

The depression, however, forced politicians to reconsider lower tax rates; national income fell, government expenditures rose, and the federal coffers became emaciated. Mellon admitted that deficits could be expected for 1930–31 but still denied that a tax hike was needed. Congress, reassured by Mellon that the deficit would not amount to more than $200 million, did not provide for additional revenue. Yet, the final tabulation showed a deficit for the fiscal year 1931 of more than $900 million.[3]

The administration had been less than candid concerning the likelihood of a budgetary deficit. When Jim Watson sought to boost GOP stock for the 1930 elections with a veterans' bonus, the president rejected the proposal because, among other reasons, the budget already had "incurred a probable deficit." Hoover kept this intelligence from the public and the lawmakers until after the 71st Congress adjourned. In late March, 1931, Director of the Budget Bureau J. Clawson Roop confirmed the worst expectations; between increased expenditures from previous commitments for public works and agricultural relief and unanticipated reductions in revenue receipts, the budgetary deficit for the current fiscal year amounted to approximately $760 million.[4] The White House could correct the deficiency if it convened the new

[2] Sidney Ratner, *American Taxation: Its History as a Social Force in Democracy* (New York, 1942), pp. 400–443 *passim*.

[3] *Ibid.*, pp. 443–45; Roy G. and Gladys C. Blakey, *The Federal Income Tax* (New York, 1940), pp. 301–3; also see Randolph E. Paul, *Taxation in the United States* (Boston, 1954), pp. 144–62.

[4] Herbert Hoover to James E. Watson, July 21, 1930, Container 1–L/312, J. Clawson Roop to Hoover, March 31, July 3, 1931, Container 1–E/80, Hoover MSS.

Congress for the purpose of raising taxes, but nothing could compel Hoover to do that. Hoover believed that it would be practically impossible to get an acceptable revision of tax schedules. The administration feared that congressional radicals would "make an onslaught on the higher brackets of the income tax," a deficit solution which would "accentuate the present trouble." For the time being, "flat opposition to any tax legislation" represented the wisest course for Hoover. Administration spokesman would educate the public on how "our taxation system has failed us" while insisting upon economy reductions in government expenditures even as they cautioned industry against cost and manpower liquidation.[5]

Thus, from 1929 to 1932, there were no alterations in the tax schedules and, significantly, national income between these years declined from $87.8 billion to $42.5 billion.[6] The inevitable 1932 consequence of this indifference to the revenue-expenditure disparity had to be considerable agitation for higher rates on existing taxes or new taxes to supplement inadequate duties, or possibly both. In the normal course of events, politicians and economists revived discussions of the feasibility of a sales tax.

State governments had been confronted by revenue crises for the past twenty years. The real estate tax, which accounted for most state and local receipts, could no longer be increased without eliciting enraged protests from county and town governments accusing the state governments of infringing on their resource; moreover, property owners insisted that all governments should leave them alone. Prior to World War I fifteen states had adopted some form of income tax. But the 16th Amendment and the war stamped the income tax as a federal device; the high rates passed by Congress deterred the states from putting a similar levy on their books. In the words of State Senator George Woodward of Penn-

[5] Diary, May 26, 1931, Stimson MSS; Hoover to Roop, September 2, October 12, Roop to Hoover, December 2, 1931, Container 1-E/80, Hoover MSS.
[6] Paul Studenski and Herman E. Krooss, *Financial History of the United States* (New York, 1952), p. 353.

sylvania, the war "made the very name 'income tax' distasteful" to state legislators.[7]

The southern states, acutely aware of their industrial retardation, launched a drive in the twenties for expanded public improvements and considered financing them with a sales tax. States which adopted the levy like Georgia and West Virginia, attracted the attention of their sister states who wondered if the sales tax would provide the desperately needed revenue. These experiments were encouraging although their results were inconclusive. The governor of West Virginia proudly enumerated several advantages which his state's sales tax had over other fiscal devices. At a meeting of the National Tax Association in September, 1929, R. C. Norman, tax commissioner for Georgia, gave his state's case for the sales tax when he candidly explained (1) "the business interests of Georgia . . . wanted it" and "they were tremendously opposed to a net income tax"; (2) "we were faced with a four and a half million dollar deficit at the end of the present year, and we had to have some immediate revenue"; and (3) the Georgia constitution limited the state property tax to five mills, although county and municipal governments had no limit on their property taxes.[8] Other states shared Georgia's problems. A year later the NTA, after a roundtable discussion on sales and excise taxes, concluded "that real property was being excessively taxed and that selected commodity taxes offered the way for relief to general property."[9] A consumer tax might give the states their needed revenue.

Ineluctably federal needs clashed with those of the states. Congressional conservatives in both parties opted for a sales tax to bolster depleted federal revenues in the autumn of 1931. Senator

[7] National Tax Association, *Proceedings of Twenty-second National Conference 1929* (Columbia, S.C., 1930), pp. 187–88.
[8] William G. Conley, "How West Virginia Found New Revenue," *Review of Reviews*, LXXXII (October, 1930): 120–22; National Tax Association, *Twenty-second National Conference, 1930*, p. 413.
[9] National Tax Association, *Proceedings of Twenty-third National Conference* (Columbia, S.C., 1931), p. 335.

David Reed of Pennsylvania initiated the public debate by pro-
prosing that Congress adopt a sales tax of one-half of 1 per cent.
This proposal, coming from a "protégé" of Secretary Mellon,
signalled for Democrats and progressives a new tax struggle remi-
niscent of those of the twenties. "It is part and parcel of Mellon's
great policy of revising the upper brackets 'to stimulate business,' "
Felix Frankfurter knowingly warned.[10]

Indeed, administration Republicans sought to keep income tax
rates low and spread the tax burden as widely as possible. In cabinet meetings the Secretary of the Treasury argued that he already
had proved during the Coolidge years that the government could
squeeze no more income from the higher brackets without de-
tracting from capital investments. That bitter enemy of the income tax, Senator Moses, told readers of a national magazine how
he had discovered "a form of taxation which is at once simple and
productive, easily administered, found equitable wherever it has
been applied and more readily absorbed than any other form of
tax. . . . It requires no army of tax eaters to enforce it . . . and it
produces a golden stream for the treasury." This fiscal miracle was
the sales tax. Then came the traditional brief: "It is based upon
the surest foundation for one's ability to pay—namely one's ability
to buy," Moses said; "and he who buys most, pays most—as he
should. Under such a tax the rich are soaked, and the poor do not
escape."[11]

The Moses sophistry on the sales tax may have reminded tax
experts of a proposal made a decade before by a freshman representative from New York, Ogden L. Mills, for what he called a
"spending tax." Mills, like Mellon, had prefaced his advocacy of
the sales tax with an attack deploring high income taxes, repeating
the familiar argument that income levies froze capital and diminished government revenues rather than expanding them. Mills

[10] Blakey and Blakey, p. 303; Felix Frankfurter to Edward P. Costigan, October 7, 1931, Costigan MSS.
[11] Diary, May 26, September 8, 1931, Stimson MSS; George H. Moses, "Death
—and Taxes," *Saturday Evening Post*, June 27, 1931, p. 97.

insisted that his "spending" tax, while admittedly a sales tax, followed the principle of a graduated tax because its rate increased with the amount of money spent. The spending tax, said Mills, was "in effect a tax on money spent for consumption, without being regressive in character or laying a disproportionate burden on those least able to bear it, and without being open to the serious evils which arise from the pyramiding of the tax." He insisted that his virtuous tax would "promote thrift and discourage extravagance."[12] Mills did not get his tax, nor did he go unnoticed in Washington. In 1927 Mellon recommended that President Coolidge appoint the New Yorker as Under Secretary of the Treasury, a post which Mills still held in 1931.

Ogden Livingston Mills was a politically intelligent aristocrat. His mother was a descendant of Chancellor Robert R. Livingston, his grandfather made the family fortune in the Gold Rush of 1849, his cousins were the Reids who published the New York *Herald Tribune*, his first wife was a Vanderbilt and his second wife a Fell of Philadelphia. Mills had served as a New York state senator for five years, as an infantry captain in World War I, and for three terms in the House of Representatives, all with considerable distinction. As a congressman he won great respect for his tax acumen in the House Ways and Means Committee. In 1926 the Republicans gave Mills the impossible assignment of defeating Al Smith for the governorship of New York. The following year, at the age of 42, he became second in command in the Treasury Department.

"Little Oggie," as liberal reporters derisively dubbed Mills, became the voice of the Treasury, conducting its relations with the press and Congress. He increasingly expanded his role as a confidant of President Hoover as it became apparent that the aging

[12] National Tax Association, *Proceedings of Fourteenth National Conference 1921* (New York, 1922), pp. 328–31. Mills explained how the spending tax would be graduated: "The tax is imposed at the graduated rate, which increases 1% for every $2000 spent up to $18,000, and thereafter 1% for each $1000 spent up to $50,000. All spendings in excess of $50,000 are taxed at the rate of 40%." He specified certain purchases which would be exempt from the tax.

Andrew Mellon lacked the younger man's political savvy and alertness.[13] In February, 1932, Hoover transferred Mellon to the Court of St. James and promoted Mills to the post which the new ambassador had held for more than a decade. Many observers believed that Hoover merely had ratified an existing situation.

Republicans considered Mills a distinct political improvement over the aloof Pittsburgh banker. His experience on the Ways and Means Committee superbly prepared him to guide the administration's fiscal program through Congress. He knew how to negotiate with the House Democrats and had their respect. To a friend of the Speaker, it appeared that Mills and Garner were "fast personal friends." Mills seemed exceptionally adroit with southern Democrats. When the 72nd Congress opened with the chairman of Ways and Means, "Billy" Collier of Mississippi, too ill to preside, Charles Crisp of Georgia became the acting chairman and floor manager of the revenue bill. Republicans could count on Crisp as one of the most conservative of Democrats on the committee. And it is probably no coincidence that Crisp, ambitious to go to the Senate, elicited several political favors from the Treasury in 1932, ranging from a government job for a friend to allocating funds for a federal court house in his home town, Americus. He received the credit when the government decided to build the Atlanta Post Office with Georgia marble instead of cheaper Indiana limestone.[14]

Mills took the Treasury portfolio at a time when the administration lacked a fiscal program. In fact, Hoover was at odds with leading cabinet members over whether the budget should be balanced. According to Henry Stimson, Hoover in May, 1931, believed that the budget could not be balanced until the nation returned to prosperity. "The President likened it to war times,"

---

[13] Edward Tracy Clark to Calvin Coolidge, November 11, 1931, Clark MSS.
[14] "The Reminiscences of Marvin Jones," COHC, p. 512; diary, December 17, 1931, Stimson MSS; Charles Crisp to Ogden Mills, February 4, 1931, Mills to Crisp, February 26, 1932, Mills MSS; also see Mills to Crisp, July 15, August 2, 1932, Mills MSS; Atlanta *Constitution*, July 1, 1932. When Richard Russell defeated Crisp in the Senate primary, Hoover appointed Crisp to the Tariff Commission.

Stimson wrote. "He said in war times no one dreamed of balancing the budget. Fortunately we can now borrow. . . ." In September Mellon opposed borrowing on bonds but his opinions counted for less than before with the president. The president hoped to finance his public works program with bond issues but found that other administration men sided with the orthodox Mellon. They suspected that Hoover had succumbed to Jim Watson's entreaties to avoid additional taxes as bad politics in an election year.[15] Stimson, however, along with Mills and Arthur A. Ballantine[16] of the Treasury Department, argued that while nothing could balance the budget in 1932, some new taxes should be levied if only to use the budget "as an educational instrument so that we could get the minds of the people behind solid finance." As late as November, 1931, Ted Clark observed the conflict within the administration. "Mills and Arthur Ballantine have been working for weeks on the tax program," Clark told Coolidge, "but felt very doubtful whether their program had the President's support because he might have one of his own." Nonetheless, three months later Mills stated in clear, absolute terms, "The committee on Ways and Means and the Treasury Department are in complete accord as to the necessity of balancing the budget during the next fiscal year so as to eliminate any further increase in our public debt. There can be no question as to the soundness of this position. It admits of no compromise."[17] The White House had decided to tax a year after it had argued against more taxes.

It is a great tribute to Mills's political sagacity and persuasiveness that he not only convinced the president to make balancing the budget an issue when nobody believed it could be done anyway, but he also turned this issue into a litany between the administration and the Democratic leadership. In the latter instance,

[15] Diary, May 26, 1931, Stimson MSS; Clark to Coolidge, November 11, 1931, Clark MSS.
[16] Ballantine is an enigma. In 1921 he opposed Mills's sales tax scheme and wrote one of the best briefs against it, "The General Sales Tax Is Not the Way Out," *Annals*, XCV (May, 1921): 212–20. Nevertheless, I do not know of other instances of his opposition to the Mellon-Mills tax policies.
[17] Diary, September 13, 1931, Stimson MSS; Clark to Coolidge, November 11, 1931, Clark MSS; Mills to Crisp, February 16, 1932, Mills MSS.

Mills removed the burden of raising additional taxes from the shoulders of a weary administration and placed it in the hands of a Democratic leadership gullible enough to accept political dynamite. The Democratic leadership advocated a Republican sales tax, which it ironically had beaten over ten years before, and echoed the administration's "balance the budget" slogan. In March Mills declared, "The so-called manufacturers sales tax was not recommended by the Administration, or by the Treasury Department. It was inserted by the Ways and Means Committee on its own initiative." Indeed, when Crisp requested that Mills suggest how additional revenue could be obtained, Mills replied that he preferred a limited group of excise taxes to a general sales tax.[18] The Democrats, fearing the opprobrium of not raising enough revenue to balance the budget, decided on a broad sales tax. Nothing could have pleased Mills more.

The Democrats were badly muddled over national finances. Garner had not conclusively decided on balancing the budget or raising taxes, but suggested that both would be attempted. Pat Harrison of Mississippi, ranking Democrat on the Senate Finance Committee, first hoped that the Democrats could avoid a deficit by issuing bonds but later showed a readiness to tax. Harrison, never a radical, indicated that Democrats would follow the administration's lead in taxation, promising that the Democratic tax plan would "not disturb business any more than Mr. Mellon's plan will."[19]

Probably the most influential man in writing the Ways and Means bill was Bernard Baruch. On the subject of finance, no Democrat could afford to ignore Baruch's counsel. What he desired fitted Republican plans perfectly: if it could not be done by bonds or retrenchment, balance the budget with a sales tax. "The sales tax may be unpleasant," Baruch conceded, "but we are in an unpleasant predicament, and it must be met by heroic measures."

[18] Mills to Charles O. Karpf, March 17, to Crisp, February 16, 1932, Mills MSS.
[19] John N. Garner to William G. McAdoo, January 11, 1932, McAdoo MSS; Pat Harrison to Robert J. Bulkley, December 12, 1931, to R. A. Montgomery, February 5, 1932, to Bernard Baruch, December 18, 1931, Pat Harrison MSS.

The financier counselled Henry Rainey, "A balanced budget is the first and greatest requisite of reconstruction. This is your policy and I think it well to announce it now." At the same time, Baruch told Harrison, "we should try to keep the onus where it now is—on the Republicans." Above all, he dreaded an unbalanced budget more than he feared the additional taxes; "we have to meet our budget," he declared with finality.[20]

Another influential Democrat, publisher William Randolph Hearst, wanting congressmen to see Canada's sales tax in operation, offered them an all-expenses-paid working vacation north of the border during the fall of 1931. Fifty representatives and four senators accepted the invitation. On January 2 Hearst launched a Garner-for-president drive and the connection between his support of the sales tax and the Speaker could not be ignored.[21] At the same time other prominent Democrats like John Raskob and Jouett Shouse discovered the virtues of a sales tax.

Despite his enormous influence, certain southern and western Democrats distrusted Baruch's fiscal ideas. Baruch seemed to forget that his party had instituted the progressive income tax and had defended it throughout the twenties. Like Mills, Baruch spoke of the dangers of destroying personal initiative and capital. No such trepidations restrained Tom Walsh, who bluntly told Baruch that he wanted to soak the rich. The suggestion of a sales tax outraged Walsh. "The most profound thinkers among our economists assign as the first reason for the business depression the inability of the consuming masses to buy," the Montana senator declared. The national wealth was great, and if it "or the one-third part of it, had been distributed among them there would be no depression."

[20] Baruch to Harrison, December 11, 1931, Pat Harrison MSS; Baruch to Thomas J. Walsh, September 29, 1931, T. J. Walsh MSS; Baruch to Frank Kent, December 23, 1931, to James M. Cox, January 6, to Henry T. Rainey (telegram), January 5, 1932, Baruch MSS. Later, on the House floor, Henry Rainey described how Baruch's personal economist had convinced him that the budget needed to be balanced with a sales tax. *Congressional Record*, 72nd Cong., 1st sess., p. 6357.
[21] *Congressional Record*, 72nd Cong., 1st sess., pp. 1808, 6657; William Randolph Hearst to Robert L. Doughton (telegram), October 28, 1931, Doughton MSS; W. A. Swanberg, *Citizen Hearst* (New York, 1961), pp. 435-36. For more on the Garner candidacy, see Chapter 7.

In the fall of 1931 Walsh wanted "to get after that accumulated wealth by taxation instead of imposing a further burden upon the consuming masses through a sales tax. . . ." Senator Elmer Thomas implied that Republicans had deceived Baruch and other conservative Democrats with "high-powered salesmen."[22] Still, these dissents never dissuaded Baruch and the Democratic leadership.

Because most party leaders favored the levy, some form of sales tax seemed a certainty as the Ways and Means Committee deliberated the revenue bill in January. Even Senator Tom Walsh admitted that "it may be that we shall be obliged to have a luxury sales tax" but vowed to resist a general tax. On January 25, Crisp, speaking for his committee, announced, "We are going to report a tax bill which will balance the budget, place as little burden as possible on industry and impose taxes on articles of wide use and distribution." The latter part of this declaration dispelled any doubts about a sales tax in the revenue bill. By early February, progressives like Tom Amlie, although they sought higher income and corporation taxes, knew for certain that the revenue bill would contain a sales tax. "We are not getting the help from the Democrats on our stand on taxation that we should receive," Amlie ruefully acknowledged.[23]

Republicans, of course, were cheered by the unusual turn of events. "Every citizen should contribute a just share toward the support of his government," the Republican Washington *Post* piously declared; "the sales tax gives him the assurance that he will not be obliged to give more than his just share." One such citizen, Roy Chapin of Hudson Motors, told his Washington lobbyist that the tax was "proper since the lower income brackets pay nothing

[22] Carter Glass to Baruch, October 1, 1931, Box 280, Glass MSS; Walsh to Baruch, October 6, 1931, T. J. Walsh MSS; Elmer Thomas to Baruch, March 30, 1932, Baruch MSS.
[23] Walsh to McAdoo, November 9, 1931, McAdoo MSS; New York *Times*, January 25, 1932; Thomas Amlie to Will M. Cowles, February 5, to M. A. Bredeson, February 6, 1932, Amlie MSS.

to the maintenance of the National Government."[24] In a cabinet meeting on March 1, Ogden Mills proposed that the administration extol the Ways and Means Committee and emphasize the importance of balancing the budget. Mills did not believe that the committee's proposals would balance the budget, but as long as everyone else thought so, Congress would hesitate before it passed extravagant legislation. Thus, Mills sought to head off relief legislation by reminding Congress that excessive spending would create an undesirable deficit.[25] Baruch's personal emissary, Hugh Johnson, had assured Mills that the House Democrats would seek higher taxes and, if the Secretary recommended proposals for balancing the budget, Baruch "would in no event be placed in the role of an adversary of the Treasury. . . ."[26] Thus, Democrats had assumed the impossible task of balancing the budget with additional levies in an election year. In turn, Mills saluted the Ways and Means Committee for its "courageous and determined" action in adopting the sales tax to balance the budget; in particular he lauded Crisp for "a patriotic task thoroughly well done." Myers and Newton later wrote, "It was an example of what could be accomplished through united bi-partisan effort, and the country was encouraged."[27]

In February Hoover was at high tide with the 72nd Congress; Washington languished in the era of cooperation. No issues divided Republicans and Democrats except who deserved credit for the RFC and Glass-Steagall laws. On February 21 House Democratic leader Henry Rainey called the sales tax the "backbone" of a "non-partisan" bill. Four days later John Nance Garner gave the sales tax his blessing.[28]

[24] Washington *Post*, February 15, 1932; Roy Chapin to Pyke Johnson, February 17, 1932, Chapin MSS.
[25] Diary, March 1, 1932, Stimson MSS.
[26] Hugh Johnson to Baruch, February 2, 1932, Baruch MSS.
[27] New York *Times*, March 6, 1932; Mills to Crisp, March 11, 1932, Mills MSS; William Starr Myers and Walter H. Newton, *The Hoover Administration: A Documented Narrative* (New York, 1936), p. 182.
[28] New York *Times*, February 22, 26, 1932.

Despite this harmony, one House Democrat dared to oppose the bipartisan leadership. Only Robert L. Doughton was willing to violate unanimity on the Ways and Means Committee's revenue bill. On March 4 the committee had formally incorporated the undesirable duty by a 21-to-4 vote, but the other three negative votes forsook opposition to the engrossed measure, leaving Doughton with the courage of his loneliness in the committee. Hundreds of letters from his North Carolina constituency attested that his decision was the popular one.

Doughton, instinctively hating the sales tax, had not always been so convinced that 1932 was the year to resist it. Although he considered it "subversive of every sound principle of taxation," he did not ignore the fact that the government's revenues were being exhausted. He doubted that, given the great decline in incomes, the government could find sufficient receipts with present taxes. A sales tax, therefore, though undesirable and unprincipled, might be "the least burdensome way the money could be raised." As late as March 2, Doughton thought it "regrettable . . . that a sales tax appears imperative."[29] Nor was he a politician who went against his party's leadership. The taciturn Doughton had spent a score of years in the House without drawing much attention to himself. Commenting on an editorial entitled "Doughton's Dander Up," he confessed, "It is true that in the past I have not assumed or manifested any great fighting qualities."[30] But circumstances now were different. On March 4 "Muley Bob" requested a constituent to compile material in opposition to the tax. The next day he told another, "I am opposed to a general sales tax and do not think I can support this measure in its present form." After grave indecision, Doughton decided only days before the committee reached its verdict.[31]

29 Doughton to Josephus Daniels, March 26, to G. C. Courtney, January 18, to Thomas H. Webb, February 18, to O. M. Mull, March 1, to W. Lunsford Long, March 2, 1932, Doughton MSS.
30 Doughton to W. E. Sherrill, March 26, 1932, Doughton MSS.
31 Doughton to A. S. Carson, March 4, to Thurmond Chatham, March 5, 1932, Doughton MSS. Also, on Doughton, see Clinton W. Gilbert, "American Representative," *Colliers*, May 14, 1932, p. 22.

But Doughton never became a pariah. In spite of the over-whelming endorsement which the committee and the administration gave the tax, many in the House pounced on it at the outset of debate. The New York *Times* reported on March 10 that "a storm of vocal opposition was still raging today and apparently growing in intensity." When Henry Rainey began polling his Democratic membership, he admitted that he could find only two who supported the revenue bill without reservations. Clarence Cannon of Missouri voiced a popular sentiment when he de-nounced the sales tax as "reprehensible at this time of national distress."

For a few days it was an inchoate opposition. The only organ-ized group against the sales tax was the "Allied Progressives," composed of about fifteen insurgent Republicans from Wiscon-sin and the middle border states and led by New Yorker Fiorello La Guardia. If La Guardia's leadership of the Wisconsin group appeared anomalous, then so did his entire political career. The East Harlem politician had been, at various times in the twenties, the only Republican in the House from New York City, the only progressive from east of Lake Michigan, the only Republican ex-pelled from the party and branded a socialist, and now the leader of La Follette progressivism in the lower chamber. By his own admission, La Guardia was "doomed to live in a hopeless minority for most of my legislative days." He enjoyed this role and his out-spokenness, courage, and articulate indignation made him strange-ly popular in the capital. Reporters liked him because he never made for bland coverage; "colorful" was an overused adjective for this diminutive barrel of energy.[32] Amid the business politics of the twenties, he dared to demand government ownership of all natural resources. During the depression he bitterly assailed the Hoover administration's relief policies, insisting that the federal govern-ment had an obligation to the unemployed. The basically conserv-ative Bob Doughton denied that an alliance with the radical La

[32] Duff Gilfond, "La Guardia of Harlem," *American Mercury*, XI (June, 1927): 152–58; Thomas L. Stokes, *Chip Off My Shoulder* (Princeton, N.J., 1940), p. 166.

Guardia against the sales tax hurt his cause; "everyone who knows him gives him credit for being an able, diligent, and conscientious Representative," declared the North Carolinian.[33]

But Doughton and La Guardia were not formidable enough to worry party leaders. What bothered them was the horde of mail bearing anxious protests from constituents. This pressure became intense. Richard M. Kleberg, the only Texan besides Garner committed to the sales tax, admitted on the floor that almost all his mail attacked the levy. "In all the years I have been here we have never had such a tense situation." Homer Hoch, a Republican serving his seventh term, told his fellow Kansan, William Allen White; "I have never worked so hard in my life. . . . Our correspondence reflects the mood of the people, and has really become a terrific burden."[34]

Initially, the House Democratic leaders were complacent about the uproar; Rainey simply shrugged off the scattered opposition. For several days the House chieftains calmly listened to righteous denunciations of the sales tax and watched La Guardia and Doughton form a coordinated, bipartisan opposition. "*The Wall Street Journal* said this morning that we who are opposing this sales tax would be defeated because we are not organized," Mississippi's John Rankin shouted in the House on March 15. "Well, we are going to organize and we are going to do it this afternoon." This was a turning point. Fifty Democrats caucused under Doughton's leadership while La Guardia's progressives met concurrently and sent their felicitations to Doughton's "courageous and public-spirited Democrats." Labelling the sales tax fight "desperate," Doughton predicted, "While we may not kill it, we will shoot it up so badly I think it will never get through the Senate."[35]

---

[33] Fiorello La Guardia, "Government Must Act," *Nation*, CXXVI (April 4, 1928): 378–79; *Proceedings of a Conference of Progressives*, March 11 and 12, 1931 (Washington, D.C., 1931), pp. 75–77; Doughton to C. R. Propst, April 16, 1932, Doughton MSS.

[34] New York *Times*, March 5, 9, 10, 11, 1932; Washington *News*, March 11, 1932; *Congressional Record*, 72nd Cong., 1st sess., p. 6253; Homer Hoch to William Allen White, March 17, 1932, White MSS.

[35] *Congressional Record*, 72nd Cong., 1st sess., p. 6159; New York *Times*, March 16, 17, 1932; Doughton to W. H. Jones, March 16, 1932, Doughton MSS.

The Democratic leadership fought the fire of rebellion with the water of conciliation. Crisp exempted canned foods from the sales tax, and other exceptions to the levy were discussed, thus stimulating talk that the sales tax would be "exempted to death." Even so, this compromise did not placate insurging Democrats. When Rainey and Bertrand Snell polled their respective memberships on the sales tax, Snell counted 150 Republicans for it but Rainey could do no better than sixty or eighty. John Rankin's forecast that two-thirds of the House Democrats would reject the sales tax appeared to be irrefutable. Vainly Rainey attempted to convince his fellow Democrats that the sales tax was painless; "the science of levying and collecting taxes is the science of getting the most feathers with the least squawking of the geese," he said.[36] His colleagues could appreciate this; the squawking they heard from their home barnyards told them that the science was not being properly applied.

The first test of the rebellion's strength came March 18 on an amendment to increase income taxes; the House passed it 121 to 81 amidst joyous foot-stomping by the insurgent congressmen. They greeted an amendment raising surtaxes close to the wartime levels with applause, yells, and whistles and it won, 153 to 87. The leadership's floor managers, Crisp and Rainey, were unnerved by the brashness of their fellow Democrats. Crisp testily demanded a recess because the House was not "in proper frame of mind to legislate today." Rainey dubbed the body "a runaway House" and ominously added: "We have made a longer step in the direction of communism than any country in the world ever made except Russia." Despite many congressmen who remained uncommitted, the rebels had the momentum; the usually pessimistic Doughton privately declared, "I believe now we will succeed."[37]

The progressive-Democratic coalition confidently asserted itself during the next few days. By 139 to 103 it erased a clause from

[36] New York *Times*, March 16, 1932; Atlanta *Constitution*, March 17, 1932; Washington *Post*, March 17, 1932; *Congressional Record*, 72nd Cong., 1st sess., p. 6354.
[37] New York *Times*, March 19, 1932; *Congressional Record*, 72nd Cong., 1st sess., p. 6512; Doughton to Harold F. Coffey, March 19, 1932, Doughton MSS.

the revenue bill providing for crediting domestic corporations with taxes paid by foreign branches; only thirteen Democrats voted for the clause. The "runaway" House resounded with exclamations like "conscript wealth" and "soak the rich." In desperation Crisp made further sales tax exemptions, a maneuver that placated La Guardia who announced he was "gratified with the concessions made." But when Doughton turned down the proposals as unsatisfactory, La Guardia quickly backtracked, saying: "I feel that I should go along with Mr. Doughton. . . . The concessions made are not enough to satisfy a majority of the House." Doughton's determined Democrats then buttressed their demands, raising estate taxes by a 190 to 149 vote.[38] Every ballot committed more representatives to a stand on taxation. The House headed for a showdown.

The struggle reached a climax on March 24 as the House prepared to vote on the sales tax provision. Before packed galleries both sides roared at each other for two hours. During one heated moment, a man from Michigan invited a Texan to "step outside," a fracas which only stirred the air. As the debate concluded, Doughton, now "quite hopeful that we have it defeated," and Crisp delivered summaries for their respective positions, and the House voted. It was a teller vote and Doughton stood in the well of the House as a tabulator, patting each anti–sales tax representative on the back as he passed. By 223 to 153, the sales tax went down to defeat amid rebel yells and whistling. The House was in near pandemonium.[39]

Rarely had Washington seen such an upset. Doughton later jubilantly wrote, "This was one case where the leaders were on one side, and the rank and file on the other. . . ." For once Hiram Johnson found himself cheering Democrats; "the revolt was the most amazing I have ever seen here," the Californian exclaimed.

---

[38] New York *Times,* March 20, 22, 23, 1932.
[39] *Ibid.,* March 25, 1932; New York *World-Telegram,* March 24, 1932. Only forty-five Democrats voted for the sales tax; about one-third were from New York City.

To the New York *World-Telegram*, "the Sales Tax rebellion was against labels . . . sectionalism . . . political tradition and prejudice . . . dominating wealth . . . 'respectability,' [and] government by bosses in favor of government by the people." Most congressional leaders at first said little or nothing in public. President Hoover, through Silas H. Strawn, president of the United States Chamber of Commerce, who had been visiting him at the time of the vote, "expressed keen disappointment."[40]

The sales taxers blamed the rebellion on the aggressive La Guardia, but their accusations only helped to magnify the progressive's role out of proportion. La Guardia had captured most of the newspaper headlines while the dour Doughton's role was relegated to lower paragraphs. Yet, as Arthur Mann has pointed out, "once the stampede began Fiorello *was led by it*." This was most apparent when La Guardia had to recant on his acceptance of Crisp's concessions because Doughton sought total defeat of the sales tax. La Guardia's prominence, however, suited the purposes of the sales taxers who sought to discredit rebel Democrats. John McCormack of Massachusetts professed to be appalled that "here we have the Democratic Party being led by a Republican. . . ." Ogden Mills twitted Joseph Pulitzer that Democrats had "accepted the leadership of that distinguished Republican from New York, Mr. La Guardia."[41] Perhaps he did persuade some progressives and fewer Democrats, but the decisive leadership came from Doughton and Rankin who, aided by an avalanche of mail, massed the Democratic rebels against the levy.

Then, too, the outcome might have been different had the Democratic leadership acted more swiftly. Garner's attitude toward the sales tax had been at best nebulous. His commitment to its passage in 1932 contradicted his own long-standing opposition

[40] Doughton to Santford Martin, March 26, 1932, Doughton MSS; Hiram Johnson to C. K. McClatchy, March 25, 1932, Johnson MSS; New York *World-Telegram*, March 31, 1932; New York *Times*, March 25, 1932.

[41] Arthur Mann, *La Guardia: A Fighter against His Times, 1882–1933* (Philadelphia, 1959), p. 305; *Congressional Record*, 72nd Cong., 1st sess., p. 6503; Mills to Joseph Pulitzer, March 19, 1932, Mills MSS.

to such fiscal devices.[42] Throughout the floor fight Garner delib- erately absented himself from the chamber which he headed. When the first series of revenue bill votes placed the sales tax in jeopardy, the situation required the Speaker to use his prestige as leader if he wanted the tax. Garner, still refusing to be drawn into debate, announced on March 18 that the method of raising revenue was "inconsequential and insignificant" as long as the budget was balanced. Refusing elaboration, he thus severely dam- aged the argument that a sales tax alone would balance the bud- get. When Crisp heard Garner's remarks, he "sat back in his seat, chagrin and disappointment in his face." To Frank R. Kent, writ- ing in the Baltimore *Sun*, Garner's statement "had a rather Cool- idgean flavor [which] lacked clarity, candor and force."[43]

After the House routed the tax, Garner held an impromptu press conference to concede that "the House does not want the sales tax." But, "in five minutes," he boasted, "I could put down a list of taxes that would yield $900,000,000 without including the sales tax."[44] A few days later Garner at last took the floor. "I am now opposed to a sales tax," he informed the applauding rebels. "But, gentlemen, if I find it impossible to balance the Budget and restore the confidence of the world and our own people in our Government without some such tax I would levy any tax, sales or any other kind in order to do that. I think more of my country than I do of any theory of taxation that I may have, and the coun- try at this time is in a condition where the worst taxes you could possibly levy would be better than no taxes at all."[45] Garner's argu- ments were not new but his techniques were. To demonstrate his leadership of the House, he asked all who believed with him in a balanced budget to rise from their seats. Not one representative,

---

[42] Ray T. Tucker, "Tiger from Texas," *Outlook and Independent*, CLVI (November 26, 1930): 492–94; Paul Y. Anderson, "Texas John Garner," *Nation*, CXXXIV (April 20, 1932): 465–67.

[43] Washington *Herald*, March 19, 1932; Washington *News*, March 19, 1932; Baltimore *Sun*, March 20, 1932.

[44] New York *Herald Tribune*, March 25, 1932.

[45] *Congressional Record*, 72nd Cong., 1st sess., p. 7028.

whether Republican, party faithful, or party pariah, remained seated; his "camp meeting" oratory had captured the House for the moment. Elmer Davis wisecracked, "La Guardia shooed 'em one way last week, Garner shooed 'em the other way this week...."[46]

It appeared that Garner had turned the tide. Across the nation editorials cheered the Texan for corralling a runaway legislature. House leaders of all persuasions urged their followers to exercise calm but swift action. Garner now rarely left the floor as he drove the House to finish writing the revenue bill. Showing fatigue, the legislators passed amendments in rapid succession. Amendments changed the revenue bill so rapidly that congressmen found it difficult to keep up with their own handiwork.[47]

Garner had attempted to divert concern from taxation to a balanced budget but, while he altered the mood of the House, he had not changed its mind. Balloting for the first time by roll call on amendments to the bill, the House on April 1 rejected the 2¼ per cent sales tax proposal; the 236 to 160 vote finished the sales tax in the House.

To some conservatives, the tax bill revolt portended a larger upheaval. They believed the sales tax defeat heralded a mass assault on taxable wealth. The White House, Ted Clark said, feared that the revolt had been inspired by men who sought "to change the basis of our taxation and to expropriate wealth." Senator Walcott and other GOP tories shared this perspective. Albert Johnson, a Washington Republican serving his tenth term in the House, declaimed that it was part of "a desire to actually take away the property of the rich. Socialism and then some!" A New Jersey Republican, Charles A. Eaton, viewed the insurrection with a patrician's horror. "Uncertainty and madness" prevailed, said Eaton; why should the American people "surrender to a

[46] New York *Times*, March 31, 1932. Marvin Jones later claimed that he did not stand although the newspapers reported that all representatives did. "The Reminiscences of Marvin Jones," COHC, p. 660.
[47] New York *Times*, March 31, 1932.

spirit of defeatism and proletarian dependence upon the government[?] Where is the old American self-reliance, courage, and initiativeness[?]"[48]

Other sales taxers viewed the rebels as fleeing from economic common sense. A sales tax would balance the budget and a balanced budget was a springboard to prosperity. "Nothing is more important than balancing the budget with the least increase in taxes," Herbert Hoover had said on March 8. Dire consequences awaited an unbalanced budget. "Is it necessary to balance the budget?" Samuel B. Hill, a Washington Democrat asked rhetorically, answering himself, "My God, do not let the whole thing crash around our ears." It was "the cornerstone of recovery and employment," as far as Charles Crisp was concerned. The budget seemed to be an irrational factor in considering the revenue bill. Distinguished Americans like Walter Lippman and Newton D. Baker agreed that the sales tax was wrong in principle; they condemned a deficit as a political expediency, but they justified the expediency of the regressive sales tax because it might balance the budget.[49] Obviously, an orthodox logic required a balanced budget above everything else.

Many anti–sales tax congressmen, nevertheless, doubted the need to balance the budget for 1932. This was a mild revolution in the economic thinking of American politicians. "When the depression began in 1929, federal budget policy was firmly anchored to the idea that the budget should be balanced annually," an economist has written. "If anyone had suggested that large peacetime deficits were imminent, he would have received scant

---

[48] Clark to Coolidge, March 25, 1932, Clark MSS; *Congressional Record,* 72nd Cong., 1st sess., p. 6675; Charles A. Eaton to William Starr Myers, March 28, 1932, Myers MSS.
[49] Myers and Newton, p. 182; *Congressional Record,* 72nd Cong., 1st sess., p. 6351; Charles Crisp, "Does the Credit of the United States Depend on a Balanced Budget?" *Congressional Digest,* XI (May, 1932): 140; Walter Lippmann to Newton D. Baker, May 6, Baker to Lippmann, May 9, 1932, Baker MSS. For a good example of how the balanced budget argument influenced a conscientious congressman, see Harold McGugin to White, March 15, 1932, White MSS.

hearing." But times had changed minds. Several lawmakers, *sans* John Maynard Keynes, advocated a dose of deficit spending as a common-sense solution to the depression. To them, the expediency of deficit spending had a logic of its own. Representative John W. Flannagan of Virginia wondered if it was realistic to balance the budget at a time when dollars were scarce. Moreover, any crisis justified a deficit. "What nation ever attempted to balance its budget during time of war?" inquired O. H. Cross of Texas; "I assert that an unbalanced budget now and then is not an unmixed evil." The slogan had been "overplayed," Missouri's Ralph Lozier affirmed.[50] Even Joseph W. Byrns of Tennessee, chairman of the powerful Appropriations Committee, scoffed at the need to erase a deficit with a consumption levy.[51]

Many sales tax opponents viewed the budget-balancing thesis as part of a conspiracy by wealth to substitute a sales tax for higher income and corporation taxes. "It's a wonder they don't put a tax on tickets to the breadline," quipped Socialist chieftain Norman Thomas. Similar sentiments were expressed in the House. "They want to lift the burden from the great incomes to the wage earner, the farmer, the small tradesman, the masses of the people," said Clarence Cannon; "they want to shift the weight of taxation from the rich to the poor. And they know they can do it with a sales tax." Cannon did not identify "they"; he did not have to. "The tax dodgers of the higher brackets," La Guardia declared, "have been urging a sales tax ever since we had an income tax. We are not going to give it to them now." The regressive quality of the sales tax was obvious. T. Alan Goldsborough of Maryland

[50] Lewis H. Kimmel, *Federal Budget and Fiscal Policy, 1789–1958* (Washington, D.C., 1959), p. 143; John W. Flannagan, "Does the Credit of the United States Depend on a Balanced Budget?" *Congressional Digest*, XI (May, 1932): 139; *Congressional Record*, 72nd Cong., 1st sess., p. 6367; Ralph Lozier to Mrs. T. A. Dodge, April 4, 1932, Lozier MSS.

[51] *Congressional Record*, 72nd Cong., 1st sess., p. 6810. Other representatives who doubted the necessity of balancing the budget were William P. Connery of Massachusetts, T. Alan Goldsborough of Maryland, Malcolm C. Tarver of Georgia, Wright Patman of Texas, and William Nelson, Clyde Williams, and James F. Fulbright of Missouri, among others.

snapped, "The sales tax is just one other thing to make the rich richer and the poor poorer."[52]

The reasons the House voted against the sales tax are almost as numerous as the congressmen opposing it. Although most prominent journals in the nation considered it essential to the country's welfare,[53] La Guardia and Doughton had no trouble finding popular approval for their opposition. Consumers who would bear the burden of the levy formed the biggest protest group. The American Federation of Labor, the New York State Power Authority, Consumers' Research, and four farm organizations were all concerned with its effect on the purchasing dollar. Retailers, wholesalers, manufacturers, and service industries individually and collectively protested the effect a sales tax would have on their businesses.[54] At a time when consumer purchasing power had declined sharply, the sales tax threatened to depreciate the consumer's few remaining dollars. If Baruch, Mills, and other Wall Streeters did not appreciate the significance of this, thousands of merchants and industrialists did; and, although they understood little about contracyclical fiscal policy, they knew that they would see fewer customers if Congress added a sales tax to their prices. Under these circumstances, no matter what financiers said, a balanced federal budget had no merit if it cut sales.

The defeat of the sales tax also reflected a growing national resentment against all taxes as well as those which directly diminished purchasing power. Columnist Mark Sullivan speculated that Americans were most hostile to taxes which they felt immediately, like real estate levies; the sales tax likewise fell into that catgory. Over two months prior to the House rebellion, Anne O'Hare McCormick had similarly portrayed local moods. "Wherever you go you run into mass meetings called to protest against taxes," she

52 New York *Times*, March 13, 1932; *Congressional Record*, 72nd Cong., 1st sess., pp. 5284, 5889, 5709, 6035.
53 "The 'Soak-the-Rich' Drive in Washington," *Literary Digest*, April 2, 1932, p. 8.
54 New York *Times*, March 15, 16, 18, 1932; F. J. Schlink to Fiorello La Guardia, March 26, 1932, La Guardia MSS; Frank P. Walsh to George W. Norris, March 12, 1932, Norris MSS; *Congressional Record*, 72nd Cong., 1st sess., pp. 6400–6401, 6148–49.

wrote. "Opposition has seldom been so spontaneous, so universal, so determined. The nearest thing to a political revolution in this country is the tax revolt." The depression made people sullen; taxes outraged them and congressmen felt the heat of their fury. During the House onslaught against the sales tax, Claude Parsons of Illinois suggested this epitaph for the common man:

> He was taxed on boots, was taxed on shoes, was taxed
> on suits and taxed on booze,
> Was taxed on socks, was taxed on hose, was taxed on
> everything that grows.
> A tax attacked him when he was born, attacked him till
> he felt forlorn.
> If they increase, as in this bill, it won't be long
> until they will
> Impose a tax on growing corn and on the toots of
> Gabriel's horn.[55]

Then, too, the sales tax fight became tied to the competition between federal and state governments for taxable sources. Two economists cogently described this massive problem in 1932:

> Formerly the federal government relied almost solely on the tariff, except in war periods, and the states and their subdivisions depended almost wholly on the general property tax. Both federal and state governments have expanded their services and have extended their tax levies to more and more subjects or objects of taxation. Instead of having separate sources as formerly, each of them is now adding taxes to subjects and objects already heavily taxed by the other. . . .
>
> It is clear that both federal and state taxes have to come out of the incomes of the people; the pressure of one governmental jurisdiction affects the ability to meet the exactions of the other. The needs of federal and state (including local) governments are unprecedented and the current incomes of the people are not what they once were.[56]

[55] New York *Herald Tribune*, March 25, 1932; Anne O'Hare McCormick, *The World at Home* (New York, 1956), p. 93; *Congressional Record*, 72nd Cong., 1st sess., p. 6379.
[56] Roy G. and Gladys C. Blakey, "Revenue Act of 1932," *American Economic Review*, XXII (December, 1932): 640.

Two governmental units often shared the same tax base. Anyone concerned with revenue resources for state or local governments found the problem nearly insuperable unless the several governments agreed on prescribed jurisdictions. Governor Franklin D. Roosevelt of New York deplored the fact that "federal and State Governments vie with each other in taxing the same source." The situation called for restraint and precedent to arbitrate the competitive claims of various governments. "In matters of taxation," the Atlanta *Constitution* declared at the height of the sales tax struggle, "the federal and state governments should act on the broad principle of reserved rights."[57]

Many congressmen sympathized with the plight of the state and local governments. "We have more than one budget to balance," Samuel B. Pettengill of Indiana reminded his fellow lawmakers. "Are you not running a risk," asked the freshman Democrat, "that for every benefit you seek to obtain for the Federal Government you are creating a more dangerous credit structure for the municipal corporations of the country?" Farm belt states like Kansas, Nebraska, and Iowa had been considering instituting income taxes in 1931 because property taxes were too high while revenues were too low. However, their populations would not tolerate a state levy on top of the existing federal income tax. Inevitably, these and other states were turning to the sales tax. Some congressmen anticipated that the sales tax might become the states' favorite fiscal device. Even as Doughton fought the federal sales tax because he despised its regressive nature, he conceded: "As the states are so desperately in need of additional revenue, it is probable that most of them will have to resort to a Sales tax in some form in the near future." Marvin Jones later recalled that he rejected a national sales tax because "some phases of taxation must be left to the states. . . ." This view was not limited to one party or section. Jesse P. Wolcott, a Republican tyro from Michigan,

57 New York *Times*, February 20, 1932; Atlanta *Constitution*, March 22, 1932. Also see National Industrial Conference Board, *Federal Finances, 1923–1932* (New York, 1933), p. 108.

told the House, "If there is going to be a permanent sales tax, it should be left to the States. . . ."[58]

Congressmen from a few southern states already experimenting with sales taxes were concerned that Washington would infringe on their productive duty. Five of the nine states that had a sales tax by the end of 1932 were southeastern states. In 1932, Mississippi, a chronically impoverished state, increased its revenues by as much as 25 per cent with a sales tax. Mississippi politicians boasted that their example would be followed by wealthier states which faced mounting deficits.[59] Mississippians were attached to a sales tax by expediency, not principle. "The legislature of my State is now struggling with a sales tax," John Rankin told skeptical congressmen when he assailed a federal sales tax. He justified his state's sales tax because it would "save our farms and our homes" from higher property taxes. If Mississippi had the wealthy resources of the federal government, Rankin declared, it "would never impose a sales tax." West Virginia's Carl G. Bachmann read telegrams from manufacturers in his state who insisted they could not afford a double sales tax. Bachmann, the House GOP whip, feared that West Virginia would "bear an additional burden" if Congress approved a federal sales levy.[60]

At times some congressmen resolved the sales tax issue into a struggle for states' rights in fiscal affairs. "If a sales tax could ever be justified at any time," D. D. Glover of Arkansas proclaimed, "it should be reserved to the States." "The Federal Government

[58] *Congressional Record*, 72nd Cong., 1st sess., pp. 6278, 6384; New York *Times*, March 8, 1931; Doughton to Ira T. Johnston, March 24, 1932, Doughton MSS; "The Reminiscences of Marvin Jones," COHC, pp. 660–61.
[59] Howard W. Odum, *Southern Regions of the United States* (Chapel Hill, N.C., 1936), p. 127; Richard Woods Edmonds, "A New Source of State Revenue," *Current History*, XXX (November, 1930): 244; Alfred W. Garner, "A Note on the Mississippi Sales Tax," *Southern Economic Journal*, I (January, 1934): 24–27; "Sales Tax Hailed as State-Saver," *Christian Century*, L (March 8, 1933): 338; Sennett Connor, "Mississippi Tries the Sales Tax," *Review of Reviews*, LXXXVI (October, 1932): 28–29; "Mississippi Trying the Sales Tax," *Literary Digest*, May 21, 1932, p. 9.
[60] *Congressional Record*, 72nd Cong., 1st sess., pp. 6160, 6177–78. Mississippi politicians must have felt some chagrin in the midst of the tax debate when a mob protesting the sales tax invaded the state capitol in Jackson and booed

is here again seeking to invade the province of the States," William W. Arnold of Illinois warned. The future of state and local government seemed to be at stake. Cross of Texas cried out that the tax would "still further trample upon the rights of the States. Yes; enact it into law and further reduce your State to the status of a Province."[61]

The sales tax embittered and estranged Democratic congressmen from the House leadership and from national spokesmen of the party. When Jouett Shouse, chairman of the Democratic National Executive Committee, pleaded for approval of the sales tax early in the struggle, his words went unheeded. Shouse mobilized the Democratic presidential candidates of the twenties in behalf of the tax. James M. Cox praised Garner for "sensible and courageous leadership" and admonished the legislators, "We must trust our leaders, as the private trusts his general. . . ." But few Democrats listened to Shouse, Raskob, Cox, John W. Davis, and Al Smith any more than they did to Garner and Rainey. The day before the first sales tax vote, Davis, horrified by La Guardia's apparent command over the Democrats, told Shouse that Congress had "already spilled all the beans." "Sanity seems to have adjourned," Cox moaned; "the time has come for plain speaking on the part of our leaders."[62]

Both Democratic camps treated each other as apostates. Garner, in his "camp meeting" speech of March 29, had appealed to Democrats to follow their "organization," never admitting that most of the faithful believed party loyalty meant the opposite of what the Speaker wanted. Doughton and others viewed Garner as a traitor whose position threatened to wreck the party. "It looks as though our National Democratic leaders have betrayed us," Doughton told Josephus Daniels; Garner and Rainey "stand on the Republican platform on the Sales tax. . . . It looks like we are

Governor Connor, a strong proponent of the state's levy. New York *Times*, March 17, 1932.

61 *Congressional Record*, 72nd Cong., 1st sess., pp. 6263, 6251, 6367.

62 New York *Times*, Washington *Post*, March 14, 1932; John W. Davis to Jouett M. Shouse, March 23, Shouse to Davis, March 25, Cox to Shouse, March 26, 1932, Shouse MSS.

headed for destruction. . . ." Lozier of Missouri noted, "A large majority of the Democratic membership of the House is exceedingly hostile to the program of Garner-Crisp-Rainey and a little oligarchy that have undertaken to commit the Democratic Party to unDemocratic and unAmerican tax formulas. . . ."[63] These atavistic Democrats considered a sales tax as tantamount to forsaking Jefferson and embracing Hamilton. The sales tax, Doughton said, was "diametrically opposed to well established principles as expressed in party platforms, party action, and party leadership from the days of Thomas Jefferson." Several Democrats, like Mississippi's Ross A. Collins, recalled the recent Democratic platforms which denounced GOP fiscal policies and the sales tax. "Old-time Democrats would never have let this thing come on Capitol Hill, let alone permitting it to come into this House," John Rankin exclaimed. At the height of the Democratic rebellion, a Republican laughingly asked a reporter, "Well, has Garner returned to the Democratic fold yet?"[64]

The sales tax rebellion ended the incongruous Republican administration–House Democratic leadership alliance. For three months the Democratic legislative captains had assisted the GOP in passing a bipartisan program and were willing to initiate a revenue bill more than acceptable to the administration. But the Democratic rank and file had had enough of a partnership which yielded unpalatable legislation. As the rebellion gained momentum, W. L. Nelson of Missouri proudly proclaimed on behalf of his compatriots, "No longer can there consistently be made the charge that Congress lacks the courage of its convictions, or that the average member is a rubber stamp." Hiram Johnson attributed the revolt to the Democrats' irritation over their role as a "mere timorous following of the Republican Party." Mark Sullivan credited the Democratic rebels with "an attempt to change the course of the party in the middle of the session after the course,

[63] *Congressional Record*, 72nd Cong., 1st sess., p. 7028; Doughton to Daniels, March 26, 1932, Daniels MSS; Lozier to P. M. Litton, March 26, 1932, Lozier MSS.
[64] Doughton to Daniels, March 26, 1932, Daniels MSS; *Congressional Record*, 72nd Cong., 1st sess., pp. 6259–60; New York *Times*, March 17, 1932; Washington *Post*, March 22, 1932.

during the first half of the session, had been set by the leaders in the conservative direction." The restlessness in the ranks was so evident that Henry Rainey humorously remarked, "If we had brought out a bill with high income tax rates it would have been beaten. We could have substituted the sales tax and the House would have passed it."[65]

Rainey's jest detracted from the large popular endorsement of the rebellion. The Democrats' behavior was not peevishness, as Rainey suggested, but represented a genuine response to constituent irascibility. No other issue attracted a fraction of the mail which poured into Congress against the sales tax. The *Congressional Digest* observed, "Men who have served in the Senate and the House for years are on record as saying that never in their experience has their mail been so heavy as it has been during this session. If they wanted to have a breathing spell their only chance was to remain away from their offices for a day or so, for if they entered their offices it was a foregone conclusion that they would find a pile of letters and telegrams awaiting them." In the words of one editorial, the plain people have "for the first time, made their needs and desires felt through their Representative in Congress."[66]

The House rebellion taught Senate Democrats several valuable lessons. Joe Robinson would not repeat Garner's blunders. The Speaker had blundered at the outset by permitting the Ways and Means Committee to write a Democratic revenue bill without consulting a party conference in the House. As Josephus Daniels put it, "His majority is so slight that he could not afford not to take the party in his confidence and make concessions in the caucus or conference rather than have the bill so radically changed on the floor." Robinson agreed: "The lack of cohesion is damaging," he said, and promised that "the mistake will not be repeated in the Senate." The Senate Democrats would agree on a tax bill

[65] *Congressional Record*, 72nd Cong., 1st sess., p. 5934; Johnson to Mc-Clatchy, March 25, 1932, Johnson MSS; New York *Herald Tribune*, March 21, 1932; "The Month in Congress," *Congressional Digest*, XI (June, 1932): 182.
[66] "The Month in Congress," p. 182; Portland (Mo.) *Evening News*, March 26, 1932, in scrapbook, La Guardia MSS.

before they took it to the floor so that commentators like Walter Lippmann could not say, as was said of the House Democrats, "They were newborn babes [who] alarmed the country by the exhibition of their own confusion."[67]

Robinson received early warnings that many Democratic solons would reject a sales tax. On March 10, Democrats C. C. Dill of Washington, Tom Walsh of Montana, and Kenneth McKellar of Tennessee ripped into the fiscal device on the Senate floor. For the time being Robinson defended the sales tax with the usual balanced budget argument, but as the hostile attitudes of others became evident, he fell silent. When Huey Long, a Louisiana novice, lambasted the sales tax for an hour and a half on the Senate floor, he won a prolonged standing ovation.[68] Even if the House had approved the sales tax, most Senate Democrats would not have had any part of it.

For that matter, several Senate progressives were as afraid of the sales tax as their Democratic counterparts. "It is not necessary to balance the budget this year," said George Norris; and Bill Borah added, "A just and equitable system of taxation is more important." Arthur Capper, the farmer's friend, preferred nuisance taxes to a general sales tax. John Blaine's mail ran so heavy against the tax bill that he printed a form letter to explain his own stand on it. Conservative Republicans wanted the sales tax but after April 1 they conceded the cause was hopeless. A Washingtonian noted, "The senators aren't interested in the manufacturer. Its their constituents they want to hear from." In May William Allen White advised a Kansas Republican, "Don't let them kid you on the sales tax. There is dynamite in it in the country."[69]

[67] Joe Robinson to Baruch, March 25, 1932, Baruch MSS; Nevin E. Neal, "A Biography of Joseph T. Robinson," Ph.D. dissertation, University of Oklahoma, 1958, p. 374; Daniels to Baruch, March 29, Robinson to Daniels, March 25, 1932, Daniels MSS; Walter Lippmann, *Interpretations, 1931–1932* (New York, 1933), pp. 106–7.

[68] New York *Times,* March 11, 22, 1932. A good example of some Democratic thinking in the Senate on the sales tax can be found in the "T" folder, Box 148, McKellar MSS.

[69] Baltimore *Evening Sun,* April 1, 1932; *Capper's Weekly,* June 18, 1932, in scrapbooks, Capper MSS; form letter, March 14, 1932, Blaine MSS; Johnson to Chapin, May 11, 1932, Chapin MSS; White to Hoch, May 28, 1932, White MSS.

For two weeks the Senate Finance Committee listened to Ogden Mills and special interest groups assail the House excise taxes and then ended public sessions to slug it out behind closed doors. David Reed carried the sales tax banner with the aid of Reed Smoot and David Walsh,[70] their strategy calling for the elimination of a big excise tax like that on automobiles and thereby forcing a general sales tax to replace the lost revenue. Mills and Ballantine hovered around the committee to lend what assistance they could to Reed. To their dismay, the committee, led by Texan Tom Connally, reversed its field and boosted income tax rates to replace a few deleted excise taxes. Then it whipped the Reed motion to restore the general tax, 12 to 8. Smoot, angered by the upset, called in Mills to negotiate the matter; the Secretary arrived looking like "a litigant who wanted to compromise, and was willing to compromise if you could give him the judgement." Mills was determined, the committee was fatigued, and in rapid order excises disappeared and income schedules were lowered. Nobody liked the bill, but Hoover had issued two public demands to the committee to expedite the measure. With some relief, the committee turned the revenue bill over to the Senate.[71]

Conservatives had not quit on a sales tax. Encouraged by Baruch, Hoover continued to call for a balanced budget although, Ted Clark noted, it was "more a matter of a slogan than an actual belief." Most senators ignored the slogan and Idaho's Borah jocularly threatened to introduce a resolution expelling the next senator who mentioned balancing the budget. But the administration felt encouraged when the Senate rejected amendments to boost income tax rates. The GOP then switched strategy and, instead of trying to eliminate excise taxes, it endeavored to write new ones. The scheme was a simple one: "Our hope," explained Henry Stimson, "is that by the time they have put on all these

---

[70] David Walsh was the only Democrat to advocate the sales tax in the Senate, a move apparently tied to Al Smith's candidacy for the party's presidential nomination.

[71] Blakey and Blakey, *Federal Income Tax*, pp. 321–26; New York *Times*, May 6, 1932; William Starr Myers (ed.), *The State Papers and Other Public Writings of Herbert Hoover* (Garden City, N.Y., 1934), II: 175–80.

bad taxes, it will provoke so much opposition that they will go back to the sales tax." Pat Harrison immediately perceived this and, on May 25, he demanded a vote on the committee's bill, which Reed, Moses, and Fess blocked. The Democrats settled for turning back GOP attempts to reduce the tax bill to an absurdity.[72]

Hoover hoped to propagandize the Senate into believing that the sales tax would win. This was difficult because every claim that sentiment had turned in favor of the tax brought a challenge by Harrison to put it to a vote; the administration did not want this so soon. The sales taxers claimed to be within a few votes of victory and Hoover's man on the Ways and Means Committee, Charles Crisp, added fuel by announcing that thirty House sales tax opponents had changed their minds. Both La Guardia and Harrison scoffed at these assertions. After Hoover conferred with forty-one editors and publishers, reports circulated that he had told them that the sales tax would be restored in the Senate. Actually, he had implored them to endorse the tax.[73] David Reed and Reed Smoot exuded confidence and told Hoover that sentiment continued to build for the sales tax. Harrison's patience grew thin and again, on May 28, he dared the Republicans to let the Senate ballot on it. "You haven't got the votes," the Mississippian shouted at them.[74]

To prove this, Harrison, Connally, and Robert La Follette circulated a round-robin declaration pledging the signers to oppose the sales tax. In a couple of days they had fifty-five signatures, including thirty-five Democrats. Finally, Hoover conceded defeat. On May 31 he dramatically addressed the Senate. After two weeks of trying to "wear down the resistance of the obstructionists," Hoover now told the senators that "time is of the essence"

[72] Baruch to Hoover, May 10, 1932, Baruch MSS; Clark to Coolidge, May 6, 1932, Clark MSS; *Congressional Record*, 72nd Cong., 1st sess., pp. 11519, 11129–30; diary, May 24, 1932, Stimson MSS; New York *Times*, May 26, 1932.
[73] Washington *Post*, May 27, 1932; Harrison to David H. Harts, May 26, 1932, Pat Harrison MSS; New York *Times*, May 26, 1932; Theodore G. Joslin, *Hoover Off the Record* (Garden City, N.Y., 1935), pp. 233–35.
[74] New York *Times*, May 27, 28, 29, 1932.

to pass a tax bill. A haggard-looking Chief Executive informed the Senate that he never favored the sales tax, would accept the excise taxes in order to balance the budget, and wanted economy in government and expanded public works. When the president departed, Walsh of Massachusetts, in a last-ditch attempt, proposed an amendment for 1¾ per cent sales tax; the Senate defeated it, 53 to 27.[75] The sales tax was dead.

Generally speaking, the same influences which defeated the sales tax in the House prevailed in the Senate. But the decisive factor in the Senate was the House's obdurate opposition to the tax. In April Joe Robinson confided to Baruch that Senate approval of the levy had been "rendered impossible . . . by the breakdown in the House of Representatives." A month later, after conferences with Garner and Doughton, Robinson reported that sentiment in the lower chamber had not changed; Senate passage of the tax would create an impasse in Congress. Pat Harrison, who in March had shown a willingness to go along with Baruch and Hoover, switched after the House attitude became evident. "I thought it would be a waste of time, in view of the overwhelming defeat of the sales tax in the House, for the Senate to pass the proposal," he explained. Other Southerners for the tax were restrained by the House's adamance. "I am still altogether disposed to support a tax of some kind," Carter Glass declared in the waning days of the Senate debate. However, an attempt to win it, the Virginian said, "would entail a delay of weeks in the passage of the revenue bill [and] those of us who are intent on a speedy passage . . . will be compelled to vote against the . . . sales tax." Walter George of Georgia hesitated until the middle of May before he declared against the tax. The senators were anxious to put the revenue bill behind them, no matter what it contained. "Debate now prolongs the agony and makes matters worse," Josiah W. Bailey wrote. "Would it not be better to pass the bill as it comes from the Committee rather than have sixty days agitation?"[76]

[75] Joslin, pp. 228–30; Myers, II: 197–203; New York *Times*, June 1, 1932.
[76] Robinson to Baruch, April 18, May 27, 1932, Baruch MSS; Harrison to Harts, May 26, to Warren M. Wells, June 4, 1932, Pat Harrison MSS; Glass to

The self-preservation efforts of certain businessmen had hurt the sales tax in both houses. Ogden Mills blamed them for the death of the sales tax. "The House was not demagogic," he angrily told the automobile industry's lobbyist. "It was business. Businessmen all over the country wrote in opposing this tax. Every Chamber of Commerce was against it. They killed it and I have no sympathy for them. Let them pay."[77] Examples of business selfishness were plentiful. Max Factor vehemently protested that an excise tax on cosmetics would be disastrous to the industry. H. J. Heinz assured senators that he welcomed taxes on everything except all fifty-seven varieties. Tammany Hall Democrats were goaded into a vain fight against a stock transfer tax when the New York exchange threatened to move to Canada to evade it.

In the end, there was something for everyone to dislike in the tax bill. As Hoover signed the Revenue Act of 1932 on June 6, he admitted (with "tongue in his cheek," said Joslin) that "many of the taxes are not as I desired." The act called for surtaxes as high as 55 per cent on incomes over $1 million; corporation income taxes of 1¾ per cent; estate taxes of up to 45 per cent on estates in excess of $10 million; and manufacturers' excise taxes on such diverse products as crude oils, coal, lumber, copper ore, tires, toiletries, jewelry, automobiles, radios, refrigerators, sporting goods, firearms, cameras, matches, candy, chewing gum, soft drinks, and gasoline.[78]

The Revenue Act of 1932 probably was the most important piece of legislation passed by the 72nd Congress. Its rates were comparable to those of World War I and, according to one economist, it "essentially set the tax structure for the entire period up to the second world war."[79]

John Stewart Bryan, May 28, 1932, Box 1, Glass MSS; *Congressional Record*, 72nd Cong., 1st sess., p. 10292; Josiah Bailey to Malcolm Muir, May 9, 1932, Bailey MSS.
[77]Johnson to Chapin, May 9, 1932, Chapin MSS. At about this time Hoover complained that the strong banks refused to help the weak ones, preferring to leave all aid to the RFC. Diary, May 19, 1932, Stimson MSS.
[78] Joslin, p. 242; New York *Times*, June 4, 1932.
[79] E. Cary Brown, "Fiscal Policy in the 'Thirties': A Reappraisal," *American Economic Review*, XLVI (December, 1956): 868–69.

Also, the sales tax rebellion, among its several consequences, represented a monumental victory by the states over the federal government in the area of taxation. There would be no further significant attempt by the national government to employ this fiscal device which states and cities would resort to in greater numbers in the next thirty years.

Politically, the sales tax rebellion revealed latent sectional antagonisms. What little opposition the Hoover program encountered prior to March had come mostly from southern and western Democrats. The division was pronounced on the sales tax. Eighty-six per cent of all southern congressmen voted to expunge the sales tax on April 1. Only conservative Virginia voted for the tax, 5 to 4. About half of the southern states were unanimously against it. The midwestern states overwhelmingly rejected the tax except for Kansas, Illinois, and Michigan. In the latter two states, Chicago and Detroit congressmen provided the margin for the sales tax, illustrating an urban-rural split. Western Democratic senators and representatives turned down the sales tax along with numerous Republican kinsmen. On the other hand, the East strongly endorsed the tax, New York, Pennsylvania, and Massachusetts approving it in the House, 33 to 7, 19 to 9, and 13 to 2 respectively. In the May 31 vote in the Senate, not one eastern solon voted against the tax, and not one Southerner voted for it. Over all, party affiliation counted for less than sectional representation.

The sales tax rebellion was a remarkable political upset which had been stimulated by widespread popular dissatisfaction. After the sales tax had been conclusively beaten, lobbyist Pyke Johnson wrote Roy Chapin to explain why his industry faced an automobile excise tax instead of sharing a broadly based sales tax: "If we have been unable to carry through it has been because the necessities of the country weighed against everything else in the minds of the legislators and I know nothing we might have done which would have changed their course. . . . We lost in the House because the swell of protest against the sales tax was overwhelming in bitterness and intensity from business, labor and agriculture alike." The lawmakers were not interested in what big business wanted. "To them this tax bill has been the symbol of the struggle between those who have and have not," Johnson said; "they have truly reflected what has been the predominant sentiment in this country." The automobile manufacturers brought the auto excise upon themselves by rejecting higher income taxes. The lobbyist closed with some advice to his client: "Go back to the people for your strength. Only through them can you hope to win the majority to the viewpoint of the minority. . . ."[80]

The sales tax rebellion was a turning point in the 72nd Congress' history. The conservative leadership suffered its first major setback because legislators demonstrated greater concern for purchasing power than for the federal budget. Conservatives still held sway on Capitol Hill, but the rebellion had taught them that they could not preach Mellon economics as the gospel. Congress increasingly was losing faith in Hoover's recovery policies. The initiative in the session's next phase belonged to those progressives and Democrats who sought federal relief for the unemployed.

[80] Johnson to Chapin, June 1, 1932, Chapin MSS.

☆ ☆ ☆ ☆ ☆

6

THE DRIVE
FOR RELIEF

Several progressives in both parties desired congressional action to initiate economic recovery. Senators Wagner, Norris, La Follette, Cutting, and Costigan agreed that the primary issue in 1932 was unemployment relief. This is what Wagner had sought in his three bills of 1930–31.[1] Public works could ameliorate unemployment, some senators believed, if started quickly, thereby creating new purchasing power. They rejected the Hoover administration's obsession with local and private initiative (impossible without capital or confidence), its dread of radical financing, and its mania for economy and balanced budgets. Instead of being immobilized by the fear of legislating without precedent, they argued that Congress must mobilize remedial legislation to overcome despair.

The idea that the federal government should regulate fluctuations of the business cycle did not originate in the depression. Prior to World War I, few people thought of federal public works as a depression preventative. But after the armistice, fears of mass unemployment led to suggestions that public works be used to forestall it.[2] In 1919 Iowa's Senator William S. Kenyon introduced a bill to have federal public works programs expand and contract in opposite rhythm with the economy. When the

[1] See Chapter 2.
[2] An example of this was the pamphlet entitled "Public Works or Public Charity," published by the War Committee of the Union League of Chicago, author and date not given. It was subtitled, "How to meet the labor crisis arising from the demobilization of troops and war workers."

downturn failed to develop, Kenyon's proposals failed to emerge from committee.[3] But the crisis which Congress needed to interest it in such radical proposals finally came and in 1921 a conference on unemployment, summoned by President Harding, recommended that the national government adopt the policy of increasing public works expenditures during depressions and reducing them in prosperous times. Kenyon's bill won committee approval in February, 1922, only to have the Senate send it back for further hearings, where it died. By this time the apparent prosperity of the twenties made men like Kenyon seem like incurable pessimists, and little more was heard about stabilizing employment via federal public works.[4]

A major objection to Kenyon's bill had been the great authority it bestowed on the president. Similar proposals failed in Congress during 1925 and 1926. Then, in 1928, Senator Wesley L. Jones of Washington introduced a bill which permitted the president to allocate public works money only with congressional approval. However, even this check failed to satisfy the Senate.[5]

The election of Herbert Hoover sent one of the most prominent public works advocates of the twenties to the White House. As Secretary of Commerce he had promoted the 1921 Conference on Unemployment and had endorsed the Kenyon bills. In late 1928 President-elect Hoover suggested a $3 billion reserve fund to be used for public construction if unemployment rose.[6] In July, 1929, Hoover recommended that a presidential committee, with the aid of the National Bureau of Economic Research, examine the planning of public works and their relation to unemploy-

---

[3] Jack F. Isakoff, "The Public Works Administration," *University of Illinois Bulletin*, XXIII (November 18, 1938): 9–11. Kenyon called for the creation of a U.S. Emergency Public Works Board to cooperate with state and local governments in administering $100 million for public works, a meager sum by later standards.

[4] *Ibid.*, pp. 11–12.

[5] *Ibid.*, p. 12; see also "Public Works for Periods of Depression Stabilize Prosperity," *American Labor Legislative Review*, XVIII (December, 1928): 414–16.

[6] Arthur M. Schlesinger, Jr., *The Crisis of the Old Order* (Boston, 1957), pp. 85–87; "Hoover's 'Plan to Keep the Full Dinner-Pail Full,' " *Literary Digest*, December 8, 1928, pp. 414–16.

ment.[7] By the time the committee's report became public in 1930, the depression had made the findings more pertinent than anticipated. But the report warned the government against emergency public works programs since "future projects of permanent public improvements are so well defined it is unnecessary to resort to make shifts for additional work." The committee did not oppose federal public works to stabilize unemployment; rather, it valued only those in process or in the files to deal with the immediate problem. Because construction projects are slow to affect the economy, it reasoned, the real task lay in "promptly and comprehensively expediting the work on projects already planned, rather than in initiating new undertakings. . . ." The committee cautiously concluded that "long-range planning and budgeting are necessary if the full value of public works as a stabilizing influence is to be developed."[8]

Hoover concurred with the report. The president was willing to complete the works in progress but he refused to engage in long-range planning, as evidenced by his coolness to Wagner's employment stabilization bill.[9] At the depression's outset, Hoover asked a cooperative Congress for additional funds for works already under way. Throughout 1930 and 1931, the administration said, allocations mounted and projects were accelerated.[10] In December, 1931, another presidential committee examining the impact of public works on the economy repeated many of the arguments against an emergency program for depression relief and added a plea for increased business initiative to cope with the

[7] Among the members of the Committee on Recent Economic Changes of the President's Conference on Unemployment were Eugene Meyer, John J. Raskob, and Owen D. Young. Doing the research were economists Leo Wolman, Edwin F. Gay, and Wesley C. Mitchell. U.S. Department of Commerce, *Planning and Control of Public Works* (Washington, D.C., 1930).

[8] *Ibid.*, pp. 4–6.

[9] See Chapter 2.

[10] William Starr Myers and Walter H. Newton, *The Hoover Administration: A Documented Narrative* (New York, 1936), pp. 25, 34, 44, 55, 114; Ray Lyman Wilbur and Arthur Mastick Hyde, *The Hoover Policies* (New York, 1937), p. 393; Herbert Hoover, *Memoirs: The Great Depression, 1929–1941* (New York, 1952), pp. 42, 57; Isakoff, p. 13.

problem of unemployment.[11] Various scholarly authorities seconded the administration's reluctance to take the lead with works
programs. "Public works can not be extemporized," admonished
one student of the problem. Another asserted that "a general return of the unemployed to their jobs will come because business
has revived and not through their employment on public works."[12]
Business confidence pre-empted pump-priming in the minds of
free-market advocates.

Whereas some congressmen tied the issue of federal public
works to unemployment, the White House linked it to the problem of economy in government. In his State of the Union address
on December 8, 1931, Hoover recommended the creation of a
"Public Works Administration" which would unify the various
agencies then engaged in construction operations. The president
made it clear that his proposal had nothing to do with unemployment: "Great economies, sounder policies, more effective coordination to employment, and expedition in all construction work
would result from this consolidation." Stimulating employment,
he said, required voluntary measures, credit expansion, and the
action of local governments. In the words of his press secretary,
Theodore Joslin, "He was convinced that the problem of relief
... was very different from that involved in general employment."
If Washington extended job relief, it would be tantamount to a
demoralizing dole.[13]

[11] Myers and Newton, p. 156; New York *Times*, December 22, 1931.

[12] Otto T. Mallery, "Program of Public Works," *Survey*, LXV (March 1,
1931): 605; Leo Wolman, "Unemployment," *Yale Review*, XX (December,
1930): 241. The arguments against large emergency public works programs
were succinctly summarized in one article: "The works thus improvised were
able to absorb only a small percentage of the unemployed. . . . Their cost is
very high on account of the inefficiency of workers unaccustomed to their
tasks. . . . In many, even in most cases, they demoralize workers by paying
them wages higher than those they have earned. The work thus performed is,
as a rule, of questionable use to the community." Georg Bielschowsky, "Business Fluctuations and Public Works," *Quarterly Journal of Economics*, XLIV
(February, 1930): 288.

[13] William Starr Myers (ed.), *The State Papers and Other Public Writings
of Herbert Hoover* (Garden City, N.Y., 1934), II: 52, 54; Theodore G. Joslin,
Hoover Off the Record (Garden City, N.Y., 1935), p. 119.

In other words, Hoover's Public Works Administration amounted to little more than a bureaucratic shake-up designed to instill economy and efficiency in governmental building programs. Again on February 17, 1932, Hoover told Congress that his PWA would be strictly a government reorganization device incorporated into the economy bill of 1932. Public works advocates in Congress accused Hoover of a subterfuge to sidetrack the issue of unemployment. "Punk and Piffle, let's feed the hungry," exclaimed Fiorello La Guardia; "employment and starvation are the paramount issues before Congress. The President seems to be indulging in a game of legislative solitaire." In April an irate House, fresh from the tax rebellion, reduced most of the economy bill to a small portion of what Hoover had wanted and eliminated the PWA.[14]

Demands for federal public works to provide employment mounted during the winter of 1931–32. The clamor for Washington to increase its role in construction increased in proportion to the decline of state and local funds. In 1932 total public construction was nearly a billion dollars lower than it had been in 1930, despite increased federal participation. Responding to the rising toll of unemployed in construction and affiliated industries, Democrats hammered out their own federal building programs. Robert Wagner introduced a resolution for a $2 billion public works program to be executed under the employment stabilization act passed the previous February. Al Smith suggested that Congress institute a highway-building program. In January a group of economists under the aegis of William Randolph Hearst declared that a public works program of $4 to $6 billion was both feasible and necessary. In some quarters the mood of urgency had developed into a "do anything but do it now" attitude. William Allen White insisted that he was "not for doles, but for jobs." Nevertheless, he warned Senator Costigan, "I shall be for the dole if this effort to produce jobs seems to fail. We cannot afford

[14] Myers, II: 114; New York *Times*, February 18, April 25, 29, 1932. Garner labelled Hoover's economy bill "idiotic and astounding," and objected to the PWA because it would place greater authority in executive hands.

to be squeamish with self-respecting men and women who are hungry."[15]

Support for giving the urban jobless federal employment often came from rural legislators like Senator Arthur Capper. The Kansas Republican was the leading spokesman for the farm bloc and his distrust of the cities showed itself when he theorized that federal relief to the "graft ridden big cities" would aid corrupt political machines like New York's Tammany Hall rather than their distressed constituents. Capper, nevertheless, was weary of the administration's drift and resolved to endorse unemployment relief. "Here is something we cannot safely, nor humanely, leave to chance," he insisted. His plan, admittedly, would aid his farmers by distributing their surplus wheat to the hungry. In addition to jobs and succor, Capper would inaugurate a federal unemployment insurance system. He seemed to sense that the time was ripe for the farmer to make common cause with the urban worker.[16]

Also from an agrarian state, Robert M. La Follette, Jr., of Wisconsin, had long stressed the need for economic planning. The elder La Follette had been a champion of political reform for a quarter of a century before he died in 1925. What the younger La Follette lacked in his father's charisma and eloquence, he made up in intellectual sophistication while retaining "Battle Bob's" ineluctable passion for reform. Young Bob impressed Washington with his earnest and didactic manner. "Even at thirty-five," reporters observed, "he is to-day the most constructive and cohesive force among the insurgents. He has the clearest conception of economics among them."[17] The depression convinced him that broad changes in American society were imperative. Crises like the present one were products of an unequal distribution of the

[15] Schlesinger, p. 231; New York *Times*, December 15, 1931, January 9, 10, 1932; William Allen White to Edward P. Costigan, August 23, 1931, Costigan MSS.
[16] Arthur Capper to White, December 30, 1930, White MSS; "In Appreciation," November 8, "We Face a Serious Emergency," December 27, 1930, "The Man and His Job," March 7, 1931, *Capper's Weekly*, in scrapbooks, Capper MSS.
[17] [Robert S. Allen and Drew Pearson], *Washington Merry-Go-Round* (New York, 1931), p. 190.

benefits of American capitalism. No good reason existed for the periodic decline of the nation's economy if men could master their circumstances. He sought the creation of public planning to control the business cycle. He personally surveyed urban unemployment in 1931 and demanded that Congress provide relief for the cities. When the administration ignored him, La Follette attacked Hoover for lacking "the understanding or the courage to press toward the goal of alleviating the distress of the unemployed or reducing the number out of work."[18]

To establish the inadequacy of governmental knowledge to control the economy, La Follette, aided by two docile senators, Morris Sheppard and Henry Hatfield, held hearings in the autumn of 1931 on a bill for the establishment of a National Economic Council. The parade of witnesses was impressive but the results had to be inconclusive; the hearings were on a bill proposed in an old Congress calling for an executive agency probably not wanted by the Chief Executive.[19] Unlike others who emphasized that relief must come via employment on public works, La Follette cared little for the devices used as long as relief was provided.

La Follette found the perfect collaborator in the freshman senator from Colorado, Edward P. Costigan. Because of his assertiveness and governmental experience, some Democrats expected Costigan to become a commanding figure in the Senate. The lean, gaunt, dark Coloradan had been a Bull Moose Republican before President Wilson appointed him to the Tariff Commission where he served until 1928. Born in Virginia, raised in

[18] Edward N. Doan, *The La Follettes and the Wisconsin Idea* (New York, 1947), pp. 163–64, 171; "La Follette Routs the 'Old Guard,'" *Literary Digest*, January 15, 1930, p. 13; New York *Times*, January 8, 9, 1930; Robert M. La Follette, Jr., "The President and Unemployment," *Nation*, CXXXIII (July 15, 1931): 62.
[19] U.S. Congress, Senate, Subcommittee of the Committee on Manufactures, *Hearings on S. 6215, A Bill to Establish a National Economic Council*, 72nd Cong., 1st sess., 1931. Among the witnesses were Frances Perkins, Henry I. Harriman, John Maurice Clark, Father John A. Ryan, Leo Wolman, Gerard Swope, Eugene Meyer, Albert H. Wiggin, Alfred P. Sloan, Jr., Daniel Willard, Sidney Hillman, Charles E. Mitchell, John L. Lewis, and Melvin A. Traylor.

Colorado, and educated at Harvard, the aristocratic Costigan presented a suave, aloof facade, but friends knew him as a determined crusader for social justice.[20] He maintained that government should be concerned with the needs of all men rather than "enlarge the profits and the privilege of the few" as it had in the twenties. He called himself "a Republican by antecedents with Democratic propensities" and many reformers envisioned his role as that of a welding agent for bipartisan progressivism. Still in 1931 a newcomer to the Senate, Costigan indicated a tentative willingness to follow the lead of La Follette, twenty years his junior.[21] On November 11, 1931, La Follette, Costigan, and Representative David J. Lewis of Maryland[22] met in Costigan's office with members of the most important welfare organizations in the country to determine the need for federal unemployment relief. Only the American Red Cross refused an invitation to be represented because it felt that it would be "impolitic." At a time when the administration insisted on private and local relief, the organizations engaged in that activity freely conceded that they lacked the funds for it. They pointed out that relief costs had risen geometrically in the last few years while their resources sharply declined. Only an unknown minority of relief cases could be handled by private agencies.[23] For La Follette and Costigan, the findings were enough to warrant bills for relief and hearings

[20] George Creel to Costigan, November 9, 1930, Costigan MSS; Fred Greenbaum, "Edward Prentiss Costigan: A Study of a Progressive," Ph.D. dissertation, Columbia University, 1962; "They Stand Out from the Crowd," *Literary Digest*, May 4, 1935, p. 22; New York *World-Telegram*, January 27, 1932; William McLeod Raine, "Costigan of Colorado," *Nation*, CXXXI (October 29, 1930): 465–66.
[21] Edward P. Costigan, "A National Political Armistice?" *Atlantic Monthly*, CXLVII (February, 1931): 260; Costigan to Creel, January 14, 1931, to Robert M. La Follette, January 20, 1931, Costigan MSS.
[22] Lewis, at 62, had returned to the House in 1931 where he had served a western Maryland district from 1911 to 1917. Beginning at the age of nine, he had worked in the coal mines while studying law and educating himself until he was admitted to the bar when he was 23. Like Costigan, he was a Wilsonian Democrat who had been on the Tariff Commission from 1917 to 1925.
[23] Transcript of "Conference on Federal Unemployment Relief," November 11, 1931, Costigan MSS.

by La Follette's subcommittee of the Senate Committee on Manufactures in late December.[24]

The hearings contradicted the administration's relief policies. In November, when Costigan requested data on unemployment and relief funds from the President's Organization on Unemployment Relief, chairman Walter S. Gifford replied in generalities. He assured Costigan that all localities were prepared for the winter and that fund quotas had "gone over top." Again the Coloradan patiently prodded Gifford for information; this time Gifford ignored him. At the hearings on January 8, Costigan pursued Gifford with questions which revealed that federal relief would be the administration's very last resort. A state would have to be "absolutely broke" and without any further means of raising revenue, Gifford conceded, to qualify for federal aid. He acknowledged that conditions were bad and getting worse, and that his organization had no sound information on unemployment or available relief. Gifford, president of American Telephone and Telegraph, was satisfied that private and local facilities would handle the situation. Costigan, losing his patience, snapped, "You are always hopeful." Unruffled, Gifford replied, "I find it pleasant, Senator, to be hopeful."[25] Silas H. Strawn of the U.S. Chamber of Commerce was one of the few to appear before the committee to object to federal relief for the jobless.[26]

La Follette and Costigan collected a sizable amount of testimony revealing that private contributions for relief counted for little and that, while the state and local governments were the most involved parties in relief, their financial sources could not keep pace with public needs. Social workers, economists, and

[24] Although the two senators introduced separate relief bills, they were so similar that there never seemed to be much doubt that they would be incorporated after joint hearings were held. See Josephine C. Brown, *Public Relief, 1929–1939* (New York, 1940), p. 103.
[25] Costigan to Walter S. Gifford, November 3, Gifford to Costigan, November 9, Costigan to Gifford, November 12, 1931, Costigan MSS; U.S. Congress, Senate, Subcommittee of the Committee on Manufactures, *Unemployment Relief*, Hearings on S. 174 and S. 262, 72nd Cong., 1st sess., 1931–32, pp. 309–33 *passim*.
[26] Senate, *Unemployment Relief*, pp. 357–58, 378.

local government officials attested to this. The stories of hardship told by social workers would remain the most vivid protraits of human misery inflicted by the depression. Again and again senators would refer to this record for evidence to justify federal relief. In late January the Manufactures Committee sent the La Follette–Costigan bill to the Senate floor.

The progressives' bill, coming during the period of bipartisan cooperation, held the distinction of being the first measure considered in almost two months of the 72nd Congress which did not have administration approval. If, after a tough fight, it won Senate and House acceptance, it probably would be squelched by a presidential veto, even though the measure was neither exorbitant nor threatened state sovereignty. At a time when some people discussed projects costing $3 or $5 billion, the La Follette–Costigan bill would make 40 per cent of only $375 million available to states on a population basis, with the remainder to go into a reserve fund to be allocated according to need. Conservatives objected to its direct relief features and before it reached the Senate floor, the bill became a hotly discussed topic. Both Senate leaders, Robinson and Watson, wanted to recommit the bill; Costigan vowed to resist such a move. Many Republicans wanted to kill it outright; many Democrats hoped to make it more palatable by de-emphasizing public works and strengthening the states' jurisdiction.[27] On February 1 the Senate began its debate.

After months of being bottled up, the genie of federal relief had escaped; to exorcise it, conservatives employed the dreaded word "dole." Most senators in 1932, regardless of party, were more concerned with a man's spirit than his stomach. They considered charity more debilitating than hunger. To give a man sustenance without requiring a day's labor was a social wrong. Against this emotional argument the progressives were helpless. The epithet, "dole," had haunted the committee hearings, forcing relief advocates like Paul U. Kellogg, editor of *The Survey*, to confront it: the hostility to direct aid, he argued, based itself upon

27 New York *Times*, January 19, 22, 31, February 1, 1932.

arguments which were a combination of "dope, emotion, and class interest." If unemployment relief was a dole, then so were the RFC and the moratorium. Moreover, as a New York newspaper bitterly cracked, "sneers about a dole will not feed hungry men and starving babies."[28]

During cross-examination in the committee Costigan had demonstrated a prosecutor's talent for inquiry; on the Senate floor, La Follette, senior in legislative service, led the fight. In a three-hour opening speech, La Follette employed all the data he could muster to underline the urgency of relief. He informed the Senate that a personal poll of American city governments had revealed that 305 metropolises wanted direct federal assistance to cope with their relief problems. The bill was not a dole, he maintained: "It proposes only to distribute funds through agencies of relief now in existence and cracking and groaning under the load they are attempting to carry."[29]

Divisions among relief advocates further impaired the cause. They all wanted a bill, but they disagreed on the La Follette–Costigan proposal. Several Democrats wanted more local self-help and public works in the bill. On February 3 a trio of Democrats, Hugo Black, Thomas Walsh, and Robert Bulkley, submitted their own plan with the semiofficial approval of their Senate leadership. They changed the $375 million in grants to loans to those states which could demonstrate that relief funds could no longer be borrowed. Another $375 million would be allocated for work relief, thus removing any possible dole stigma. But Wagner pointed out that many states already had reached their constitutional limitations on debts and could not assure the repayment of loans. On February 11 Wagner put forth his own amendment to deduct the loans from annual roadbuilding grants to the states beginning in 1937. The three versions concurred that the states no longer could finance their own unemployment relief and, for some indiscernible reason, agreed on the figure of $375

[28] Senate, *Unemployment Relief*, p. 85; New York *World-Telegram*, February 2, 1932.
[29] New York *Times*, February 2, 1932.

million.[30] Still, there would have to be greater accord to pass any relief bill over strong bipartisan opposition.

On February 10 the fight over the La Follette–Costigan bill produced what one conservative journal described as the most exciting debate of the session. Before crowded galleries that included a smiling Bernard Baruch, Simeon Fess calmly initiated an attack on the bill, but soon his fists were vehemently pounding a desk until his knuckles were bloodied. The little Ohio regular emphasized the dole argument with such fierceness that William Borah could not resist taunting him. Borah professed not to see the difference between state and federal aid to families although Fess insisted that only state relief was proper. The Idaho solon chided the administration for its readiness to lend money to corporations but not to individuals. "It is a conflict of materialism of one side, and humanity on the other," he asserted; "I am endeavoring to place the individual human being on the same level as a corporation in the United States." He denied that federal aid to persons constituted a dole. In an obvious reference to the RFC, he insisted, "If you ask what evils may flow from such a precedent I shall ask what evils will flow from the practice of giving bankers money from the treasury."[31]

La Follette and Costigan expertly marshalled their available forces. Organized labor supported their bill as it had Wagner's the year before, William Green assailing the Black-Walsh-Bulkley measure as "a mere subterfuge" and pleading for the progressives' version. Following an all-day conference in Washington on February 9, more than 100 labor leaders marched to the White House to express their approval of the La Follette–Costigan bill; Hoover received their statement without comment. On January 29 Costigan fired off a telegram to Governor Franklin D. Roosevelt urging him to use his influence with New York's senators; FDR responded with a telegram to Wagner.[32]

But S. 3045—the La Follette–Costigan bill—clashed with the

---

[30] *Ibid.*, February 3, 4, 12, 1932.
[31] *Ibid.*; Washington *Post*, February 11, 1932.
[32] New York *Times*, February 5, 10, 1932.

Black-Walsh-Bulkley substitute in mid-February and more senators expressed their reservations by seeking amendments. By the time they came to a vote, the two bills were nearly identical. Both provided $375 million for road-building and the same sum for relief. Yet, there were two vital differences: the original called for relief in the form of outright grants administered by a federal agency; the substitute made loans to be repaid or deducted from future highway grants to the states with administration by state agencies.[33] Most progressives opposed the substitute and states' rights Democrats retaliated by blocking the original.[34]

Wagner and La Follette should have united on one bill but Wagner sought a distribution of funds based on a 1930 census of the unemployed while La Follette pointed out that their numbers had sharply increased in two years. La Follette seems to have encouraged voting against all amendments until only his bill remained. On February 15 the Senate rejected the substitute bill, 48 to 31. The next day, after debating it for four hours and deftly killing three amendments, the Senate turned down the original bill, 48 to 35. Only fifteen senators, all Democrats voted for both the original and the substitute.[35] If the La Follette progressives and

[33] We are indebted to Walsh of Montana for this brief analysis. *Congressional Record*, 72nd Cong., 1st sess., p. 3938.

[34] *Ibid.*, pp. 4023, 4046–48. La Follette claimed that by forcing the states to compensate the federal government for loans, relief ultimately would be financed by state property taxes instead of federal income taxes. On the other hand, Black of Alabama protested federal bureaucracy encroaching upon the states.

[35] New York *Times*, February 14, 15, 16, 17, 1932; *Congressional Record*, 72nd Cong., 1st sess., pp. 3911–14; Washington *Post*, February 17, 1932. Of the fifteen for relief, five were nonprominent Southerners. Others who supported both bills included Bulkley, Wagner, and Tom Walsh, sponsors of versions which La Follette and Costigan would not accept.

Also, it should be noted that just five Democrats voted against both bills. They were Josiah Bailey of North Carolina, Hubert Stephens of Mississippi, Millard Tydings of Maryland, and David Walsh and Marcus Coolidge of Massachusetts. Bailey's vote was anti-urban because he believed that the cities, whether Chicago or Charlotte, were shirking their responsibilities in relief and they had the greatest wealth. Walsh's opposition to federal relief in 1932 contradicted his advocacy of it the year before; La Follette excoriated Walsh for this inconsistency. Walsh did not reply then but later told Edward Keating that he feared for local responsibility. Josiah W. Bailey to Josephus Daniels, February 20, 1932, Daniels MSS; *Congressional Record*, 72nd Cong., 1st sess., pp. 4039–41; David I. Walsh to Edward F. Keating, February 27, 1932, Keating MSS.

the substitute-bill Democrats could have united behind one relief bill, it probably would have passed.[36]

The Republicans were determined opponents to any federal relief for the jobless. Some thirty Republicans rejected both bills and when administration stalwarts like Simeon Fess and David Reed doubted the need for relief, it augured a presidential veto. As Key Pittman remarked, it was futile to pass a bill that would be vetoed, knowing that the majority lacked the strength to override the veto.[37]

Outside of Congress, relief opponents waged a vigorous campaign. Many conservatives insisted that federal succor in any form would harm, not help, the states. In the words of James A. Emery of the National Association of Manufacturers, "Federal aid impairs the fundamental political relations of the States and the nation, lessens their sense of responsibility, checks their action and reduces them to mendicant provinces awaiting Federal philanthropy." Sometimes sophisticated men permitted their instinctive dislike of charity to distort their reasoning. Walter Lippmann approved of federal aid to states that had exhausted their financial resources; but, he said, "these states cannot be the great industrial states where there is the largest amount of unemployment. The industrial states are the richest states, and if Federal aid is to be extended, they must not expect to receive aid but to give it."[38] In other words, the states with the greatest difficulties had to help the states with the least and expect nothing in return. The Minneapolis *Journal* declared that the La Follette–Costigan bill would have created a "Dole Bureau"; the Boston *Transcript* said that it "would have cost Congress the confidence of the business world."[39] All of these themes were decisive despite the massive

[36] Twelve Democrats voted for the substitute and against the original; ten progressives voted against the substitute and for the original. These two groups, along with the core of fifteen, probably would have passed a relief bill they could agree on, presuming that there were still thirteen and seventeen nonvoters as on the two ballots.

[37] *Congressional Record*, 72nd Cong., 1st sess., p. 4050.

[38] New York *Times*, February 6, 1932; Walter Lippmann, *Interpretations, 1931–1932* (New York, 1933), p. 139.

[39] Quoted in the Washington *Post*, February 20, 22, 1932.

evidence of distress compiled by the Manufactures Committee. Abstractions were deemed more important than conditions.

"The Forty-Eight who voted against relief have not heard the last of it," the New York *World-Telegram* forecast. "They will hear from the hungry again."[40] In March support for federal relief began to crystallize. The fact that many states and cities bordered on insolvency was no longer neglected. Congressmen did not need the progressives to inform them that their local governments could not finance relief or that millions of people needed help; their mail effectively established these points. In April Tom Amlie noted, "In the last few weeks I believe that there has been a growing realization on the part of Members of the House that the situation we are facing is extremely grave. This fact alone, in my opinion, is encouraging." He thought that if the La Follette–Costigan bill could be revived, it would pass.[41]

Still, any attempt to enact such legislation would encounter resistance from the White House. The day after the Senate defeated the La Follette–Costigan bill, Robert Wagner introduced a new relief bill which incorporated the most acceptable features of the moribund S. 3045. Democrats in the House mustered behind a road-building works bill but ran into administration intransigence. The GOP warned that the works would damage the economy program.[42] In early March Hoover conferred with those lawmakers whom he considered "represented the important Congressional committees concerned with relief and recovery" and told them that he wanted their "frank advice" as to whether he should continue relief through his committees, "appropriate

---

[40] New York *World-Telegram*, February 17, 1932. Felix Frankfurter wrote Senator Costigan a personal note: "President Eliot, you will recall, used to say that a real man devoted to a cause, after its defeat, asks 'When will the fight begin again?' Well, that was a grand fight you waged and such a fight is never lost. In one form or another you continue this fight during all your Senate days. Your presence in the Senate is an enormous reinforcement for the causes that matter—courage and wisdom in dealing with human affairs in public life." Frankfurter to Costigan, February 17, 1932, Costigan MSS.

[41] Thomas R. Amlie to Charles P. Hackett, April 23, to Claude Downs, April 29, 1932, Amlie MSS.

[42] New York *Times,* February 18, 28, 1932.

funds for direct doles," or expand public works beyond his program. The meeting might have been fruitful if the participants
had included such men as La Follette, Costigan, Black, Bulkley,
Wagner, or Tom Walsh. But the president had not sought an
exchange of ideas on relief, merely a confirmation of his own ideas.
He could expect this from his conferees, Senators Watson, Reed,
Fess, Robinson, and Glass and Representatives Garner, Snell,
Hawley, Crisp, and Steagall. Only Garner, according to Hoover,
held out for "nonproductive" public works.[43]

Spring came to Washington in 1932 and found a Congress too
fatigued to appreciate it. The few months that had passed since
December 7 had been the most enervating that many of the lawmakers had ever known. Pat Harrison, in Congress for over two
decades, could say without reservation that "this has been the
most strenuous session we have ever had. . . ." The circumstances
were extraordinary and had produced problems which were, Representative Ralph Lozier commented, "more complicated, controversial, embarrassing, hatred creating, [and] passion producing.
. . ." "Most of us are tired beyond description," Hiram Johnson
told C. K. McClatchy. When legislators reflected on previous
years, they remembered little to compare with the situation they
faced after three winters of depression. John B. Kendrick, who
had represented Wyoming in the Senate for three terms, thought
the first session of the 72nd Congress "has been the most trying
. . . of my entire experience." Key Pittman recalled the turbulence
of a wartime Senate and sadly decided that "conditions of the
War were nothing like these."[44] A newcomer to that austere body,
Josiah Bailey, was shocked by the demands made upon him; he
complained that he was "working about twice as hard as I did
when I was running [for the Senate]." Congress looked forward
to adjournment sometime in June. "We're all ragged here, physi-
cally and mentally," the volatile Hiram Johnson wrote. "Nerves

[43] Hoover, *The Great Depression*, p. 153.
[44] Pat Harrison to Phillips Jay, May 25, 1932, Harrison MSS; Ralph Lozier to
W. W. Smith, May 28, 1932, Lozier MSS; Hiram Johnson to C. K. McClatchy,
June 26, 1932, Johnson MSS; John Kendrick to N. A. Pearson, April 25, 1932,
Kendrick MSS.

are so raw that anything may take place in Congress. . . . The urge is not infrequent these days to punch somebody in the eye."[45]

The burden of the depression problems upon the legislators was staggering. North Carolinians crowded Bailey's office seeking advice, jobs, or relief. "The demands made upon me have been almost more than I could bear." Bailey wrote. "Everybody wants the Government to save his home, if he had one, and those who do not have homes want jobs. If I could just meet their wishes, I would be a very happy man, but it depresses me mightily to go through a long series of disappointments every day. I feel pretty badly broken down." His mail was so heavy that Tom Amlie estimated it would require two stenographers working eight hours a day to answer each letter individually. "This job here is terrible," said Amlie, a conclusion without dispute in Congress.[46]

Moreover, spring brought no regeneration of hope since many of them expected conditions to worsen. "Desperate" was a word they used again and again to describe the national economic condition and the Washington mood. "There is a great deal of hysteria and loose talk around here," Amlie observed in late April. Washington seemed to have lost any sustaining courage or will to believe that prosperity would return in due course. Instead, some politicos privately predicted that the bottom had yet to be reached. "I fear that our greatest danger from an economic standpoint is yet ahead of us," Bob Doughton wrote; "I hear many expressions of apprehension from those in high authority." Speaker Garner was more specific. He quietly forecast on April 22 that within the next sixty days the nation would be plunged into a new financial panic "in spite of anything accomplished or that anyone can do." That same day Josiah Bailey was equally pessimistic: "I have been driven to the conclusion that the Ad-

[45] Bailey to William Bailey Jones, April 5, 1932, Bailey MSS; Johnson to McClatchy, June 5, 1932, Johnson MSS.
[46] John R. Moore, "Josiah W. Bailey of North Carolina and the New Deal, 1931–1941," Ph.D. dissertation, Duke University, 1962; Bailey to Daniels, undated, ca. 1932, Bailey MSS; Amlie to George Garrigan, March 15, 1932, Amlie MSS.

ministration's last card will be as vain as all the others, and there-fore, we are rapidly approaching a very grave crisis." Members of the Senate Banking and Currency Committee were talking ex-pectantly of more disasters to befall the nation.[47] Pessimism per-vaded the Capitol.

Even the administration believed that a new crisis, not prosper-ity, was just around the corner. Ted Clark noted that a feeling of foreboding had infiltrated the White House. President Hoover began a luncheon conversation on May 16 by telling Henry Stim-son that he anticipated a crash within the next three weeks.[48] In early June Charles G. Dawes resigned as president of the Recon-struction Finance Corporation, issued a chary public statement, and headed back to Chicago to resume the management of his bank. Two days before his departure, Dawes allegedly told a senator that the country soon would experience a final crash. Dawes had gone back to put his house in order.[49] The rhetoric of confidence had become submerged in a welter of despair.

If a turning point in the depression was imminent, few people believed that it would be for the better. "The outlook for the Country is very gloomy," said Bailey; "we have reached the point now where nothing will serve save a very severe shake-down and rebuilding almost from the ground up." Great changes would soon take place in the land. "Seemingly, we are in the incipient stages of a rapidly developing social and economic revolution," Ralph Lozier remarked. According to Tom Amlie, "We have by no means reached the middle of the depression. . . ." The situa-tion would deteriorate further and bring unforeseen conse-quences. William Allen White wondered if America could

[47] Amlie to E. A. Polley, April 28, 1932, Amlie MSS; Robert Doughton to T. C. Bowie, May 6, 1932, Doughton MSS; John N. Garner to Daniels, Bailey to Daniels, April 22, 1932, Daniels MSS; Johnson to McClatchy, May 14, 1932, John-son MSS.

[48] Edward T. Clark to Calvin Coolidge, May 27, 1932, Clark MSS; diary, May 16, 1932, Stimson MSS.

[49] Amlie to Garrigan, June 8, 1932, Amlie MSS. A few weeks after the Dawes resignation, the RFC loaned his bank $90 million. Schlesinger, p. 238. See also memorandums for June 26, 1932, Binder 46, G. L. Harrison MSS.

survive a fourth winter of depression without a revolution. Newton Baker articulated the thoughts of enlightened conservatism
when he told Daniel Willard,

> I have great respect for the President and for the earnestness and
> devotion with which he is trying to fight his way through in the
> dark, but . . . from the crash in 1929 until now, the President
> has quite genuinely believed that "prosperity is just around the
> corner." In the meantime, we have turned a number of corners
> without finding it. The real problem in America is not to feed
> ourselves for one more winter, it is to find what we are going to
> do with ten or twelve million people who are permanently dis-
> placed. . . . I am far less worried about left wing radicalism than
> I am about right wing lack of foresight.[50]

Amid these trepidations the pressure for federal relief swelled.
On May 1 a group calling itself the Joint Committee on Unemployment met in Washington and demanded jobs for the jobless.
"What has thus far been done in Washington is in the nature of
a palliative," economist E. R. A. Seligman told Senator Wagner;
"I think that we are ready for something positive, and we must
not forget the great dangers of inaction and further drifting."[51]
Charity had been exhausted, William Allen White advised Senator Capper: "We can no longer depend on passing the hat, and
rattling the tin cup. We have gone to the bottom of the barrel.
I know this is true for Kansas. . . ." When the La Follette subcommittee of the Senate Manufactures Committee reconvened to
consider a new relief bill in May, Edward P. McGrady of the
American Federation of Labor depicted the jobless as being on
the verge of revolution. "There are another two B's besides balancing the Budget, and that is to provide bread and butter," declared the labor leader. The newspapers were filled with reports
from private organizations, cities, counties, and states that relief

[50] Bailey to Jones, April 5, to J. H. McAdam, April 12, 1932, Bailey MSS;
Lozier to W. C. Michaels, June 10, 1932, Lozier MSS; Amlie to Chris Morison,
March 7, 1932, Amlie MSS; White to Capper, May 25, 1932, White MSS; Newton
Baker to Daniel Willard, August 8, 1932, Baker MSS.
[51] New York *Times*, May 1, 4, 1932. Seligman had a financing plan calling
for peace bonds like the war's emergency loans.

had become too immense a task to be handled by them. Incidents of violence involving civil authority increased in frequency. As Mayor Cermak of Chicago told the House Banking and Currency Committee, either the federal government would send relief or it would send troops.[52]

May became the month Congress embraced federal relief. "The movement for Federal aid apparently was gaining ground in the Senate, particularly among the Democrats," the New York *Times* observed early in the month. "Sponsors of the movement were talking more optimistically than at any previous time this session." Schemes for succor came from all quarters. A Wagner bill already was under consideration. On May 6 Costigan and Representative Lewis jointly introduced a plan to give the states $500 million for public works to be paid for by a bond issue. Senator John H. Bankhead of Alabama called for an immediate appropriation of $100 million for the jobless to be distributed by the president. Senator Royal Copeland revived his idea to permit the RFC to give loans to the cities for relief of the unemployed.[53]

Conservative Democrats did not want the relief movement to get out of their control. During the summer of 1931 Bernard Baruch's factotum, Hugh Johnson, had toured midwestern industrial centers, discussed economic conditions with manufacturers and bankers, and returned appalled by the extent of unemployment and the lack of job relief. Plants like Ford's, Johnson reported, were shutting down or laying off workers in large numbers; iron and steel orders were sharply reduced and, except for public works, there was little construction in operation or planned. Nevertheless, Baruch emphasized state relief until January, 1932, when he told Joe Robinson that he was giving the matter of federal relief "a great deal of study." In March Baruch and Johnson unveiled for Robinson a plan for "self-liquidating"

[52] White to Capper, May 17, 1932, White MSS; U.S. Congress, Senate, Subcommittee of the Committee on Manufactures, *Federal Cooperation in Unemployment Relief*, Hearing on S. 4592, 72nd Cong., 1st sess., 1932, pp. 36–37; Irving Bernstein, *The Lean Years* (Boston, 1960), pp. 465–67.
[53] New York *Times*, May 7, 10, 11, 1932.

public works.[54] Fearing that a progressive or Hoover plan would take the political initiative from the Democrats, Baruch and Robinson quickly publicized their relief scheme in early May. They no longer insisted that relief belonged to the states. As he announced the Baruch plan on May 11, Robinson declared, "The time has arrived when action should be taken by the Federal Government."[55]

The next day the president detailed his own plan, one which harmonized with Baruch's. Hoover drew a sharp distinction between "productive" and "unproductive" public works. The issuance of bonds to pay for the latter, he cautioned, would be a "direct charge upon the taxpayer or upon the public credit." He would expand the RFC to handle the financing of public works. The works had to be income-producing or "self-liquidating" because payment for their use would balance their costs. Toll bridges, power-producing dams, municipal waterworks, and slum clearance were prime examples of productive works. When progressives argued that nonproductive works at least would provide employment, Hoover retorted that the number of jobs created would not be worth the expenditure.[56]

Hoover and the progressives agreed solely on the need for a resumption of investment to create work and restore public confidence. On the other hand, the area of agreement broadened considerably between the White House and the conservative Democrats to include a balanced budget and pay-as-you-go works. Walter Lippmann derided the progressives' visions. "It is a vain hope to think that a major deflation can be stopped by the relatively small influence of the most grandiose public works scheme," he wrote. "The Robinson-Hoover plan is, therefore, a truly statesmanlike effort to deal by sound principle with a problem which will otherwise surely provoke the adoption of entirely

[54] Hugh Johnson to Bernard Baruch, August 3, Baruch to Joe Robinson, December 11, 1931, telegrams, January 22, March 7, telegram (not sent), March 8, Arthur Krock to Baruch, May 17, 1932, Baruch MSS.
[55] New York *Times*, May 12, 1932.
[56] Myers and Newton, pp. 201–11.

unsound principles." Only business' recovery could raise employment and Lippmann feared that federal competition would damage state financing and frighten business investment away. In brief, Lippmann accepted most of Hoover's tenets as valid, although he wondered if they would triumph. Unless the conservative plan prevailed, "something much more contemptuous of 'fine spun theories of financing' will certainly be substituted for it."[57]

A tacit coalition existed between Democratic leaders and Republicans on public works as it had through most of the session. Robinson, who had been, said Henry Stimson, "pretty faithfully working with Hoover," believed that the president would cooperate with conservative Democrats. The Chief Executive concurred with Baruch on the need to prevent Congress from passing what Baruch called "a worse program coming from log-rolling for government work."[58] In an election year, however, such bipartisan collaboration, even among conservatives, had little chance of enduring through June and July. Both parties wanted credit for remedial legislation and this alone dispelled any enduring bipartisanship.

As the New York *Times* editorialized, the Hoover and Robinson plans, by only conceding the necessity of federal aid, represented "in substance, if not in form, a victory for Senator La Follette and Senator Wagner." Senator Costigan rejoiced that "the prospects of helpful legislation have greatly brightened within the last week." "Certainly Congress must not adjourn without preparing a relief fund," declared Senator Arthur Capper. Across the Capitol, three representatives, Clyde Kelly of Pennsylvania and James Mead and Fiorello La Guardia of New York, announced that they represented a bipartisan group dedicated to keeping Congress in session until a relief bill passed.[59] Thus, by

[57] Lippmann, pp. 79–91.

[58] Diary, May 17, 1932, Stimson MSS; Robinson to Baruch (telegram), May 12, Baruch to Krock, May 16, Robinson to Baruch, May 16, 1932, Baruch MSS. Baruch told Mark Sullivan that he was willing to do everything he could "to hold the Democrats to this limited program." Mark Sullivan to Larry Richey, May 26, 1932, Sullivan folder, Box 26, Richey MSS.

[59] New York *Times*, May 14, 15, 1932; Costigan to Dr. Sherwood Eddy, May 17, 1932, Costigan MSS; Capper to White, May 20, 1932, White MSS.

mid-May the question was not whether to legislate federal aid, but what form it should take.

When John Nance Garner announced his own relief bill on May 19, there were not less than five major relief bills for Congress to consider, with perhaps dozens of variations to come in the form of pet amendments. Among the major bills there was no sharp disagreement. The amount to be spent varied from President Hoover's $1.8 billion to Senator Wagner's $2.4 billion. With the exception of Senator Robinson's proposal, they agreed that the RFC would distribute the bulk of funds. Most agreed on financing with bond issues but differed on sums. Only the La Follette subcommittee's and Garner's versions contained grants or works which might be tagged "doles."[60] Ample opportunity remained for conflict on particulars.

With four of the five proposals bearing a Democratic stamp, the administration had been placed on the defensive. Hoover maintained silence for a few days but as Snell, Watson, and Mills assailed the Democratic plans, there could be little doubt of his hostility. On May 22 the White House blasted the Democrats as profligates. "We cannot thus squander ourselves into prosperity," the president proclaimed. The Garner plan, calling for numerous post offices to be built throughout the nation, most rankled Hoover. On May 27 he told his cabinet that he had prepared "a hot message for Garner"; later, at a news conference, he denounced the Garner bill: "This is not unemployment relief. It is the most gigantic pork barrel bill ever proposed to the American Congress. It is an unexampled raid on the public treasury."[61] Similarly, the president restlessly probed for a way to stymie the Senate Democrats. He thought of a series of bitter attacks to drum up public support for his program. He considered inviting forty or fifty senators to the White House to ask for their resistance to the Garner plan, deliberately snubbing the other senators. Finally, on May 31 Hoover went to the Senate to plead for a

[60] New York *Times*, May 21, 1932.
[61] *Ibid.*, May 22, 23, 28, 1932; Myers, II: 189–95, 196; diary, May 27, 1932, Stimson MSS.

balanced budget and less spending. ". . . The course of unbalanced budgets is the road of ruin," the president warned.[62]

Because of its unblushing extravagance, the Garner relief bill sometimes embarrassed its supporters. Its public works proposals seemed designed more for electing Democrats than providing jobs. Many people, regardless of party, branded it "pork barrel" legislation and cited the plethora of post offices and other nonproductive works that augured a presidential veto. "The Garner bill is worse than nothing," William Allen White gibed. Democrat Ralph Lozier believed that the bill would help the construction and ancillary industries more than the unemployed. Also, the costs would require additional taxes which the common man would bear. For a newspaper like the Washington *Post*, which had not acclimated itself to any form of federal aid, the Garner bill was "vicious," "wicked," and "monstrous."[63]

But Garner was determined to see his bill approved by the House. "If the President suggested this plan it would not be pork-barrel—it would be statesmanship," the Speaker snapped. No "ham, a slice of or a smell of 'pork' " would Garner permit in his bill. The sales tax rebellion had taught Garner the need to secure a commitment from the Democratic membership, and on June 3 he caucused the House Democrats to rally them behind his relief bill. Several Southerners were unhappy about it; led by tight-fisted Joe Byrns of Tennessee, they assailed portions of it as wasteful. Edward H. Crump, the Boss of Memphis, diligently tried to mollify his kinsmen. The first vote on the bill went in Garner's favor, 98 to 43, but this was not enough to bind Democrats to it. On the second vote, Byrns threw in with Garner and the caucus endorsed the bill, 123 to 18. The Speaker triumphantly

[62] Clark to Coolidge, May 27, 1932, Clark MSS; Myers, II: 197. Hiram Johnson, on the subject of economy, once wrote: ". . . We're such a fickle and volatile people that we are quite likely to become asphyxiated by the emanations from our own expressions and phrases. . . ." Johnson to McClatchy, April 24, 1932, Johnson MSS.
[63] White to Henry Allen, May 29, 1932, White MSS; Lozier to Samuel W. Sawyer, to T. O. Stanley, May 30, 1932, Lozier MSS; Washington *Post*, May 25, 1932.

emerged from the four-hour conference predicting that the House would pass it in four days.[64]

To facilitate action by the House, Garner decided that the lower chamber would debate and vote on his bill on June 7 under a rigid rule limiting discussion to three hours. Republicans were infuriated but the Democrats scorned objections, pointing out that the GOP had pushed the Hawley-Smoot tariff under a similar procedure. The rule stipulated that only members of the Ways and Means Committee could offer amendments. The Republicans frantically tried to devise some strategy of resistance while a few Democrats voiced disgust.

The debate on the rule forecast the furor over the bill. William Bankhead, who led off the procedure fight, candidly acknowledged that the limit on debate was "very strong-arm and drastic"; but he reminded everyone that it had been used before in emergency and wartime conditions. Circumstances in 1932, the Alabaman said, were more desperate than those of 1917. Republican Earl Michener appealed to progressives to be consistent in their opposition to gag rules, but La Guardia immediately shot back that "in deciding between relief for human suffering and my preference for parliamentary procedure, I must decide in favor of alleviating human suffering." Michener's appeal for rules, the New Yorker declared, cloaked an opposition to relief at a time when relief was more imperative than parliamentary procedure. Thirteen Republican progressives joined with the Democrats to pass the rule, 205 to 189.[65]

The oratory that followed ranged freely from eloquence to vituperation with even some poor, sardonic verse mixed in, as in these lines from a New York Republican:

> Odor of pork is in the air.
> A Democratic Speaker is in the chair.
> Hog Callers, calling in despair.
> Pigsties, post offices everywhere.

[64] New York *Times*, May 28, June 1, 4, 1932.
[65] *Ibid.*, June 8, 1932. That same day the House passed a law deporting alien communists. *Congressional Record*, 72nd Cong., 1st sess., pp. 12097–99.

The Democrats had the momentum. John O'Connor of New York decried Hoover's "self-liquidating" requirement for public works as "somewhat similar to that old bromide about 'balancing the budget.' " By 216 to 182, the House approved the Garner bill.[66]

Washington's attention then centered on the Senate where Wagner's bill ran into more effective GOP opposition. W. Warren Barbour of New Jersey incorporated the Hoover proposals into a bill to counter Wagner's and Ogden Mills assisted with an appearance before the Senate Banking and Currency Committee on June 7. A clash between the Secretary of the Treasury and the New York senator aptly defined their differing relief philosophies. "I'm trying to put men to work and you won't cooperate," Wagner brusquely accused. "I want to break the ice by lending to industry so that somebody will begin to spend money," Mills retorted. The exchange tersely summed up the history of the 72nd Congress. But the next day the committee rejected the Barbour version, 9 to 6, and sent the Wagner bill to the Senate floor, 7 to 4.[67]

Wagner divided his proposals into two separate bills and on June 10 the Senate debated the section that empowered the RFC to make loans totaling $300 million to the states, the amount to be apportioned according to each state's 1930 population and to be administered by the states. Wagner shrewdly made the federal corporation the dispensary of relief while the population criterion satisfied more senators than that of need. Also, senators preferred state administration of funds because they feared federal bureaucratic interference in state relief.[68] Loans would be made only when the states could establish their incapacity to give relief and they would be repaid by deducting from federal funds to the states for road-building rather than plunging the states further

---

[66] *Congressional Record*, 72nd Cong., 1st sess., pp. 12189–90, 12191, 12197–99, 12199–12244 *passim.*

[67] New York *Times*, June 8, 9, 1932.

[68] Robert Wagner to Alfred E. Smith, June 13, 1932, "Special Correspondence," Wagner MSS.

into debt. In sum, the Wagner bill reflected the mind of an artful legislator as well as a determined welfare advocate.

When the Senate voted 72 to 8 for the Wagner bill on June 10, it demonstrated, as Senator Costigan noted, "that legislation which was taboo in January is sanctified in June." In essence, it represented a victory for the objectives of the La Follette–Costigan bill. Wagner freely admitted that his bill was a variation of the February attempt at relief. Many senators who desired a more radical bill without Wagner's compromises frankly and hopefully predicted that the loans would never be repaid. M. M. Logan of Kentucky could see nothing amiss if Congress wished to make a "donation" to the states. Costigan candidly described the loan provision as a "subterfuge." The progressives wanted the Wagner bill but viewed it as, in Hiram Johnson's words, "a mere drop in the bucket." "My first criticism of this measure," said La Follette, "is that it comes belatedly from a grudging government." The bill was "inadequate in amount and wrong in principle." Perhaps the unanticipated endorsement of the bill by Republican conservatives bothered the progressives. Frederic C. Walcott of Connecticut, an old colleague of the president's from war relief days, endorsed it along with the author of the administration's substitute, Warren Barbour.[69]

The second Wagner proposal straddled a line between lawmakers irreconciled to federal relief and those who sought liberal allocation of aid. This measure, calling for $3 billion to be loaned by the RFC for self-liquidating public works, became the subject of a hotter, lengthier debate. The progressives endeavored to increase the appropriation but Wagner feared that Hoover would veto a bill with greater funds.[70] On June 22 La Follette proposed spending more billions than Wagner for public works and the

---

[69] *Congressional Record*, 72nd Cong., 1st sess., pp. 12526, 12513, 12517, 12530, 12545–47, 12535–37. The eight votes against the bill came from Republicans Warren Austin and Porter Dale of Vermont, Hiram Bingham of Connecticut, Felix Hebert and Jesse Metcalf of Rhode Island, George Moses of New Hampshire, and David Reed of Pennsylvania and Democrat Thomas Gore of Oklahoma.

[70] *Ibid.*, pp. 13340–56 *passim*.

Senate overwhelmingly rejected this, 56 to 12.[71] That same day
the Senate defeated an amendment by Moses of New Hampshire,
57 to 19, to strike out a provision for a $500 million bond issue
for public works. Moses objected to the works, not the financing.
The vote evidenced strong White House disapproval of the bill
as most Republicans close to the president went with Moses.[72]
The next day the Senate turned down a Moses amendment to
place the administration of public works solely in the hands of
the president, 50 to 20. Then, without a roll call, the Senate passed
the second Wagner relief bill.[73]

Congress now faced the touchy problem of adjusting the
Wagner and Garner bills while accommodating the White House.
The Senate's bills, although conservative enough for the New
York *Times* to find them "a great improvement over Speaker
Garner's,"[74] still remained far from satisfactory to President
Hoover. On June 24 Hoover cavalierly declared he was glad to
see Congress adopt some of the RFC provisions "for which I
have been contending" and "in line with major objectives I have
been advocating." Nevertheless, he made it clear that the bills
were unacceptable because they contained "pork barrel char-
acteristics," and would incur a budgetary deficit. Hoover insisted that relief allocations should be based on actual need rather
than population. The president served fair warning that unless
"these destructive factors and delinquencies" were rectified in
conference, a veto would be forthcoming. Wagner irately retorted that the president was a Johnny-come-lately public works
advocate although he may have believed in such measures "within
the silence of his own heart." The New Yorker accused Hoover
of being "petty," "not quite candid," and denied that his bill
would unbalance the budget.[75]

[71] *Ibid.*, p. 13702; New York *Times*, June 23, 1932.
[72] *Congressional Record*, 72nd Cong., 1st sess., p. 13671. Only two Democrats,
Gore and Logan, voted for the amendment.
[73] New York *Times*, June 24, 1932.
[74] *Ibid.*, July 11, 1932.
[75] Myers, II: 214–16; *Congressional Record*, 72nd Cong., 1st sess., pp. 13944–
45; New York *Times*, June 24, 25, 1932.

The congressional session had run later than expected and everybody was exhausted. For months congressmen had talked wearily about adjourning by June 1, but by the last week of that month it appeared doubtful that they could leave Washington before July. One example of the frayed nerves occurred when John Nance Garner went to Bertrand Snell's office to suggest that they, as party leaders, might better handle the House end of the works bill conferences with the Senate than the appointed conferees. Snell rejected the Speaker's idea, preferring regular channels. The gentlemen exchanged words, then began pounding a desk with their fists and filled the office with loud epithets that sent secretaries running into the halls. "I hate a man without guts," Garner bellowed. Snell countered, "Well you've run aplenty yourself this season." For a moment Garner could not find a come-back, and when he did, reporters regretted that it was unprint-able. The Speaker stormed from Snell's office, his ruddy face more crimson than ever. On the floor of the House Garner and Snell exchanged barbs of little consequence as Garner resignedly ap-pointed five members of the Ways and Means Committee to rep-resent the lower chamber at the conference.[76]

In the latter part of June, the Democrats opened their con-vention in Chicago to nominate a candidate against Hoover, and Washington grew so politically charged that an easy agreement on the relief bill appeared remote. Nor could Congress adjourn without producing a bill modeled on Hoover's requirements. The conferees worked slowly while the Democratic convention distracted them. Finally, on July 1, the day the Democrats nomi-nated Franklin D. Roosevelt for president, the conferees an-nounced a compromise bill. But the compromise was doomed. Watson and Snell both forecast a veto because the White House perceived "objectionable features" in it.[77] Negotiations between the administration and congressional Democratic leaders proved fruitless. On July 6 Hoover personally blamed Garner for the impasse and accused the Speaker of wanting to turn the RFC

[76] New York *Times*, June 25, 1932.
[77] *Ibid.*, July 2, 4, 5, 1932.

into "the most gigantic banking and pawnbroking business in all history." Garner, now the Democratic nominee for vice-president, became a hero in the House for standing firm before Hoover. He was through with "class legislation," he told cheering Democrats and progressives. Snell answered that Garner was demagogic and suddenly a woman in the public gallery shouted, "Remember November"; the Republican leader halted and looked up in astonishment while Democrats laughed uproariously.[78]

Most House Democrats and progressives were committed to the Garner bill in spite of Senate and White House opposition. The House passed the conference bill on July 7, 202 to 157, the negative votes almost unanimously Republican.[79] Republicans continued to object to Title II of the bill which called for expanded RFC loans to local governments and industries. Many House Democrats viewed it as necessary to supplement the weakened credit facilities of banks. Senate Democrats, however, still hoping for a bill acceptable to Hoover, vainly sought to talk the Speaker out of a certain veto. Some Democrats suggested that Garner's stubbornness made Hoover seem more conciliatory, to the political advantage of the White House. As Joe Robinson observed, "I fear Garner is letting the President take relief legislation which Wagner and I with other Democrats have worked so hard to pass."[80]

The defection of Garner to the spenders had upset the coalition of Republican and Democratic leaders. The Senate Democratic leadership frantically sought to repair the economy dike against the flood of expenditure bills. The concept of self-liquidating public works, agreed to by Hoover and Robinson, conformed to that of balancing the budget. As it had on the sales tax, the Senate Democratic leadership cast its lot with the White House. But Garner had lost command of his House following once before on the budget issue and was determined not to repeat

[78] *Ibid.*, July 6, 7, 1932; Myers, II: 222–26.
[79] One hundred sixty-six Democrats, thirty-five Republicans, and one Farmer-Laborite voted for it; 155 Republicans and two Democrats were against it.
[80] Robinson to Baruch, July 7, 1932, Baruch MSS.

that mistake. This time the Speaker spearheaded the House attack against the conservative alliance. Not even the threat of an executive veto could deter the passage of a spending bill which Hoover and Baruch had hoped to thwart with a commitment to a balanced budget.

Congress soon tired of debating a bill destined to be vetoed. Charles McNary announced that he would vote for the bill in order to get a quick veto and repassage. Josiah Bailey forecast that Congress would pass the measure with the understanding that Hoover would reject it. Indeed, the Senate passed it on July 9, 43 to 31, and two days later Hoover, as anticipated, vetoed the Garner-Wagner bill.[81] The president, in an abrasive veto message, detailed the wrongs of the measure as well as his familiar recommendations: ". . . I can not approve the measure before me fraught as it is with the possibilities of misfeasance and special privileges, so impracticable of administration, so dangerous to public credit and so damaging to our whole conception of governmental relations to the people as to bring more distress than it will cure."[82] A week later Congress passed a compromise relief bill, adjourned, and five days later Hoover quietly signed the Emergency Relief and Construction Act.

The relief act was a Pyrrhic victory for the Hoover administration. "We finally won our point for the reproductive public works," the president exulted in his memoirs. He had opposed any federal relief at first, insisting on voluntary or local action. But the Emergency Relief and Construction Act heralded, in the words of one scholar, "the entrance of the federal government into the field of relief." As expected, the loans never were repaid and thus became the grants which Wagner, La Follette, and Costigan desired.[83] Hoover got his type of financing and the relief

---

[81] New York *Times*, July 8, 9, 10, 1932; Bailey to R. C. Moore, July 9, 1932, Bailey MSS. The Senate's division was fourteen Republicans and twenty-nine Democrats for the bill, twenty-five Republicans, five Democrats, and one Farmer-Laborite opposed to it.

[82] Myers, II: 233; New York *Times*, July 15, 16, 1932.

[83] Hoover, *The Great Depression*, p. 148; Edward Ainsworth Williams, *Federal Aid for Relief* (New York, 1939), p. 49; Paul Studenski and Herman E. Krooss, *Financial History of the United States* (New York, 1963), pp. 357–59.

advocates won the works projects Hoover had earlier opposed. The Hoover-Robinson advocacy of federal relief had been a "sudden, remarkable somersault," in the words of an excited Hiram Johnson. Wagner, La Follette, and Costigan had charted a new role for Washington. Near the end of the session, Arthur Capper observed that the relief bill would be "of a kind that would have seemed fantastic and unreal even six months ago."[84]

Hoover seems to have lost valuable time in his fight against the depression and the Democrats. Conservatives no longer could sustain the moribund belief that relief was solely the function of state and local government. Hoover protested that the government could do little to promote prosperity without industry; but many people insisted that the government could quicken the pace of production. No longer could Hoover justify intransigence on abstract principles of preserving states' rights and individual initiative. Perhaps, in the words of an admirer, "if any one attitude lost the election in 1932, it was Hoover's refusal to use federal resources in direct relief."[85] Hoover and the fear of his veto power had blocked a concerted drive by progressive Democrats and Republicans to use federal funds to stimulate the economy. Only after worsened conditions had disintegrated his arguments did the president retreat and, with a veto, dictate the terms of his defeat.

As Hoover signed the Emergency Relief and Construction Act, a symbol of the forces that changed his mind sat encamped on Anacostia Flats in Washington—the Bonus Expeditionary Force. The rag-tag army of unemployed World War I veterans had come to Washington to collect a bonus for their wartime services that was not due until 1945. The White House opposed the payment for the usual budgetary reasons. Nevertheless, on June 15 the House voted 211 to 176 in favor of Wright Patman's bill to pay the bonus. The conflict among progressives represented the

[84] Johnson to McClatchy, May 14, 1932, Johnson MSS; Capper to White, June 1, 1932, White MSS.
[85] Harris Gaylord Warren, *Herbert Hoover and the Great Depression* (New York, 1959), pp. 206, 208.

divided sentiments throughout Congress: Fiorello La Guardia viewed the bonus as unnecessarily favoring one group of the un- employed; Tom Amlie liked the dividend because he doubted that any other unemployment relief bill would be as effective; and La Follette, fighting for a public works bill, eschewed the vet- erans' bonus because it would force his measure to be scuttled by an economy-minded Congress.[86]

The bitterness and hope of the veterans was revealed while the Senate debated the bonus bill on June 17. The old soldiers lob- bied fiercely and derided their opponents, as in this parody:

Hoover is our shepherd
We are in want
He maketh us to lie
Down on the park benches
He leadeth us beside the still factories
He disturbeth our soul
He leadeth us in the path of destruction for his party's sake
Yea, though we walk through the valley of depression
We anticipate no recovery for those who art with us
Thy politicians and diplomats frighten us
Thou preparest a reduction of our salary in the presence
    of our enemies.

Our expenses runneth over
Surely poverty and unemployment will follow us
And we will dwell in mortgaged homes forever.[87]

But the Senate rejected the bill, 60 to 20, and the veterans ac- cepted the news with dignity. A bugle sounded, they sang "Amer- ica," and, in orderly fashion, 20,000 tattered and disheartened veterans marched off to their encampment. It was, said Arthur Vandenberg, who voted against the bonus, "the most amazing, colorful, ominous, tragic and yet thrilling experience of a life- time. . . . The final climax to the 'siege of Washington' has yet to

[86] Arthur Mann, *La Guardia: Fighter against His Times, 1882–1933* (Phila- delphia, 1959), p. 308; Amlie to E. J. Mallory, June 13, to Donald P. Fina, June 24, 1932, Amlie MSS.
[87] "Bonus—1932," found in Rainey MSS.

be written."[88] Meanwhile, the budget-minded lawmakers continued to prevail in Congress.

The attitudes of the lawmakers toward their experience of the last eight months varied sharply. Republicans tended to deprecate the work of the 72nd Congress' first session as much as Democrats hailed it. Progressives had a confluent sense of accomplishment and frustration. There had been numerous triumphs for the progressives: they had written a progressive revenue act, passed the Norris–La Guardia anti-injunction law and the Emergency Relief and Construction Act, and sent George Norris' lame-duck amendment to the states. In March, as Norris embarked on another futile drive for federal operation of Muscle Shoals, even so staunch a Democrat as John Garner privately expressed admiration for the Nebraskan: "Surely his statesmanship has been established so far as the judgment of this Congress is concerned." But the mavericks bemoaned the greater tasks that were neglected. "It has been the most horrible session since the war, and [possibly] any during the war," Hiram Johnson gloomily commented. Fear had reigned over mastery: "Every individual in authority during the last session has conjured up ghosts of disasters and ruin until I think the whole of Washington got a sort of shell shock which rendered it incapable of thinking, or acting intelligently. The Congress has done more things with less knowledge in this session than in any other sessions ever held."[89]

Stout conservatives shared Johnson's hyperboles and morose view of recent events, albeit from a different perspective. The direction set by the White House and Capitol Hill frightened old tories like Carter Glass: "I do not think Congress did one sound or orthodox thing nor did the President recommend one thing which was not tainted with State socialism. The Democrats went along with him only because they refused to be put in the attitude of obstructionists, but I am perfectly confident that the

[88] "The Bonus Expeditionary Force," Scrapbook 4, Vandenberg MSS. For more on the B.E.F., see Schlesinger, pp. 256–65.

[89] Garner to Daniels, March 7, 1932, Daniels MSS; Johnson to McClatchy, July 17, 1932, Johnson MSS.

precedents set by the legislation enacted will ultimately do more harm to the country than the depression which it was designed to cure." It seemed as if there had never been another congressional session like this one. "In my thirty years of experience in Congress," Glass concluded, "I never had my endurance taxed as at this last session. . . ."[90]

The administration and its allies excoriated the record of the Congress. "With the adjournment of Congress in July, 1932," Hoover wrote in his memoirs, "the whole country drew a sigh of relief. Confidence began to return."[91] Only the administration appeared to have retained its sanity and clear vision. "How Congress qualifies for a very high ranking in a mad world," Ogden Mills remarked. The Newark *News* headlined, "Congress Quits its Job and Everybody is Happy." The Troy (N.Y.) *Record* declared, " It has been a long time since any Congress had made such a mess of things as this." Everything that Congress had touched independently had been despoiled, it argued; "all the good work it did during its session was forced upon it by the President." The trouble with Congress, the *Saturday Evening Post* advised, was that the legislators necessarily had parochial attitudes. "We should not ask too much of Congress, for even our modest expectations are too likely to be disappointed." Republican newspapers like the Washington *Post* believed that, on the basis of actions during the last year, "President Hoover has acquired a significant advantage in the coming political contest."[92]

The jeers notwithstanding, the first session of the 72nd Congress had accomplished much when Democrats followed the president. "Few Congresses in recent years have enacted more important legislation during a period of six or seven months than has the present one," E. Francis Brown commented; "yet upon its head has been visited the opprobrium of the Nation. . . . Congress has been cast for the role of the scapegoat, a part which

[90] Carter Glass to Clarence H. Poe, July 29, 1932, Box 299, Glass MSS.
[91] Hoover, *The Great Depression*, p. 163.
[92] Ogden Mills to Garrard Winston, May 13, 1932, Mills MSS; "Congress's Terrific Blow at the Depression," *Literary Digest*, July 30, 1932, pp. 1-2; "Parochial Politics," *Saturday Evening Post*, July 12, 1932, p. 20.

any impartial examination shows to be wholly undeserved." Brown argued that the 72nd Congress had "avoided an undue amount of oratory and has worked with dispatch." This is most apparent when contrasted with the 71st which, although loaded with an overwhelming majority from the president's party, consumed more than a year in deliberating a tariff bill that never fully satisfied the Chief Executive. Ironically, virtually without a majority to rely upon in the 72nd, Hoover won most of his program. The moratorium, the RFC, and the Glass-Steagall act were decisive victories early in the session, and even after the sales tax rebellion, Congress gave Hoover the substance of what he wanted. Representative of this was the Home Loan Banking Bill passed on the last day of the session, together with the relief bill, as the president requested. Hoover complained of "heartbreaking delays all along the line," but the remarkable aspect of the first session was that so little had been left over for the second session. The 72nd had delivered in some form almost everything that Hoover had asked for during its first session, a noteworthy feat for any Congress, particularly in a presidential election year with an incredibly divided legislature.[93] Most of the "defeats," which Hoover said later he had suffered, concerned RFC powers, farm and home credit extension, and sundry minor parts of his program.[94]

The 72nd Congress, spurred by conservative Democratic leaders intent on throttling imprudent spending which contradicted the economic principles of the previous decade, had written a surprising record of cautious achievements. ". . . Retrenchment, revenue and relief . . . were the all-dominating three Rs of the tempestuous session just ended," columnist Frederic William Wile wrote. Garner's turnabout in favor of heavy spending came in recognition that an election year in a crisis demanded

[93] This point was privately and publicly emphasized by French Strother, a White House secretary. See "Robert P. Lamont" folder in Box 9, "Review of Reviews" folder in Box 12, and Strother to White, July 27, 1932, in Box 15, Strother MSS.

[94] E. Francis Brown, "Congress Plays Its Part," *Current History*, XXXVI (July, 1932): 464–65; Hoover, *The Great Depression*, pp. 121–23, 163.

opposition to the status quo. The most embattled moments of the session, the sales tax rebellion and the drive for unemployment relief, were in response to the exigencies of popular pressure. The Omaha *World-Herald* summed up the 72nd Congress' first session in this way: "The wonder is not that it did so badly, but that it did so well; not that it denied the President so much, but that it yielded him so much; not that it was so hopelessly divided, but that, on recurring great occasions it got together and functioned."[95]

[95] Both quoted in "Congress's Terrific Blow at the Depression."

☆ ☆ ☆ ☆ ☆

7

THE MOST AVAILABLE MAN

PROPONENTS OF FEDERAL RELIEF believed that the one prominently mentioned candidate for president in 1932 who might provide active leadership was Franklin D. Roosevelt. They had little choice. The GOP would renominate Hoover; Democratic possibilities like Smith and Garner offered little more than the incumbent. On the basis of his record as governor of New York, Franklin D. Roosevelt became the hope of progressivism in 1932.

If congressional caucuses had nominated the presidential candidates in 1932, the results would have been the same as at the Chicago conventions. Ignoring a handful of malcontents who would deny Herbert Hoover an opportunity to succeed himself, Republicans almost indifferently concluded that the party would do worse if it turned its back on the Chief Executive. "My faith in Hoover is unshaken," Arthur Capper insisted at a time when others doubted; "I still believe he is the best man we have for the job."[1] But Democrats had a pleasanter task. An overwhelming number of Democrats in the national legislature desired Roosevelt to head their ticket. Together with a few dozen progressives, a majority of Congress preferred Roosevelt in 1932.

Unlike the Republicans, the Democrats faced the upcoming campaign with enthusiasm. The depression had begun to reverse the GOP tide in 1930 and as the crisis deepened in 1932, the confidence of the Democrats climbed. It seemed that the outcome of

[1] Arthur Capper to William Allen White, June 1, 1932, White MSS.

179

few elections had been so insured before they were held. Fourteen months before the Democrats chose their candidate, even the gloomy Cordell Hull wrote: "Only the democratic party by its failure to function, can save the republican party and its Hoover administration from overwhelming defeat in 1932."[2] It would require the most sanguine Republican to perceive a ray of hope through the overcast of circumstances. For the Democrats, the problem involved converting a sure thing into a winner.

The congressional Democrats thought they had a winner in Roosevelt. It is surprising, in retrospect, that Roosevelt did not have more challengers for the nomination in what had to be a Democratic year; perhaps this is a tribute to the strength of his candidacy. But others who sought the nomination lacked Roosevelt's availability. Al Smith wanted another crack at Hoover and when Democrats realized that the Roosevelt-Smith split was genuine, the threat of another Smith candidacy frightened more Democrats into F.D.R.'s camp. John Nance Garner was better liked outside of Congress. Newton D. Baker did not want the nomination and few congressmen thought of giving it to him, except as a last resort. A scattering of other candidates provided little choice for the politicos; Governor Albert C. Ritchie of Maryland sounded like Hoover and was known only in his state; W. H. ("Alfalfa Bill") Murray, governor of Oklahoma, provided the party with color but little more; and industrialist Owen D. Young was popular only with Democratic conservatives who were rapidly losing a strong voice in party affairs. On the other hand, Roosevelt could not miss; he had a magic name, a progressive record, had been a winner in New York, and had a properly nebulous position on prohibition and international affairs. Another Smith race could spell disaster; the Democrats believed they could not afford to lose the White House again. A majority in Congress would not be enough; committee chairmanships were fine but federal patronage was better. "I am tired of being in the minority," Key Pittman grumbled. "I want to win."[3]

[2] Cordell Hull to W. E. Norvell, Jr., April 31, 1931, Hull mss.
[3] Fred L. Israel, *Nevada's Key Pittman* (Lincoln, Nebr., 1963), p. 96.

Roosevelt was a winner in a state that counted heavily. Many Democrats welcomed F.D.R.'s ascendency in the Empire State and rejoiced that the 1928 elections had relieved them of the burden of Smith's presidential candidacy. Within a month after Smith's defeat, South Carolina's James F. Byrnes told Roosevelt, "You offer the only hope for democracy to again get control of the government." "Under your leadership," Congressman Adolph Sabath of Chicago wrote FDR, "we will have a better opportunity of success."[4] During Roosevelt's first term as governor, Democrats watched intently to see how he would handle his task. In the spring of 1930, Senator Burton K. Wheeler, a progressive Democrat, jumped the gun by hailing Roosevelt as "a General to lead the people to victory under the banner of a reunited, militant progressive party." Roosevelt's power policies appealed to Wheeler, but most of all, the Montanan said, "with him I feel sure we can win." Roosevelt repeated his electoral success even more impressively in 1930 and made believers out of some doubters. "The Democrats nominated their President yesterday, Franklin D. Roosevelt," cracked Will Rogers. Senator C. C. Dill of Washington, reassured that the New York governor was a public power man, became an enthusiastic Roosevelt-for-president partisan. But issues mattered less to other Democrats. Roosevelt could carry New York and therefore he could win; "Franklin Roosevelt will be the nominee," Key Pittman prophesied.[5]

The Roosevelt bandwagon gathered speed in 1931 as Cordell Hull of Tennessee guided its fortunes in the Capitol. Hull was, by his own admission, "the Cassandra of Congress," viewing the present with gripping desperation and the future with morbid foreboding. He had strong convictions—free trade, the Democratic party, and an amorphous "progressivism" being his articles

---

4 Earland I. Carlson, "Franklin D. Roosevelt's Fight for the Presidential Nomination, 1928–1932," Ph.D. dissertation, University of Illinois, 1955, p. 10.
5 Frank Freidel, *Franklin D. Roosevelt: The Triumph* (Boston, 1956), pp. 136–37, 167; C. C. Dill to Edward F. Keating, November 12, 1930, Keating MSS; Key Pittman to W. G. Greathouse, November 10, 1930, Pittman MSS.

of faith—all clouded with premonitions of disaster. Thus, the Democrats had to be decisive or the party "will go into dissolution after 1932," wrote Hull with his usual urgency; "it is now or never with the Democratic party. . . ."[6] And, as if afraid to permit the world to know how really bleak matters were, he admonished his correspondents with a legend on his letters, "Confidential-Destroy." Hull nonetheless put aside his misgivings and flung himself into the struggle to save the party and the Republic by directing both on a "progressive" course; his trepidations never immobilized him. Franklin Roosevelt offered hope in 1932.[7]

Besides using Hull, the governor himself often invited Democratic congressmen to visit him in Albany or at his vacation retreat in Warm Springs, Georgia. En route to Warm Springs, Roosevelt would pause in Washington to confer with Hull and other supporters like Senator Thomas J. Walsh and Representatives Henry T. Rainey and William Ayres. His backers were western and southern Democrats, a fact which comforted those who feared that Roosevelt was another parochial Tammany politician like Smith. The Bryanite Democrats wanted someone who could carry New York without being part of the Tammany machine; the Democratic National Committee meeting in March, 1931, gave Roosevelt a chance to demonstrate substance to the rumor that there was a rift with the Smith people. The Shouse-Raskob attempt to alter the party's stand on prohibition drove Southerners into Roosevelt's arms. FDR's campaign manager, Jim Farley, sat with Hull and other Dixie politicians during the meeting and reassured them that they had a New York ally. After the June governors' conference at French Lick, Indiana, newspaperman Frank Kent observed that, because of John Raskob's hostility, Democratic governors leaned to FDR's candidacy.

---

[6] Hull to Josephus Daniels, February 29, 1932, Daniels MSS.
[7] For additional insights into Hull, see his *Memoirs* (New York, 1948), p. 134; Ewing Y. Mitchell to Hull, March 5, 1932, Mitchell MSS; Hull to Daniels, February 29, March 12, 1932, Daniels MSS; Mitchell to Frank P. Walsh, January 18, 1932, F. P. Walsh MSS; and New York *Times*, March 4, 1931.

The party knew for certain now that Roosevelt and Smith spoke different languages.[8] The rush to Roosevelt began early. A week after the fateful March meeting, old Thaddeus Caraway of Arkansas told the press that he was committed to the favorite-son candidacy of his colleague, Senator Joe Robinson, but if Robinson could not make it, he wanted Roosevelt. A few months later he practically invited Robinson to leave the race when he declared that "the unanimity of public opinion" in Arkansas was pro-Roosevelt.[9] Throughout the summer and fall of 1931, others publicly or privately made known their preference. Senators William J. Harris of Georgia, Josiah W. Bailey of North Carolina, William H. King of Utah, Alben Barkley of Kentucky, Kenneth McKellar of Tennessee, and Robert Bulkley of Ohio acknowledged that Roosevelt was the man to beat. Few of them were forthright in declaring for Roosevelt. Most were more circumspect; they liked the front-runner and wanted to be on his side if he won, but as Key Pittman put it, "Experience has taught me that candidates may make and break themselves in a very few months."[10] Many politicians on the bandwagon had not settled down; they were prepared to abandon it if it broke down.

In an effort to solidify support in Congress and acquire additional adherents, FDR's representative, Homer Cummings, went to Washington in February, 1932, and conferred with as many senators as Hull could round up. Twenty-four senators representing twenty states lunched with Cummings on February 13.[11] The solons liked what they heard. Reflecting later on the confer-

8 Freidel, pp. 179–82; Frank Kent to Bernard Baruch, June 5, 1931, Baruch MSS.
9 New York *Times*, March 14, June 6, 1931.
10 *Ibid.*, June 5, August 9, 1931; Pittman to William A. Kelly, February 13, 1932, Pittman MSS.
11 Among those attending were Joe Robinson, Sam Bratton of New Mexico, Duncan Fletcher and Park Trammell of Florida, Hubert Stephens of Mississippi, John Kendrick of Wyoming, William King of Utah, Edward P. Costigan of Colorado, Walter George of Georgia, and Matthew Neely of West Virginia. Washington *Post*, February 14, 1932.

ence, Hull thought "it was really a turning point in the Roosevelt candidacy."[12]

Throughout the spring of 1932 the drive moved indefatigably forward from the New Hampshire primary on, with only minor detours in the California and Massachusetts primaries. As far as Washington was concerned, the Roosevelt performance was superb. The city swarmed with Roosevelt partisans who were selling their candidate. Washington lawyer Robert W. Woolley employed his numerous contacts to sound out congressmen on FDR and found them very receptive.[13] Frank P. Walsh, Roosevelt's power commissioner in Albany, traveled to Washington to reassure public power advocates that the governor was one of them. Walsh, a former Kansas City lawyer, also secured the help of Representative Joseph Shannon in lining up the Missouri House delegation behind Roosevelt. At the instigation of Jim Farley, Edward P. Costigan sought to persuade the Colorado state Democratic convention to instruct its national delegates for Roosevelt.[14] More congressmen, like Robert Doughton of North Carolina and W. W. Arnold of Illinois, declared for him. "In my opinion," Senator Pat Harrison pontificated, "Governor Roosevelt will be nominated on the first ballot, as he is undoubtedly the most available man."[15]

With equal confidence, however, William Gibbs McAdoo insisted that John Nance Garner was "the most available man we can nominate." Garner posed the only formidable threat to the Roosevelt candidacy in the anti-Smith West and South. Democrats who dreaded anything tainted with Tammany Hall turned to the Speaker as a natural preference to Roosevelt. Businessmen

---

[12] Rough draft of a letter, Hull to Colonel E. M. House, December 31, 1932, Hull MSS.

[13] See 1931–32 correspondence with Robert W. Woolley, House MSS.

[14] Walsh to Mitchell, March 10, 1932, F. P. Walsh MSS; James A. Farley to Edward P. Costigan, May 21, Costigan to Walter Walker, May 26, 1932, Costigan MSS.

[15] Robert L. Doughton to James M. Curley, January 26, 1932, Doughton MSS; W. W. Arnold to Franklin D. Roosevelt, May 27, 1932, Democratic National Committee file, Roosevelt MSS; Pat Harrison to W. B. Herbert, May 26, 1932, Pat Harrison MSS.

rated him as conservative enough to qualify for the job. Newton D. Baker, a former Wilson cabinet member like McAdoo, told a friend: "Of the whole lot of people talked about as possibilities Garner would make the best President. . . . He is thoroughly familiar with the times and the demands of public life, he is a wise, honest man and would make an informed and firm President." The anti-Roosevelt people who wanted any conservative but Smith were attracted by Garner. As one correspondent succinctly analyzed the Garner-for-president drive: "The . . . impulse is rooted in a deeper and stronger feeling within the party. It arises from the desire of the rank and file Democrats to get away from everything the East implies and to find a good, safe politician with an innocuous record who knows the game and how to play it. Unconsciously, what they want is a Democratic Coolidge, and they instinctively feel that Garner is their man. They are not wrong."[16]

The "era of cooperation" between the Democratic leadership of the House and the Republican administration convinced some Democrats that Garner represented their kind of statesman. William Randolph Hearst launched the Garner boom on January 2 in a radio address, commissioned an editor to write a Garner campaign biography, and directed his editors to sound out regional Democratic leaders on where they stood on the Garner candidacy. In February McAdoo inaugurated his own Garner drive. Garner, Will Rogers said, was "the man of the hour now." The 72nd Congress by March had featured a virtuoso performance by the Speaker of the House. "He has been tried in the hard crucible of the House," wrote a Democratic observer from Missouri. "He is making—if not already made—an impressive reputation. . . . His conservative control of the House under very trying conditions has duly impressed the people in New York." From Wall Street, Bernard Baruch agreed that the Texan showed "evidences of real leadership." The Garner candidacy, Brecken-

---

[16] William G. McAdoo to H. H. McPike, February 18, 1932, McAdoo MSS; Newton D. Baker to John H. Clarke, February 22, 1932, Baker MSS; Robert S. Allen, "Texas Jack," *New Republic*, LXX (March 16, 1932): 119–21.

ridge Long forecast, "will grow and grow, and he will be the alternative for the Roosevelt strength in the South and parts of the West and may easily become the compromise choice in the East and Northeast." The Speaker had provided "sensible, courageous leadership," James M. Cox declared.[17] Roosevelt men in the Senate were apprehensive. The Garner candidacy, Josiah Bailey warned, "is taking rather significantly." The Texan would be "a very strong candidate," Key Pittman noted. "He is a really remarkable man."[18]

The sales tax rebellion, however, abruptly throttled the Garner boom. Failing to anticipate such an insurrection, the Speaker had neither engaged the support of the Democratic membership behind the Ways and Means Committee's bill nor acted forcefully to nip the uprising early. "Confidentially, Garner has not enhanced his standing during the battle over the tax matter," commented Robert L. Doughton.

> He was first for a Sales tax; then indifferent; then again for it, but took no active hand in it until after the Sales tax was defeated and we were all back working together—then when it was perfectly evident that the revenue would be raised to take the place of the Sales tax, he makes a "grand-stand play" by appearing on the House floor and delivering a speech. Those here know that it did not make or lose a vote—the battle was over so far as the Sales tax was concerned, and those opposed to it were working in harmony with those who had supported it, to complete the bill.

In Capitol cloakrooms congressmen whispered that Garner had "laid down" on Charles Crisp and let him suffer the brunt of the rebellion. After evading the searching questions of reporters for

[17] New York *Times*, February 20, 1932; Baruch to James M. Cox, January 6, to McAdoo, March 3, 1932, Baruch MSS; Breckenridge Long to Desha Breckenridge, February 15, 25, 1932, Long MSS; Washington *Post*, February 13, March 14, 1932.

[18] Josiah Bailey to Daniels, February 20, 1932, Daniels MSS; Pittman to S. M. Pickett, February 1, 1932, Pittman MSS. Roosevelt supporters were afraid of going too far out on a limb. "I am committed to Governor Roosevelt but this is subject to his course and conduct," Bailey wrote. Bailey to Clarence Poe, February 24, 1932, Bailey MSS.

days, Garner finally held a news conference on March 24 which yielded little information. The newsmen noted that he no longer was the confident leader they had portrayed earlier in the session. He "seemed on the defensive. There was gone from the room that atmosphere of power which had permeated it such a short while before."[19] Thomas L. Stokes thought that no House leader had been more roughly overridden since the 1910 revolution against "Uncle Joe" Cannon. Another columnist, Frank Kent, wondered if "this marvelous leader stuff about Mr. Garner has been somewhat overplayed. . . ." The "camp meeting" speech, followed by a vote that rejected Garner's pleas for the sales tax to balance the budget, only served to indicate that his leadership had been "overwhelmingly repudiated." Across the Capitol, Joe Robinson deplored "the failure of the Democratic management in the House. . . ."[20] At the very beginning of the presidential primary season, the Garner campaign for the Democratic nomination had been dealt a setback. Until the tax defeat, a correspondent wrote, the Speaker had been "the King of the House. But . . . Jack fell down and broke his crown, and his boom came tumbling after. Whether he will be able to mend one and inflate the other remains to be seen."[21]

But Garner never could recover his lost prestige. In January Huey Long had dubbed the Speaker "the best bet" for the Democratic nomination; Garner was "courageous to a fault . . . decisive in action . . . bold." Later, in April, Long recalled, "Then I thought Garner was a man, but when he let them bring him in on the sales tax, I about gave up on that."[22] Garner became the object of derision, whether for his handling of the relief bill or the veterans' bonus bill. "Just plain stupid" was the way a pundit de-

[19] Doughton to Daniels, March 31, 1932, Doughton MSS; Washington *Post*, March 21, 22, 25, 1932.
[20] Atlanta *Constitution*, March 26, 1932; Baltimore *Sun*, March 20, 1932; quoted in the Washington *Post*, April 1, 1932; Joe Robinson to Baruch, March 25, 1932, Baruch MSS.
[21] Paul Y. Anderson, "Texas John Garner," *Nation*, CXXXIV (April 20, 1932): 467.
[22] Carlson, p. 353; Atlanta *Constitution*, May 1, 1932.

scribed his leadership; he claimed that Garner had "done more to make possible Mr. Hoover's reelection than the whole Republican National Committee." Republican verses lampooned Garner's legislative difficulties:

> The boys were waiting by the score,
> Just outside the Speaker's door.
> For Garner made a promise that
> For them he's going to the bat.
>
> But while the Vets baked in the sun,
> Jack beat it out—and did he run.
> The reason for his get-away
> Was explained by him next day.
>
> "Twas Ma that had the transportation,
> So Pa just sneaked out for the station."
> The station was a railroad siding,
> A darn good place to find him hiding.
>
> And Jack again has demonstrated
> That he's a great deal over-rated.
> How could he run this great big nation
> When he couldn't make the Union Station?[23]

Texans stood behind their native son and, in May, the Texas Society of California helped swing that state's primary to Garner. Nevertheless, after March, congressional Democrats no longer rated Garner as available.

Like Garner's, Smith's candidacy had limited appeal to Democrats. Smith's only support stemmed from New York and New England, a fact which solidified anti-eastern sentiment against him. Democrats in Congress were either vociferously opposed to his candidacy or less than enthusiastic for it. Robert Wagner maintained a discreet silence but the more conservative David Walsh announced his support for Smith. Walsh's declaration did not carry with it a conviction of Smith's availability anywhere except in the Bay State. "It would be ungrateful for the Democracy of

---

[23] Walter Lippmann, *Interpretations, 1931–1932* (New York, 1933), pp. 106, 242; "The Speaker's a Sneaker," Box 31, Reed MSS.

Massachusetts to consider any other candidate while Governor Smith is receptive," he said, and he added that Roosevelt was his first choice if Smith withdrew. Such a hedging announcement could hardly bolster Smith's stock. Obviously, Walsh and Congressman John W. McCormack, another Massachusetts man devoted to Smith personally, were doubtful about their candidate's chances. Moreover, events worked against Smith. He wanted prohibition to be the main issue of the campaign but most Democrats stressed "bread above booze" as a depression issue. "The Democratic candidate this year should have ability and availability," declared Thomas Gore of Oklahoma. "Even Governor Smith's enemies admit he has ability, but . . . [he] cannot be said to have availability."[24]

Some issue-oriented Democrats resisted the appeal of the Roosevelt bandwagon. The dean of southern conservatism, Carter Glass, rated Roosevelt as an upstart; he preferred Newton Baker or Owen Young to carry out his dogmas of fiscal conservatism. Senator Morris Sheppard of Texas would not accept Roosevelt even if Garner should falter; he wanted a devoted prohibitionist and a Southerner in the White House.[25] George Creel derided Roosevelt as "mediocre" and even doubted his honesty; the old Wilsonian inclined to Owen Young. Harlan Fiske Stone, the Republican Supreme Court justice, appraised FDR as "an utterly impossible man for President of the United States."[26]

The sternest public critic of Roosevelt was Walter Lippmann. Late in 1931 Lippmann advised Newton Baker that, based on "impressions from many long talks in the last few years," Roosevelt was "a kind of amiable boy scout. I consider it extremely important that he shouldn't be the Democratic candidate for President." Early in 1932 Lippmann characterized the New York

---

[24] Boston *Post*, January 31, Boston *Herald*, February 10, 1932, in scrapbooks, D. I. Walsh mss; Carlson, p. 288.

[25] Rexford G. Tugwell, "F.D.R. on the Verge of the Presidency," *Antioch Review* (Spring, 1956), p. 62; Carter Glass to Edward A. Christian, September 22, 1931, Box 280, Glass mss; Escal F. Duke, "The Political Career of Morris Sheppard," Ph.D. dissertation, University of Texas, 1958, pp. 402–3.

[26] George Creel to Costigan, November 9, 1930, Costigan mss; Alpheus Thomas Mason, *Harlan Fiske Stone: Pillar of Law* (New York, 1956), p. 285.

governor, in a now-famous column, as "a highly impressionable person, without any grasp of public affairs and without very strong convictions."

> For Franklin D. Roosevelt is an amiable man with many philanthropic impulses, but he is not the dangerous enemy of anything. The notion, which seems to prevail in the West and South, that Wall Street fears him, is preposterous. . . .
>
> Mr. Roosevelt is, as a matter of fact, an excessively cautious politician. He has been Governor for three years, and I doubt whether anyone can point to a single act of his which involved any political risk. . . . For Franklin D. Roosevelt is no crusader. He is no tribune of the people. He is no enemy of entrenched privilege. He is a pleasant man who, without any important qualifications for the office, would very much like to be President.

Lippmann appraised the Roosevelt candidacy as an ephemeral phenomenon born in a vacuum of Democratic leadership. Smith, Davis, Baker, and other prominent Democrats had no confidence in him. The New Yorker's strength was sectional and, like Bryan and McAdoo, had little support north of the Potomac and the Ohio and east of the Mississippi; the implication was that he would lose as they had. But why was Roosevelt the front-runner? "He has the support of many local politicians looking for an available candidate and a likely winner. . . ." Lippmann maintained his assault on Roosevelt until the convention, where he wrote a rapturous article proclaiming Baker as "the real first choice of more responsible Democrats than any other man."[27]

Few political conventions have been written about as extensive-

---

[27] Walter Lippmann to Baker, November 24, 1931, Baker MSS; Lippmann, pp. 261–62, 270–71, 303–5.
   Lippmann suggested that Roosevelt was "being used by . . . the seasoned politicians of the South [who] have few illusions as to his personal capacity. Many of the most powerful among them say frankly that he is not their personal choice and that they would greatly prefer Newton D. Baker of Ohio. But they have two interests which transcend their interest in selecting the fittest. . . . One is the determination to avoid a deadlock like in 1924 and the other is an almost hysterical desire to depose the Raskob-Smith leadership. . . ." Lippmann, pp. 298–99.

ly as the 1932 Democratic gathering, and few have such an aura of mystery. The story of how Franklin Roosevelt's nomination went through three ballots without the required two-thirds until McAdoo swung California and the Garner votes behind the New York governor is familiar to savants of American political lore.[28] But one question remains—who influenced the decisive switch to Roosevelt? Is it too apparent that McAdoo sought revenge against Smith for 1924's deadlock? Or did Hearst, out of abhorrence for Smith and Baker, decide that Roosevelt must win if Garner could not? Perhaps maverick financier Joseph P. Kennedy, who served as liaison between Hearst and Roosevelt and personally hated the Wall Street groups behind Smith and Baker, roused Hearst to rally to Roosevelt.[29] Maybe Breckenridge Long, with assurances from Roosevelt that Garner was the vice-presidential choice, contacted the Speaker via Rayburn to assure the switch to FDR.[30] But this speculation is incidental. Whoever manipulated the switch that put Roosevelt over the top, for whatever reason, merely inserted the keystone in an arch which had been under construction by the Roosevelt people and their congressional allies for more than three years. His nomination was a triumph for those who sought party harmony and victory above all else.

The nomination of Roosevelt heralded a changing of the guard in the Democratic party. The conservatives who had dominated the party in the twenties had been replaced by expedient Senate "radicals." Newton Baker, the reluctant dark horse, declared in amazement, "Think of John Davis, Carter Glass, and the whole group they represent, being pushed into the background and Dill, Wheeler, Huey Long, McAdoo and Hearst being the dominant group in a party which must save the country. . . ." To John J. Raskob, the victors were "a crowd of radicals, whom I do not at all regard as Democrats. . . ." It did not disturb Raskob that he had not been a Democrat as long as the men whom he denounced as

[28] See Arthur M. Schlesinger, Jr., *The Crisis of the Old Order, 1919–1933* (Boston, 1957), pp. 296–314.
[29] Roy W. Howard to Baker, July 12, 1932, Baker MSS.
[30] Long to Pittman, July 5, 1932, Long MSS.

perfidious to its ideals. He bemoaned the fate that had befallen his friends: "When one thinks of the Democratic Party being headed by such radicals as Roosevelt, Huey Long, Hearst, McAdoo, and Senators Wheeler and Dill, as against the fine, conservative talent in the Party as represented by such men as [Jouett Shouse], Governor Byrd, Governor Smith, Carter Glass, John W. Davis, Governor Cox, Pierre S. DuPont, Governor Ely and others too numerous to mention, it takes all one's courage and faith to not lose hope completely."[31]

On the other hand, conservatives dominated the Republican convention held two weeks before the Democratic in Chicago. But it was a dull affair lacking a contest. The party was resigned to a repeat ticket of Hoover and Curtis. "The renomination of Herbert Hoover was inevitable," James W. Wadsworth later recalled. "It is not in the cards to take the Republican nomination away from President Hoover," George Moses warned insurgents; "it is time for Hoover men to stand up and be counted, to make their opinions known." In such a moment Republicans could depend on Simeon Fess to rise. "For the sake of the Republican party, as well as the country there must be no question raised as to the wisdom of renominating the President," the Ohio senator admonished. And, in a rare moment of candor, Fess advised that "such talk is perfectly useless for no other man, unless he was a publicity seeker, would accept the nomination. Hoover is the only man that could be elected. There never has been a renomination denied to a Republican President."[32]

However, a few dissonant voices had called for a progressive rebellion against the 1928 ticket. But no effective anti-Hoover drive was launched because progressives discounted any possibility of success. Only Gifford Pinchot wanted to enter the political arena against Hoover and, ironically, Hoover took the Pennsyl-

[31] Baker to Howard, July 3, 1932, Baker MSS; John J. Raskob to Jouett Shouse, July 7, 1932, Shouse MSS.
[32] "The Reminiscences of James W. Wadsworth," COHC, p. 371; New York *Times*, July 28, 1931; Merrill A. Symonds, "George Higgins Moses of New Hampshire—The Man and the Era," Ph.D. dissertation, Clark University, 1955, p. 295; Simeon Fess to C. S. Fess, August 25, 1931, Fess MSS.

vania governor's candidacy more seriously than progressives did; a year before the convention the president feared that Midwesterners for Pinchot would embarrass him in Chicago.[33] The *Nation* ran its own Borah-for-president drive, declaring that if the Idaho senator were to enter the race, "he would arouse such a revolt as to head off renomination."[34] Borah seems to have ignored this drum-beating. Others, such as Harold Ickes and Colonel Robert R. McCormick of the Chicago *Tribune*, urged Hiram Johnson to oppose Hoover in several midwestern and Pacific coast state primaries. The 66-year-old Johnson doubted he could beat Hoover in his native California, and this made any race elsewhere out of the question.[35]

In 1928 the Republican party had shunted Calvin Coolidge aside and enthusiastically nominated Herbert Hoover for the presidency; in 1932 some GOPers wished fervently that Hoover would relinquish the party standard. If Hoover would retire, Hiram Johnson said, "he would have the undying gratitude of the rank and file of the Republican party." Although this opinion came from a long-time Hoover antagonist, there were others who agreed. A reporter quoted an anonymous Republican party official as saying that the withdrawal of Hoover would enable the GOP to "look forward to the nomination of Coolidge or of Dawes. . . . The effect would be electrical. There would be no stopping us." Republicans had become maudlin over Coolidge. Prosperity and victory did not seem elusive when silent Cal was in the White House. The formula seemed too simple to be true: restore Coolidge and prosperity with one sweep. Washington occasionally heard rumors that Coolidge would leave his New England retreat to take the party reins in '32. As early as the spring of 1930 the White House learned that a delegation of twenty businessmen

[33] M. Nelson McGeary, *Gifford Pinchot: Forester-Politician* (Princeton, N.J., 1960), pp. 387–89; Edward Tracy Clark to Calvin Coolidge, May 7, 1931, Clark MSS.
[34] "Is Mr. Hoover Inevitable?" *Nation*, CXXXIII (September 30, 1931): 322; William C. Murphy, Jr., "Borah—Now or Never," *Nation*, CXXXIV (March 2, 1932): 247–49.
[35] Harold L. Ickes to Bronson M. Cutting, January 30, 1932, Cutting MSS; Hiram Johnson to C. K. McClatchy, February 2, 1932, Johnson MSS.

had sent an emissary to Northampton to initiate the grand come-back. Some suggested that he be nominated for vice-president, but Hoover suspiciously regarded this as a furtive attempt to inject the magic Coolidge name in order to stampede the convention to the New Englander.[36]

Defeat stared at the Republicans gathered in Chicago. "The Republicans suspected that they were licked," James Wadsworth recalled of the 1932 proceedings; the campaign "was a very doubtful prospect." Just as the Democrats sought the most available man, so did the Republicans; this ruled out Hoover but Hoover ruled the convention. The president personally devised the formula for a successful convention: "full of celebrities, and all the best men in the Republican party and make a good demonstration."[37] Hoover's best men consisted of his cabinet members and Senate acolytes like Simeon Fess and Lester J. Dickinson. The gloom that pervaded the White House reached into the convention. Newsmen found the meetings insipid as the politicos and federal job holders went through the motions. The president was too great a burden for GOP candidates at all levels to carry. There was no demonstration of affection for the leader; moreover, it seemed that in all of Chicago nobody displayed his photograph. Yet, there was no hint of dissent except for a comic opera attempt to nominate a nonentity, a move promptly squelched by the presiding officers. Hoover equated unanimity with harmony. "Surely it is astonishing that in the midst of such great economic distress there should be no rumbling here of social discontent," Lippmann commented.[38] A convention's traditional function is to generate

[36] New York *Times*, November 20, 1931; "Tossing in Mr. Hoover's 1932 Hat," *Literary Digest*, January 2, 1932, p. 6; Theodore G. Joslin, *Hoover Off the Record* (Garden City, N.Y., 1935), pp. 226–27; Roy V. Peel and Thomas C. Donnelly, *The 1932 Campaign* (New York, 1935), pp. 20–21.

[37] "The Reminiscences of James W. Wadsworth," COHC, p. 371; diary, February 25, 1932, Stimson MSS.

[38] Lippmann, pp. 286–87, 289, 292–93. Lester Dickinson's keynote speech annoyed Lippmann because it came at a time when Congress was debating a nonpartisan relief bill. "After this speech, so jealous and so grasping," Lippmann wrote, "the Democrats who have been cooperating with the President would be more than human if they did not feel that Herbert Hoover was a rather difficult man to cooperate with."

enthusiasm among party workers; this one only deepened despair. Hoover and his friends waded into the campaign with a little optimism that was quickly dissipated. The president closely watched the Democratic proceedings, believing that Roosevelt probably would be the easiest man to beat. After Roosevelt's dramatic flight to Chicago and his acceptance speech, Henry Stimson, who had campaigned against Roosevelt in 1930, observed that "everybody is beginning to think that Roosevelt is going to put up a hard fight. I have thought so from the beginning." A few days after the Democratic convention ended, Stimson noted that Hoover had become wary of his opponent's appeal and was "rather blue on the subject of Roosevelt."[39]

Nevertheless, many Republicans continued to depend on what they rated as the better wisdom of the American electorate. "I can name no man better prepared, by native ability and by training and experience to guide this government through the coming four years than Hoover," Arthur Capper told his midwestern audience. The exuberant Simeon Fess proclaimed that Hoover's stock was rising and would continue to do so. Roosevelt, the Ohioan forecast, would pay "the price of Bryanism" and lose the East, but the Hoover margin in Maine in September fell by over 12 per cent from his 1928 majority and the Democratic vote for Congress rose by the same amount over the 1930 total; in fact, Republican Maine elected two Democrats for its three House seats. Fess only sneered: "Democrats elect in September and October. We do our voting in November." Uncommitted independents still would elect Hoover when they considered the alternative.[40]

Many Republicans did not share either Fess's optimism or his devotion to Hoover. Several presidential actions had alienated GOP lawmakers. Hoover had demanded "not cooperation but compliance" from the Old Guard. By delegating important tasks

---

[39] Diary, June 27, July 4, 5, 1932, Stimson MSS.
[40] "We Must Remake the United States," *Capper's Weekly*, July 2, 1932, in scrapbooks, Capper MSS; Simeon Fess to Sumner Fess, August 22, September 30, 1932, Fess MSS.

to junior senators, he had disrupted regular channels of authority. He had shown little consideration for the political needs of Republican senators who would face their constituents on election day. Ted Clark warned that Hoover could expect little help from GOP senators because of this indifference. "If Mr. Hoover cares nothing for the election of anyone except himself why should they try to insure it to their own loss?" Clark wondered.[41] Many GOP incumbents who already viewed Hoover as a liability to the ticket had no reluctance about ignoring him. They studiously avoided campaigning for Hoover or even identifying with him. Old Guard powers like Jim Watson, Reed Smoot, and George Moses, fighting for their political lives, were of no assistance to Hoover.

Other Republicans, like James Couzens and Gerald Nye, also sought to disassociate themselves from Hoover by ignoring his candidacy. In Missouri, where all candidates for Congress were running at large, Democrats discovered that some GOP politicos were telling voters that a vote for Roosevelt was all right as long as the rest of the Republican ticket was elected.[42] As early as the previous spring, William Allen White observed that any GOP candidate for the Senate in Kansas would be "in for a licking not because he deserves it but because the folks are feeling that the Republican Party is responsible and in their mad, blind rage are striking out at its leading candidates."[43] Under such conditions it was every candidate for himself.

Peter Norbeck also faced the dilemma of sharing a ticket with Herbert Hoover in 1932. Norbeck's South Dakota, which had been solidly Republican in 1928, had elected a Democrat to the Senate in 1930. Norbeck could not ignore this threat and he feared that he would go down with Hoover if he attempted to justify administration policies to rancorous farmers. When Hoo-

41 Clark to Coolidge, May 27, 1932, Clark MSS.
42 Hugh J. Savage, "Political Independents of the Hoover Era: The Progressive Insurgents of the Senate," Ph.D. dissertation, University of Illinois, 1961, pp. 269–73; M. S. Romjue to Ralph Lozier, September 26, 1932, Lozier MSS.
43 White to Charles F. Scott, April 28, 1932, White MSS.

ver's campaign managers in South Dakota requested Norbeck to endorse Hoover, the senator refused, although he did not want to offend party workers. As his biographer has written, Norbeck "decided to fight his own campaign and let Hoover do the same." Many of his supporters realistically adopted the slogan, "Elect Norbeck and Roosevelt." The strategy paid off for Norbeck. Roosevelt swept the state by 84,000 votes and took Democrats to the House with him; yet Norbeck survived by a majority of 26,000 votes.[44]

Hoover desperately craved outspoken support and did not appear able to cope with such political adversity. Stimson noted that the president was "losing his balance" and tended to view the race as cataclysmic. On August 5 Stimson told Hoover that the campaign was faring badly and the president responded that he would use the RFC to secure his re-election because it was in the national interest. This attitude startled Stimson: "I told him that he had stated the danger much more sharply and acutely than I had presented it to him; that I was astounded at what he said and didn't believe he meant it and it was only evidence to me how far he had been swung by his fatigue and the terrible strain he had been under. . . . Ogden Mills stood looking rather aghast and silent during this performance and took no part in it." Stimson had served Hoover with loyalty and devotion; yet he was shocked by his chief's despair. Hoover believed that he was indispensable in the depression crisis. "He has wrapped himself in the belief that the state of the country really depended upon his reelection," Stimson confided to his diary.

> I really believe he believed it. All through the three and a half years, I could see the question of his reelection was constantly in his mind. I really believe that he will be able to rise above it because he is a bigger man. But the thing was constantly in his mind and constantly entered into his policy. . . . I believe that if a man allows the desire for reelection to be in his mind as much

[44] Gilbert C. Fite, "Peter Norbeck: Prairie Statesman," *University of Missouri Studies*, XXII (1948): 186–90.

as it evidently was in Mr. Hoover's, it necessarily impairs his work and prevents him from being as good a President as he otherwise would be.

But others around Hoover also tended to view the election as a crusade; his defeat would yield the worst possible consequences. "The specter which we are fighting is not a matter of men or personalities," Senator Frederic Walcott told Hoover; "it is a radical form of socialism."[45]

The Roosevelt campaign suffered few of the incumbent's problems. It was confident and the candidate traveled the circuit with gusto. "It looks as if it is all over but the counting and shouting," Senator Kenneth McKellar advised FDR after the Maine vote in September; "you might save yourself the expense of your western trip except that the railroads need the money."[46] But Roosevelt, his own party united behind him, a few unreconstructed conservatives excepted, embarked on that western trip determined to take Senate Republican progressives off the fence and place them squarely behind him.

Roosevelt had been courting the progressives for several years. He had quietly supported the La Follette–Costigan bill and secretly backed Norris on the Muscle Shoals issue. At a conference of progressives in Washington in March of 1931, George Norris had declared that the nation needed "another Roosevelt in the White House," an oblique remark which all construed as referring to the man in Albany. By late 1931 most Republican progressives acclaimed Roosevelt as their candidate; La Follette told Democrats that FDR had the vision of a "political Moses."[47]

Some progressives were anxious to aid Roosevelt. Frank Walsh and George Norris, as early as March, 1932, discussed the formation of a "Roosevelt League for Progressive Democracy" through

[45] Diary, November 11, 1932, Stimson MSS; Frederic Walcott to Herbert Hoover, October 10, 1932, Walcott MSS.
[46] Kenneth McKellar to Roosevelt (telegram), September 14, 1932, McKellar MSS.
[47] Roosevelt to Walsh, April 23, 1930, F. P. Walsh MSS; *Proceedings of a Conference of Progressives, March, 1931* (Washington, D.C., 1931), pp. 126–35; R. W. Woolley to House, December 22, 1931, House MSS.

which the progressives could support FDR without committing themselves to the Democratic party. But it was not until September that Norris and others organized the bipartisan National Progressive League, dedicated to mobilizing progressives for the election of Franklin Roosevelt.[48] The men who composed the organization attested to its bipartisan nature.[49] The Speakers Bureau was run by David K. Niles, who had performed a similar service for the La Follette CPPA campaign of 1924.[50] George Norris served as chairman of the league, Edward P. Costigan as vice-chairman, and written across the top of their stationery was, "We need a Roosevelt in the White House," the words spoken by Norris at the 1931 Progressive Conference.

Roosevelt's swing through the West in late September had the air of a cautious triumphal march; the conqueror was careful of the pride of the conquered. Although Norris had committed himself, Hiram Johnson and Bronson Cutting stayed aloof. Neither had joined the league but Roosevelt smoothly brought them into his camp without embarrassing either. In California the candidate made some flattering references to Johnson and the progressive warhorse felt compelled to respond in kind. As Johnson confessed, "There isn't much doubt about my attitude. . . ." Cutting proved harder to woo. Roosevelt requested that Cutting meet with him secretly during his New Mexico tour but the senator rejected the proposal because secrecy was impossible. When Roosevelt went to New Mexico, Mrs. Roosevelt "unexpectedly" invited Cutting to talk with her. Cutting had been determined

[48] Memorandum dated March 5, Democratic National Committee file, George W. Norris to Basil Manly, September 1, 1932, National Progressive League file, F. P. Walsh mss.

[49] There were three headquarters: the New York headquarters was run by Frank Walsh, Washington by Basil Manly, and Chicago by Harold Ickes. Members of the National Committee included Representatives David J. Lewis, George Huddleston, and Robert Crosser, Senators Lynn J. Frazier, Henrik Shipstead, Elmer Thomas, and M. M. Neely, Governor Julius P. Meier of Oregon, and C. K. McClatchy and Ernest Gruening. Memorandum, September, 1932, National Progressive League file, F. P. Walsh mss.

[50] Other members of the Speakers Bureau were Senators George Norris, Thomas J. Walsh, Burton K. Wheeler, Tom Connally, and C. C. Dill, Mayor Frank Murphy of Detroit, Claude Bowers, Donald Richberg, and Edward Keating.

to sit out the campaign but he had to admit that Roosevelt was "the only practical alternative to Hoover."[51] When Norris became ill while on a speaking tour for Roosevelt, Cutting was persuaded to fill in for the Nebraskan. Johnson, too, agreed to campaign for Roosevelt in mid-October because the Democrat was "the only hope . . . of Progressivism."[52]

Threatened by the progressive defections and Democratic tide, Republicans were in a confused array. Old Guard patriarchs like Moses, Watson, and Reed Smoot were given little chance to return. Watson, although Senate majority leader, had won by only 11,000 votes in 1926 and Indiana had taken a sharp turn toward the Democrats in 1930. Smoot continued to depend on higher tariffs to put himself across. Moses ignored the depression, counted on his own prestige, and campaigned on a platform that stressed "the Constitution, the Nation and New Hampshire—always."[53] Wesley L. Jones, another venerable Senate Republican, tried frantically in the waning days of the campaign to gain the support of organized labor, yet stoutly defended the Hoover administration although certain that the Democrats would sweep the state of Washington. A Democratic victory was so sure that Fiorello La Guardia, insurgent Republican and Hoover antagonist, begged progressive Democrat Edward Costigan to forget party lines and send him an endorsement, lest progressive ranks lose a member in the House.[54]

The Democrats had wanted a strong candidate who could help Congressional candidates; Roosevelt, or the anti-Hoover vote, ran

[51] Johnson to Charles L. McNary, October 7, 1932, Johnson MSS; Cutting to his mother, September 21, October 5, 1932, Cutting MSS. However, Cutting wrote, "Voting for [Norman] Thomas is surely throwing away one's vote (though I have no doubt he would make the best President of the three)."
[52] Walsh to Cutting, October 19, Johnson to Cutting, October 18, 1932, Cutting MSS.
[53] Clark to Coolidge, November 11, 1931, Clark MSS; William G. Shepherd, "Save Smoot and Watson!" *Colliers*, September 3, 1932, pp. 14–15; Symonds, pp. 312–16.
[54] William S. Forth, "Wesley L. Jones: A Political Biography," Ph.D. dissertation, University of Washington, 1962, pp. 818–19; Wesley L. Jones to William Green, October 17, 1932, Jones MSS; Fiorello La Guardia to Costigan, September 24, 1932, Costigan MSS.

ahead of the Democratic ticket in most states outside of the South. The New Yorker polled a greater percentage of votes than Democratic candidates for Congress in such large states as California, Illinois, Iowa, Massachusetts, Michigan, Missouri, New Jersey, Pennsylvania (which he lost), and Wisconsin; he trailed congressional candidates in New York and Ohio. Whether Roosevelt carried other Democrats to victory with him is the moot point; less debatable is the point that he probably did less to deter votes from the Democratic ticket than Smith, Garner, or Baker might have.

The statistics that the Democrats gained thirteen seats in the Senate and ninety in the House do not reveal the full impact of the Democratic triumph.[55] A greater percentage of Americans went to the polls in 1932 than in any year since the world war, and not since the Civil War had the Democrats won such a large majority in the Senate or since 1890 in the House. The gains made by Democrats in 1932 far eclipsed those of 1930. Whereas Republicans won 55.1 per cent of the votes cast for major party candidates for the House in 1930, the Democracy captured 56.6 per cent in 1932, a remarkable turnabout.[56] Geographically, Democrats gained in every part of the United States and won a majority of the votes cast for representatives in every section but New England. Yet, only two years before, despite a substantial gain in the House, Democrats had still received a minority of the votes cast everywhere except in the South. The greatest gains by Democrats in 1932 came on the Pacific coast where they picked up 51.2 per cent of the votes after getting only 19.4 per cent in 1930. Indeed, the Democrats made their greatest gains over 1930 in states west of the Mississippi.[57]

The Old Guard was dealt a setback that amounted to a repudiation of its reign in the twenties. Reed Smoot had been in the Senate

[55] The 73rd Congress would have sixty Democrats, thirty-five Republicans, and one Farmer-Laborite in the Senate, 310 Democrats and 117 Republicans in the House.

[56] American Institute of Public Opinion, *The Gallup Political Almanac for 1948* (Princeton, N.J., 1948), pp. 13, 16.

[57] *Ibid.*, p. 28. In the mountain states the Democratic percentage increased from 48.5 to 57.4 and in the west north central states from 37.1 to 54.0.

for thirty years but his Utah constituency elected Democrat Elbert Thomas with 57.6 per cent of the vote. George Moses' senatorial career ended although Hoover took New Hampshire. Hiram Bingham bowed to Augustine Lonergan by 8,000 votes in Connecticut, another state won by Hoover. Jim Watson ran behind his ticket as Indiana went Democratic. In Illinois, William H. Dieterich beat Otis Glenn and the Land of Lincoln had two Democratic senators for the first time since 1861. Tasker L. Oddie was edged out in Nevada by Democrat Pat McCarran. Only six Republicans, all incumbents, won Senate seats in thirty-four contests.[58]

The election did not dismantle the Republican leadership in the House as severely as it did in the Senate; there were, however, some very noteworthy changes. John Tilson retired and his old district went Democratic in Connecticut. After holding it for twenty years, Idaho's Burton French lost his seat by a margin of 10,000 votes out of 75,000 cast. The influential Will Wood lost the second district of Indiana by 11,000 votes. Although Gilbert N. Haugen's name had been synonymous with Iowa agriculture since 1899, he lost by over 20,000 votes. The Democratic sweep in West Virginia took the House Republican whip, Carl G. Bachmann, down to a narrow defeat.

Traditionally Republican states went overwhelmingly Democratic in 1932. In the corn belt, Democratic candidates for Congress won 53 per cent of the vote in Iowa where two years before they received only 39.2 per cent. Six of the nine Iowa House seats would be Democratic although they had been unanimously Republican after the 1930 election. Kansas Democrats won a close majority of the votes, a good improvement over their 42.9 per cent in 1930. Republicans in Michigan had been accustomed to better than 70 per cent of the vote until the Democrats won a majority in 1932; in 1930 a Democrat could not win a House seat and two years later they had ten of Michigan's seventeen. Hoover won Maine but House Democratic candidates won 50.4 per cent

[58] They were Barbour of New Jersey, Nye of North Dakota, Norbeck of South Dakota, Steiwer of Oregon, Davis of Pennsylvania, and Dale of Vermont.

of the vote. Conservative Ohio sent eighteen Democrats to its twenty-two House seats, almost the reverse of 1928's outcome.

Change, that which the depression created and that which had taken place in America since 1920, was also reflected in the 1932 electoral results. District reapportionment to conform with the 1930 census undoubtedly yielded fewer GOP strongholds. The revolt of the city, first noted on a national level in the Smith candidacy of 1928, was reflected in the 1932 House returns.[59] California picked up nine new House seats and the Golden State Democrats gained ten. New Jersey got two more representatives and so did its Democrats. Where states did not redistrict and resorted to temporary at-large races, the results mostly worked to Democratic advantage: Kentucky, Missouri, and Virginia Democrats wiped out their few GOP districts with at-large races for all House seats. Illinois, Ohio, and Oklahoma put their additional seats up at-large and Democrats swept them. Only in Minnesota and North Dakota did Democrats fail to benefit by at-large races and in the former the Farmer-Labor party scored the greatest gains.

The election's very decisive pattern frightened Republicans. "Frankly, I am glad I was not running this year," Arthur Capper declared. "It was certainly a 'lack of confidence' vote for the Republicans," said Peter Norbeck, but he wondered if other Republicans would see it the same way. Although Republicans had anticipated losses, their dimensions surprised party veterans. They tended to blame the president for the havoc which had befallen the party. A New York *Times* reporter polled Republicans and discovered that "no one could be found to say a kind word about the manner in which he had exercised or failed to exercise political leadership of his party." The GOP, they argued, would have to purge itself of the Hoover command before it could face another election.[60]

[59] See Samuel Lubell, *The Future of American Politics*, 3rd ed. (New York, 1965), Chapter 3.
[60] Fite, p. 190; Peter Norbeck to Lauritz Swenson, December 29, 1932, Norbeck MSS; McNary to W. T. Stolz, November 10, 1932, McNary MSS; New York *Times*, November 10, 1932.

Nevertheless, there were defenders of Hoover who explained the outcome by pointing to the apparent irrationality of the electorate. The people were "thoughtless but passionate," Simeon Fess maintained; "judgement gave way to emotion and prejudice." The administration was dumbfounded. Henry Stimson knew that "the people of sobriety and intelligence and responsibility" had voted for Hoover, "yet we have the feeling that the immense undercurrent is against us." The people did not seem to realize, Stimson said, that "a very unworthy element of the nation is coming into control." Seeking a little consolation from the results, Secretary of Commerce Roy Chapin declared, "The mood of the country was such that . . . perhaps we are lucky that we didn't get a Socialist or Radical instead of Roosevelt."[61]

Conservative Democrats were as distressed as Republicans. Carter Glass did not regret Hoover's defeat as much as its size and side effects. On this particular occasion Glass believed that the Democratic triumph was "too great for comfort"; if interpreted as a progressive mandate, it might "lead to loose thinking and some harmful action." He was sorry responsible Republicans like George Moses were turned out and replaced by mischievous Democrats. Under such conditions, victory lost its sweetness.[62]

No election, it has often been observed, is a solemn referendum, and mandates are best interpreted by winners as what they want them to be. If Americans voted against people and programs in 1932, certainly Americans did not want another four years of Republican and Hoover leadership. But, put positively, what did they want? Apparently another Roosevelt in the White House and federal action under his and Democratic leadership is the ambiguous answer. Even so, the lame-duck amendment to the Constitution had not yet been ratified and the rejected politicians retained the responsibility for making crucial decisions for almost four more crisis months.

---

[61] Simeon Fess to Sumner Fess, November 12, 1932, Fess MSS; diary, November 8, 1932, Stimson MSS; Roy Chapin to Frederick S. Stearns, November 9, 1932, Chapin MSS.
[62] Glass to Claude Swanson, November 15, to George H. Moses, November 14, 1932, Box 299, Glass MSS.

☆ ☆ ☆ ☆ ☆

8

THE LAST LAME DUCK

THE PROSPECT of legislative success after the Old Guard rout excited federal relief advocates. "Think of the Senate without Bingham, Jones, Moses, Oddie, Shortridge, Smoot or Watson!" Bronson Cutting exclaimed,[1] disregarding the fact that the 72nd Congress had three months of constitutional life remaining during which these soon-to-be banished solons would continue as they had in July. Although the 72nd Congress had legislated the end of the lame-duck session when it sent the 20th Amendment to the states in 1932, its action came too late to prevent its own second session from convening in December. It still could be stymied in a time of great stress. Momentous decisions were required, but while the nation awaited a new administration and Congress to act on their mandates, a discarded president continued at 1600 Pennsylvania Avenue and 144 representatives and fourteen senators legislated and debated acts for which they no longer could be held accountable. About 30 per cent of the lawmakers would no longer serve after March 4. There had never been a session with so many lame ducks before this one. Accordingly, the session was doomed to be a three-month stalemate.

Postelection sessions at any time were notoriously unproductive of notable legislation. Rejected congressmen were distracted by a variety of sordid or apparently lofty influences. Some sought revenge upon congressional antagonists whose favors they no longer needed; the filibuster was a favorite weapon of those senators who

---

[1] Bronson M. Cutting to his mother, November 11, 1932, Cutting MSS.

endeavored to frustrate holdover senators for a few months. Others continued habits which had led to their defeat, determined to render a historical impression of consistency of principle in the face of public opinion. A few arranged "deals" which insured their future security, often to the detriment of the public interest. The only hope for enacting legislation lay with the politician seeking a comeback by voting the way his constituency apparently wanted his successor to vote. According to Arthur Krock, the latter lame duck was "the one most frequently observed." It seemed, however, unlikely that these lame ducks would speedily approve a remedial program. As Senator Arthur Capper noted at its outset, "This probably will be a Congress of Disapppointment."[2]

Besides, Hoover was a lame-duck executive whose mood was hardly conciliatory. He had opposed congressional activism before the election and his setback at the polls was not likely to alter his attitude. Moreover, like several congressional lame ducks, he had his eye on history and a political rejuvenation. Soon after the election, Henry Stimson detected "the spirit of the campaign on him" as Hoover prepared for the return of the 72nd Congress. The president evinced great interest when Stimson related how Grover Cleveland had rebounded four years after defeat in 1888 by avoiding controversial stands. Ever distrustful of congressmen, Hoover decided that no program was better than one which would be distorted. "I don't want them to do anything now," he told his press secretary; "whatever they might do would be bad legislation from our point of view." Hoover was not about to change his policies to suit his critics. During the session, Charles McNary noted that, concerning legislation, "You can get nothing by Mr. Hoover at this time. . . ." Senate GOP leaders forecast several vetoes which would force a special session upon the Democrats.[3]

[2] E. Pendleton Herring, "Second Session of the Seventy-second Congress," *American Political Science Review*, XXVII (June, 1933): 404; New York *Times*, November 27, 1932; "The Short Session Won't Do Much," *Capper's Weekly*, December 31, 1932, in scrapbooks, Capper MSS.
[3] Diary, November 16, 1932, Stimson MSS; Theodore Joslin, *Hoover Off the*

The Last Lame Duck

When Hoover delivered his State of the Union address to Congress on December 6, 3,000 "hunger marchers" picketed the Capitol. In the plaintive, vapid manner familiar to lawmakers after almost four years, the president sought to retrieve hope from the nation's despair. He informed them that public health was improving and Americans had "grown in their conception and organization for cooperative action for the common welfare." The latter point made his administration a valuable educational experience for the American people. Hoover seemed determined to demonstrate the correctness of his policies with a show of consistency. He intended to conclude his presidency by balancing the budget with a sales tax, cutting government expenditures, and reforming the banking system. His only allusions in the address to unemployment relief were plaudits for voluntary efforts and reproductive public works. Otherwise, the message was a hymn to American individualism and a restatement of his economic philosophy that government "should act as a regulatory agent and not as a participant in economic life." Such distinctions, one might have thought, had been blurred by Hoover's RFC and were of no interest to activist lawmakers. Indeed, congressional reaction to the speech, even when politely laudatory to the outgoing president, noted that he did not recommend a substantial program. "The message offers no formula for recovery," Senator Royal Copeland remarked as if he had expected one. To Arthur Krock, the lame-duck status of president and Congress seemed most compelling, and he forecast a lackadaisical three months; "the outlook today is for inaction," the correspondent wrote.[4]

Some Democrats, however, were actively seeking the profits of a majority before March. They vowed to oppose all nominations for government posts proposed by Hoover, in reprisal for similar tactics which, they asserted, the Republicans had used against Woodrow Wilson in 1920–21. Hoover wanted govern-

Record (Garden City, N.Y., 1935), pp. 339–40; Charles L. McNary to John H. McNary, January 25, 1933, McNary MSS; New York *Times*, December 7, 8, 1932.
    [4] William Starr Myers (ed.), *The State Papers and Other Public Writings of Herbert Hoover* (Garden City, N.Y., 1934), II: 494–505; New York *Times*, December 7, 8, 1932.

mental reorganization and economy; House Democrats would give Roosevelt almost dictatorial powers to accomplish both, authority they denied to Hoover. The Democrats were vindictive but they were rational. When Louis T. McFadden, the renegade Republican from Pennsylvania, offered a resolution in the House to impeach Hoover, the lower chamber rejected it without any debate, 361 to 8.[5]

Victory without power incurred anxiety among Democrats. The party in Congress found itself in the role of a caretaker government, responsible for cooperation with the incumbent and the president-elect on a program for recovery. The leaders extended Hoover the same cooperation, albeit more aggressive, given him the previous session. Joe Robinson promised, before the short session began, "Everything the Democrats can do to prevent obstruction or interference with the enactment of legislation to benefit the country as a whole will be done." Congress in the interregnum, the Senate majority leader declared, should "lay the groundwork necessary to national recovery." Democratic leaders were sensitive to talk of a do-nothing session. Speaker Garner eschewed the usual two-week Christmas holiday in favor of a three-day break; he reminded protesting congressmen, "A good many people with no jobs at all would be only too glad to work three days while we are off."[6]

Lacking a program or a direction, the second session rehashed several of the problems which had beset the first. Unemployment continued to attract an assortment of nostrums, none with much chance for passage. In order to create more work, Senator Hugo L. Black of Alabama pushed a bill for a thirty-hour work week which would permit access to interstate and international commerce only to those commodities produced in shops complying with the limited week. George Norris' subcommittee of the Sen-

[5] New York *Times*, December 8, 10, 1932; *Congressional Record*, 72nd Cong., 2nd sess., pp. 339–402. In addition to McFadden, others voting for impeachment were Democrats Anthony Griffin and Loring Black of New York, Thomas L. Blanton and Wright Patman of Texas, Milton Romjue of Missouri, Martin Sweeney of Ohio, and Frank Hancock of North Carolina.
[6] New York *Times*, December 2, 12, 1932.

ate Judiciary Committee held hearings on the thirty-hour bill and several union leaders appealed for its approval. Also in January, retired General P. D. Glassford, who was Washington's police commissioner during the Bonus Army March, told the Senate Manufactures Committee that unemployment among youths could be reduced by creating small camps for jobless young men which would be operated along military lines to perform socially useful tasks.[7] Both ideas would take hold in the next Congress and spark the writing of the National Industrial Recovery Act and the Civilian Conservation Corps; but the 72nd Congress had no desire to act upon them.

Unemployment insurance had a more practical appeal to lawmakers wary of government interference in the economy. The state of Wisconsin had installed an unemployment insurance system in 1932 and other states like New York were considering similar schemes. But few states had the revenue resources to undertake such a project in 1933 and inevitably its advocates brought the proposal to the attention of Congress. Two leading supporters of federal unemployment insurance were Senators Robert Wagner and Edward Costigan, Wagner favoring a voluntary system because he recognized the "need for further education" of his peers in order to achieve a compulsory program. Obviously Wagner did not expect congressional acceptance because of the majority insistence upon private, voluntary systems. Costigan discussed the proposal with several economists; Alvin H. Hanson and John R. Commons doubted the plan's effectiveness although they liked the concept in general. With a few Republicans like Arthur Capper supporting unemployment insurance, Wagner and Costigan were confident of its adoption in the near future, but not during the 72nd Congress.[8]

For the short session of the 72nd Congress, progressives had to

---

[7] Irving Bernstein, *The Lean Years: A History of the American Worker, 1920–1933* (Boston, 1960), pp. 482–84; New York *Times*, January 26, 1933.

[8] Robert F. Wagner to William Green, August 29, 1932, to George R. Fearon, February 24, 1933, Wagner MSS; John R. Commons to Edward P. Costigan, July 25, Alvin H. Hanson to Costigan, August 5, 1932, Costigan MSS; "The Man and His Job," *Capper's Weekly*, February 14, 1931, in scrapbooks, Capper MSS.

be content to improve the condition of the jobless by broadening the public works provisions of July's Emergency Relief and Construction Act. The law hindered the allotment of RFC funds by imposing stringent borrowing requirements upon the states; Wagner, La Follette, and Costigan endeavored to loosen more funds for public works. "Everything is sabotage under the present law," Congressman David Lewis complained; machinery for instituting relief was so cumbersome that it was "cheating the needy out of the national assistance intended for them, and which they so worthily deserve." La Follette and Costigan embarked on a new drive for the relief bill which had failed the previous February. They still did not expect its passage during this session, but hoped to sustain agitation for relief and further critical examination of unemployment and how the July law had failed to bring relief. Therefore, the senators reconvened the Manufactures subcommittee in January to hear testimony which would advance their case for direct federal aid to the unemployed.[9]

Wagner agreed that federal unemployment relief thus far had failed. The administration of relief by the RFC, the New Yorker told the Senate, had been "too technical, too legalistic, and particularly devoid of the spirit of enterprise in seeking ways . . . to open employment opportunities for those who are clamoring for a chance to earn a living." Wagner would permit the RFC to lend more of its funds than the $300 million allowed by the Emergency Relief and Construction Act, not require a state to declare itself nearly bankrupt in order to qualify for a relief loan, transfer the authority to make loans from the RFC to a special committee of three, and liberalize the interpretation of a self-liquidating works project.[10]

Yet Wagner and La Follette remained at odds over the crucial loans versus grants controversy, and the cause of relief suffered.

[9] Edward Ainsworth Williams, *Federal Aid for Relief* (New York, 1939), pp. 49, 56–57; David J. Lewis to Costigan, August 20, Robert M. La Follette, Jr., to Costigan, November 16, 1932, Costigan MSS; U.S. Congress, Senate, Subcommittee of the Committee on Manufactures, *Federal Aid for Unemployment Relief*, Hearing on S. 5125, 72nd Cong., 2nd sess., 1933.
[10] *Congressional Record*, 72nd Cong., 2nd sess., pp. 671–72.

La Follette approved of Wagner's proposal to raise the RFC limit to $600 million, although he accused the New Yorker of erring on the side of parsimony. Also, the son of "Battle Bob" insisted that the loans should be forthright grants to the states. "The fiction of loans to be deducted from future highway funds has vanished," he proclaimed. Probably Wagner concurred with La Follette, but he maintained that the 72nd Congress was not prepared to face such truths. As a more practical politician, Wagner preferred not to antagonize conservatives who still believed that the unemployed were people "foolish enough not to have planned for a rainy day of prosperity." On this issue Wagner preferred to deceive rather than educate. In order to attain any relief expansion before March, Wagner and La Follette would have to pool their efforts against Simeon Fess and other tories like him.[11]

The Wagner–La Follette argument flared up on the Senate floor on February 20 during debate on the Wagner amendment to the La Follette–Costigan relief bill, which was itself an amendment to the Emergency Relief and Construction Act of 1932. Wagner rejected the bill because its grants smacked of doles to the states. "I do not want to indulge in pure futilities," Wagner explained. "I do not see that it gets bread to the destitute to stand for some so-called principle of grants as against loans if, in the end, by pursuing that policy, we invite a veto and the hungry get nothing. I took a more pragmatic view of the situation. In my anxiety to see that funds were available for the needy and the destitute, I framed my legislation so as to secure congressional approval and approval at the White House." Moreover, the shrewd Wagner anticipated that most states would default on the loans, making them grants in fact. Against Wagner's "realism," La Follette and Costigan argued that RFC statistics showed that $133 million of

11 New York *Times*, January 23, 1933; Simeon Fess to Sumner Fess, December 20, 1932, February 1, 1933, Fess MSS. Fess wrote: "We have any number of dead-beats who would prefer to be kept in idleness and receive a dole from the Government than to work. There are any number of people who . . . assume that the Government is compelled to keep them whether they do anything or not. That is the viciousness of the present propaganda directed by a certain group of welfare people, who mean well, but whose efforts are poisonous to a principle of industry and frugality."

the original $300 million had not been used, indicative of state
and municipality inability to take advantage of RFC funds unless
they first swore "pauper's oaths." Injecting their own brand of
"realism," the progressives insisted that the Wagner loans would
not give effective relief; grants, notwithstanding the eleemosynary
connotation, would reach the needy in amounts which the loans
had not. They favored confronting conservative fears and daring
an executive veto; the emergency demanded it. At times the debate approached such intensity that both sides implied that the
other was sabotaging relief legislation.[12]

The Senate adopted the Wagner amendment, 44 to 28, and by
a sound margin of 54 to 16, it then approved the La Follette–
Costigan bill with the Wagner loan provision. The tone of the debate and the Wagner victory suggest that the New Yorker had
accurately gauged the conservative temper of the Senate. The bill
went to the House Committee on Banking and Currency and,
with less than two weeks of the session remaining, it died in the
House. A year had passed since the Senate killed the first La Follette–Costigan bill, but it still opposed direct relief.[13]

Both sides in the loans or grants debate may have aimed their
remarks at the incoming Chief Executive rather than the lame-
duck legislature. The antagonists, by dramatizing the urgency of
relief, undoubtedly hoped to persuade Roosevelt to convene the
73rd Congress soon after the 72nd expired. They were, however,
in earnest over their differences and sought to bolster their respective arguments with the president-elect's support. In January
La Follette had what he characterized as "a very gratifying . . .
attentive and sympathetic" discussion with Roosevelt. Costigan
wired a plea to Roosevelt early in February to enlist Wagner's
and Joe Robinson's backing for the La Follette–Costigan bill.
After the Senate passed it with the Wagner alteration, La Fol-

[12] *Congressional Record*, 72nd Cong., 2nd sess., pp. 4476, 4461–4503 *passim*.
[13] Twenty-six Democrats and eighteen Republicans voted for the Wagner
amendment, twelve Democrats, fifteen Republicans, and one Farmer-Laborite
against. Progressives formed a major portion of the resistance to the Wagner
provision for loans. Thirty-two Democrats and twenty-two Republicans favored the expansion of RFC funds for public works to $600 million; eleven
Republicans and five Democrats opposed it.

lette and Costigan urged Roosevelt to advise against House approval of the amendment because it would "merely continue mistakes, failures, lack relief standards [and] tragic consequences" would develop. On the other hand, Wagner called on Roosevelt to endorse it if only because it improved upon existing relief.[14] Roosevelt kept quiet and the matter became the province of the 73rd Congress.

Like the matter of methods for unemployment relief, the sales tax question also made its reappearance. Hoover revived the sales tax issue in his State of the Union address but Roosevelt and the Democrats decisively fought it. The White House secured assurances from Garner and Ways and Means Chairman William Collier that they would permit the House to debate it once more. Upon hearing this, Roosevelt, in one of the few times he attempted to influence legislation in the interregnum, declared his opposition to the levy. His Albany announcement knelled the end of the tax. Anti–sales tax Democrats greeted Roosevelt's action with relief. "Well, I guess that fixes it," Robert Doughton said with an air of hopeful finality. John Rankin thought that Roosevelt had "certainly pulled some of our leaders out of a blind alley." Surveying the tax's chances from the angle of a supporter, Henry Rainey observed that the opposition seemed "more solidified" in December than the previous spring. Rainey possessed a survey which showed that 125 Democrats and fifty-five Republicans who voted against the sales tax in March had been re-elected to the new Congress; thus, only thirty-eight additional votes were needed to kill the sales tax, a relative certainty in the 73rd Congress. In the other Capitol chamber, Joe Robinson advised the resolute Bernard Baruch that "violent opposition" to the tax lingered on.[15]

Vice-President-elect Garner appeared to be piqued by the president-elect's rejection of the sales tax. Prior to Roosevelt's declared opposition, Garner had conferred with him and left with

[14] La Follette and Costigan to Franklin Roosevelt, February 22, 23, 1933, Costigan MSS; Wagner to Roosevelt (telegram), February 23, 1933, Wagner MSS.

[15] New York *Times*, December 9, 25, 27, 28, 29, 1932; Washington *Post*, December 29, 1932; Joe Robinson to Bernard M. Baruch, December 19, 1932, Baruch MSS.

the impression that he would support a sales tax debate. Roosevelt corrected this misunderstanding before his public pronouncement, but then Garner, who had concurred with Hoover, found himself in the embarrassing position of telling Hoover that he could not deliver on the sales tax.

Republicans asserted that Roosevelt had betrayed Garner.[16] The charge, however, has little substance. Albany correspondent James A. Hagerty, in his dispatch on Roosevelt's statement, wrote, "With four years' experience as head of the government of the wealthiest and most populous State, Governor Roosevelt has come to believe that there should be coordination in the taxing system of the various governments, local, State and national." Roosevelt believed this before the House rebellion; earlier in 1932 he told the Yale University *Daily News* that he deplored "the levying of new taxes on the same source [by] the Federal Government and the State Governments. . . ."[17]

The overlapping of federal, state, and local taxes had disturbed congressmen considerably in the first session.[18] Henry Rainey had appointed a subcommittee of five of the Ways and Means Committee in June to study the problem and recommend which taxes should be reserved to the federal and state governments. The subcommittee avoided making any recommendations but did report that it had discovered federal and state duplications in 326 taxes; also, it noted that local taxes, in the decade beginning in 1922, had risen by 62 per cent while federal taxes had declined.[19]

Thus, the fact that the states coveted the general sales tax as a fiscal device free from federal encroachment continued to figure

[16] Bascom N. Timmons, *Garner of Texas* (New York, 1948), pp. 171–72. Hoover, in a footnote in his memoirs, quotes Timmons extensively on the Roosevelt-Garner conference but conveniently omits the passage which declared that even newsmen were aware that " 'the conferees cannot agree what they agreed on.' " See Herbert Hoover, *Memoirs: The Great Depression, 1929–1941* (New York, 1952), pp. 192–93.
[17] New York *Times*, December 29, February 20, 1932.
[18] See Chapter 7 and Jordan A. Schwarz, "John Nance Garner and the Sales Tax Rebellion of 1932," *Journal of Southern History*, XXX (May, 1964): 162–80.
[19] New York *Times*, June 17, December 1, 1932.

prominently in the reaction against the sales tax in the lame-duck session. Surveys conducted early in 1933 showed that Vermont, Illinois, North Dakota, Arizona, Utah, and Oregon had recently adopted sales taxes and the legislatures of Alabama, Tennessee, New Hampshire, Maine, Ohio, Michigan, California, and Missouri were considering it.[20] The major influences leading to its adoption were dwindling state revenues, expanded relief rolls, and the outcries of overburdened property owners who were the main supporters of local government. "In the past," said Franklin D. Roosevelt in late December, "the Federal Government has passed revenue legislation with too little consideration for State taxing systems...."[21] From now on the Democrats would remember the states' fiscal problems. Pat Harrison, in line to be the Senate Finance Committee's next chairman, displayed fair perspicacity when he declared, "There is a growing feeling that the sales tax should be left exclusively to the States."[22]

Hoover chose to disregard these insights. On January 17 he again requested Congress to pass the sales tax. He reasoned that since the excises in the 1932 revenue act were themselves "sales" taxes, it would be "good statesmanship" to broaden the burden by taxing all manufactures at a low rate. Also, he argued that the sales tax was the only likely alternative to deficit spending. The Democrats ignored Hoover's logic. Several of them stressed the tax's adverse effect on consumers; "let us talk about balanced rations before we talk about balancing the budget," quipped Huey Long. The *New Republic* remarked that Hoover behaved as if he won the November mandate. However, the Ways and Means Committee rejected the sales tax three days later, 14 to 10,[23]

[20] *Ibid.*, February 9, March 27, 1933.
[21] Between 1930 and 1937, more than half of the states adopted sales taxes of varying universality. During 1933 twelve states adopted this levy and four in 1934, bringing to twenty-three the number of states with sales taxes.
[22] AFL-CIO Research Department, *State and Local Taxes* (Washington, D.C., 1958), p. 70; Carl L. Nelson, Gladys C. Blakey, and Roy G. Blakey, *Sales Taxes* (Minneapolis, 1935), pp. 13–14; New York *Times*, December 28, 29, 1932.
[23] Myers, II: 576–81; Washington *Post*, December 27, 1932; quoted in Roy G. and Gladys C. Blakey, *The Federal Income Tax* (New York, 1940), p. 338; Herring, pp. 412–13.

although less than eleven months before the committee had approved it, 20 to 4.[24]

Although Democrats had no tax policy, Roosevelt and congressional leaders opposed deficit spending. Meeting Democratic leaders at his Manhattan home in early January, the president-elect agreed that the budget must be balanced and approved a congressional plan to do it. The scheme would raise excise taxes, lower exemptions, and double the normal income tax rates. The last proposal touched off a furor in House Democratic ranks; Garner and Rainey had to reassure their flock that income taxes would not be boosted except as a last resort. If the proposal was a trial balloon, the New York *Times* observed, "the result was a puncture." As Pat Harrison noted, Democrats preferred cutting expenditures instead of raising taxes to balance the budget. The Democrats would not tax, they would not spend; they would do nothing.[25] The tax bill remained in limbo awaiting the new Congress.

Conservatives still hoped to bind Congress to a bipartisan fiscal policy of caution and a balanced budget. Eugene Meyer wanted the Federal Reserve to prepare economic legislation for Congress in order to head off an "unsound program." George L. Harrison agreed that "a coalition program on the budget and on taxation must quickly be adopted" and advised Ogden Mills in November to confer with congressional leaders to gain their assent. Mills, although smarting from the bitter campaign, agreed that fiscal policy should not be left up to Congress alone.[26] The rout of the sales tax in December did not discourage conservatives. When the Senate Finance Committee commenced hearings in January, Bernard Baruch led off with a half-day sermon on the importance of legislative inaction and a balanced budget. "Reject all plans which oppose or postpone the workings of natural processes," Baruch admonished the senators. With the exception of young Bob La

[24] Charles Crisp, who had led the fight for the sales tax in March, had resigned from the House to accept appointment to the Tariff Commission by Hoover.

[25] New York *Times*, January 6, 7, 9, 13, 1933.

[26] Memorandum dated November 7, Binder 50, telephone conversations dated November 9, 10, 11, 1932, confidential file, Binder 46, G. L. Harrison MSS.

Follette, the committee questioned the financier in the manner of disciples before the sage. A succession of businessmen repeated Baruch's injunction to restore business confidence with fiscal conservatism. When Marriner Eccles and Keynesian J. David Stern urged a great public works program, the senators brushed aside their proposals as errant nonsense.[27]

Radicalism, however, erupted in a January filibuster which shook the Senate. It developed when an upstart from Louisiana, Huey Long, dared to question the wisdom of a banking reform bill sponsored by the Senate's unchallenged authority on banking, Carter Glass. Perhaps no other individual dominated the Senate's deliberations in this session as much as Long.

The legend of Huey Long may be as close to the truth as any legend can be. It tells of the backwoods boy who fought the bosses and the special interests of oligarchical Louisiana to become governor, build a political machine second to none, and achieve national fame as a benevolent dictator. Elected to the Senate in 1930, Long remained in Louisiana to consolidate his authority before he went to Washington in January, 1932. The Capitol soon discovered that he was not the country bumpkin it had anticipated. He was "one of the strangest beings . . . I have ever encountered," an astounded Hiram Johnson declared. "He is the apostheosis [*sic*] of vanity and egotism. He is totally irresponsible and a wholly blaviating blatherskite." Even so, Johnson acknowledged that when Long reproached Joe Robinson and the Democratic leadership for being hidebound, he endeared himself to the old progressive pariah. Most observers doubted that Long would succeed in the Senate because his free spirit demanded a degree of elbow room that the club did not readily concede to an individual member. Nevertheless, as Alben Barkley noted, "it was easy to disapprove of him politically, but hard to dislike him personally. . . ."[28] The Kingfish of the bayous seemed to work almost as hard

[27] U.S. Congress, Senate, Committee on Finance, *Investigation of Economic Problems*, 72nd Cong., 2nd sess., 1933, pp. 1–67 and *passim*.

[28] Hiram Johnson to C. K. McClatchy, April 30, 1932, Johnson MSS; Clinton W. Gilbert, "The Roosevelt Convention," *Colliers*, June 4, 1932, p. 24; Alben W. Barkley, *That Reminds Me—* (Garden City, N.Y., 1954), p. 159.

to be liked as he did to be obnoxious. He flattered people to whom he had just been introduced and later rhetorically assaulted them to make a point. Long was a bundle of paradoxes. He was "a constructive demogogue" in the opinion of Ray Lyman Wilbur. Hoover's Secretary of the Interior remembered him as "one of those strange men who in a moment can turn on a pleasant voice and good manner when, just previously, he had been boisterous, profane and vulgar drunk."[29]

Long exasperated, offended, and charmed Washington. Hiram Johnson had known all sorts of personages, but the Kingfish was, he said, "the most irresponsible, impossible and impervious individual I have ever seen. . . . No shaft penetrates his hide. He is into everything, with no real knowledge of anything. He is not without ability, and has a very great smartness and cunning." During one performance before the press, Long announced a panacea for the depression that amounted to a radical redistribution of wealth. When a reporter inquired why he had not become a Socialist, Long retorted, "Why haven't I? Why, I'm the only man who can run on the platform of Jefferson and Lincoln at the same time." The Senate lost its tedium with Long on the floor; he was, a bemused observer wrote, "the Billy Sunday of politics."[30]

The Senate leadership did not find Long entertaining when he launched his filibuster against the Glass banking bill on January 10, 1933. It all began innocently with Long announcing that he wanted "merely to elaborate" on what the previous speaker had said "in a very few words." Then, in what Glass characterized as "a rather vehement and boisterous way, with accompaniment of physical gymnastics," Long contradicted and mocked the Virginian's preachments on banking. Implying that Glass was a tool of J. P. Morgan, Long tore into his remark that small banks were no more than "pawn shops," and even claimed to know more

---

[29] "The Reminiscences of Marvin Jones," COHC, p. 763; Edgar Eugene Robinson and Paul Carroll Edwards (eds.), *The Memoirs of Ray Lyman Wilbur* (Stanford, Calif., 1960), p. 531.

[30] Johnson to McClatchy, January 16, 1933, Johnson mss; New York *Times*, January 27, 1933; Mildred Adams, "Huey the Great," *Forum*, LXXXIX (February, 1933): 71.

about banking conditions in the Old Dominion than Glass himself. Joe Robinson and other venerable Democrats also became the targets of Long's gibes. Much of the Senate and press was aghast; few could remember such an assault on party elders by a freshman solon.[31]

Long warned Glass and the Democratic leadership that he would do anything to thwart passage of the banking bill. He maintained most of the filibuster without aid from other senators because few of them had the temerity to challenge "the father of the Federal Reserve System" on the subject of banking. After talking for five hours on January 12, the weary Long sought a recess but the Senate routed the motion which would have permitted him to resume the floor the next day, 51 to 14. Carter Glass smiled for the first time since the filibuster began, but later the bored Senate surrendered to Long. Although the Senate revered its rule protecting unlimited debate, conservative Democrats chafed after several days of Long's talkathon. With criticism of the Senate mounting, Millard Tydings dramatically threatened to resign from the Senate in protest against Long's tactics, a mere gesture in a career which still had eighteen years to run. Southerners wondered about the cherished filibuster, Glass loftily insisting that he had never endorsed any because they were "totally vicious." To any suggestion that he yield the floor, Long candidly demanded that the Glass bill and "imperial finance" be sidetracked.[32] Senators began to consider cloture on January 18 and the next day they nearly won the two-thirds majority, 58 to 30.

An incongruous alliance of Democrats, progressives, and Old Guard Republicans defended the right of unlimited debate. The anomalous support of the filibuster by GOP lame ducks like Watson, Moses, and Smoot especially angered Joe Robinson. "Huey's cabinet," Robinson sneered, sought nothing other than to embarrass the Democrats. Robinson's ire seemed unjustified to George Moses: the Democrats "have been coming over to our

[31] *Congressional Record,* 72nd Cong., 2nd sess., pp. 1491–1564 *passim*; New York *Times,* January 11, 1933.
[32] *Congressional Record,* 72nd Cong., 2nd sess., pp. 1573–81, 1646–57 *passim*; New York *Times,* January 13, 15, 16, 17, 19, 20, 1933.

side for years and playing with our radicals, and now they belly-
ache when they think we are doing the same thing." Jim Watson
later claimed that he had masterminded the filibuster in order to
force the Democrats into a special session in the spring.

Hoover appears to have done little to discourage the Watson
group. He wanted the banking act, but he believed, according to
his press secretary, Ted Joslin, "it was vital to put every possible
obstacle in the path of the unruly Congress." The president found
it "expedient to encourage debate. The more the Senate talked, the
less undesirable legislation would be enacted." In fact, no legislation passed the Senate for three weeks. "Well, it's a short session
for the House," a reporter punned, "but a long session for the
Senate."[33]

The Senate had been brought to a standstill. The New York
Times lashed out at Long as "a reservoir of all that is crass" and
deplored the Senate's futility and surrender to his insults. The filibuster, Arthur Vandenberg claimed, had "maddened the entire
country."[34] Long finally capitulated after three weeks when it
appeared that the Republicans would ignore Watson and vote for
cloture. But enough time had expired to forestall any House approval. The banking reform bill died in a House committee.

Although the newspapers singled out Long for blame for Congress' inaction, clearly GOP conservatives were determined to
discredit an increasingly activist Congress, even if it meant helping
Long to filibuster. No wonder Robinson fulminated against Long.
Losing control of Congress, the GOP Old Guard sought to dis-
play the national legislature as the captive of unstable Democratic
radicals.

The Barry episode further demonstrated tory apprehension of
an activist Congress. In the February issue of the *New Outlook*,
David S. Barry, a former newspaperman and the Senate's sergeant-

[33] New York *Times*, January 20, 1933; James E. Watson, *Memoirs: As I Knew Them* (Indianapolis, 1936), pp. 304–6; Joslin, p. 339; "Huey Long's Rampage," *Literary Digest*, January 28, 1933, p. 8.
[34] New York *Times*, January 15, 17, 1933; undated and untitled entry in Scrapbook 5, Vandenberg MSS.

at-arms since 1919, wrote that there were some congressmen who "sell their vote for money" and many more "demagogues of the kind that will vote for legislation solely because they think that it will help their political and social fortunes." Barry, who would lose his Senate sinecure when the Democrats organized the new Congress, charged that the national legislature had fallen into the hands of radicals who sought to subvert the Constitution with wild remedial legislation.[35]

The Senate could not ignore this accusation of malfeasance made by an official of that body. On February 3 it convened as a court to hear Barry substantiate his accusations of vote-selling, senators acting as prosecutors and jurymen. He denied that he knew of any particular instances of illegal conduct, claiming that he had written the article to defend the Senate against commonplace insinuations that "Congressmen were crooks." Thus, the Senate had an employee who asserted that "it is pretty well known who those few [crooks] are" in Congress, although he himself did not. After two hours of interrogation and discussion, the Senate rejected George Norris' motion for immediate dismissal of Barry and sent the case to Norris' Judiciary Committee for further investigation. The Nebraskan viewed this procedure as useless and hearings on February 6 verified his doubts. Barry calmly refused to retract his unproved charges, steadfastly insisting that he had no malicious intent when he wrote the article.[36]

The Senate, not Barry, was on trial. After a tempestuous debate over Barry on February 7, it ousted the sergeant-at-arms, 53 to 17. Even so, its integrity and dignity had been successfully breached. Lame ducks Otis Glenn and Hiram Bingham depicted Barry as a maligned old man persecuted by a vindictive Senate. Norris, his face white with anger and shaking his fist at Glenn, hotly defended the Senate's action.[37] Not surprisingly, the managing editor of

---

[35] David S. Barry, "Over the Hill to Demagoguery," *New Outlook*, CLXI (February, 1933): 40; "Talk of the Nation," *ibid.*
[36] *Congressional Record*, 72nd Cong., 2nd sess., pp. 3269–82 *passim*; New York *Times*, February 7, 1933.
[37] *Congressional Record*, 72nd Cong., 2nd sess., pp. 3511–30 *passim*.

the *New Outlook* asserted that the Senate's debate over Barry had verified demagoguery on the rise in Congress; the Senate, crowed the editor, had put on a "floor show." The New York *Times* suspected that Barry's charges had some merit because the Senate "rather threw away than vindicated its dignity." Senator Henry F. Ashurst wondered if the senators were "thin-skinned." "It is no secret that there is no longer any sympathy left for Senators," M. M. Logan acknowledged of his brethren; "the public does not like them; it thinks they are living off the public in hard times." In late February Barry repeated his charges before 1,000 Brahmins in Boston's City Club and asserted he could have proved them if not for the Senate's threat to "lynch" him.[38] The Senate could not win this point of honor. Barry may have been correct in his estimation of the public image of Congress.

As March 4 approached, the impotent Congress anxiously looked forward to the new administration for stabilization out of the chaos. The nation sank deeper into the depression as some banks failed and others closed their doors rather than go under. Across the country expressions of pessimism were heard with increasing frequency. Senator "Cotton Ed" Smith of South Carolina carried his remaining cash resources in a belt strapped around his waist. The situation was not self-correcting, as Americans had wished. Instead they were confronted by surrealistic nightmare as irrationality challenged the American destiny. "These be Barbarous times," publisher Frank Knox told his wife; Roosevelt would be inaugurated "under the most ominous auspices of any President save that of Lincoln."[39]

Once again the Republic appeared to be threatened from within; once again old values seemed to be shunted aside. Few men could comprehend the changes taking place or their causes, much less adapt to them. Symbolically, one era of simplicity ended and an unknown one began when Calvin Coolidge died in January,

[38] New York *Times*, February 6, 9, 11, 24, 1933; George F. Sparks (ed.), *A Many-Colored Toga: The Diary of Henry Fountain Ashurst* (Tucson, Ariz., 1962), p. 328.
[39] Sparks, p. 331; Frank Knox to Annie Knox, March 4, 1933, Knox MSS.

1933. Prior to his passing, Coolidge had expressed the alienation from events which many of his countrymen felt:

... I feel I no longer fit in with these times. Great changes can come in four years. These socialistic notions of government are not of my day. When I was in office, tax reduction, debt reduction, tariff stability and economy were the things to which I gave attention. We succeeded on those lines. It has always seemed to me that common sense is the real solvent for the nation's problems at all times—common sense and hard work. When I read of the new fangled things that are now so popular I realize that my time is past. I wouldn't know how to handle them if I were called upon to do so.

Less than four years after he had left the White House, Coolidge declared with equanimity: "We are in a new era to which I do not belong, and it would not be possible for me to adjust myself to it."[40] Death relieved him of the burden which the living shouldered.

Others desperately sought to adjust themselves to this bewildering crisis. "Dig in," Senator John Blaine cautioned, "for after all, self-preservation has Divinity's sanction." Economic stresses seemed to have weakened the moral and political fiber of the nation beyond anything imaginable by Americans. The tribunes of the people were frightened. Like a Bourbon observing the Paris mobs, Josiah Bailey told a constituent, "I sometimes think that you and I are calmly beholding the crumbling of an ancient and great empire...."[41]

From time to time the politicians speculated on whether the situation would degenerate into absolute chaos or a dictatorship. "If this goes on we'll have an insurrection within sixty days," a newspaperman later recalled a congressman saying early in 1933. Representative E. W. Pou of North Carolina wondered if the

[40] Quoted in William Allen White, *A Puritan in Babylon* (New York, 1938), p. 439; also see Edward Tracy Clark to Bruce Barton, January 26, 1933, Knox MSS.

[41] John J. Blaine to T. E. McGillan, December 24, 1932, Blaine MSS; Josiah W. Bailey to Dr. Horace Williams, December 21, 1932, Bailey MSS.

moment had arrived "when some autocratic power should be put in the hands of somebody who can be trusted." When House Democrats proposed giving Roosevelt complete authority over government economy, talk about a dictatorship heightened considerably. "I don't think the country is yet ready for a Mussolini," Bertrand Snell angrily snapped; "if we are, we'd better go the whole route and abolish Congress."[42]

Congress' futility made it the object of considerable abuse and ridicule. The Long filibuster and the Barry article contributed much to the legislature's chagrin; other incidents added to the embarrassment. Journals were filled with stories of the profligacy of Congress. One article, entitled "Congress Cashes In," named legislators who took needless jaunts abroad on large expense accounts, tipping big and engaging in other extravagancies. Another newsman complained about the high cost to taxpayers of expensive funerals for congressmen who died in office. This *New York Times* headline must have been disconcerting in the Capitol cloakrooms: "Congressional speeches costing $4000 a day; No Government appropriation are passed."[43] When William Whittington of Mississippi proposed that representatives reduce their own salary from $10,000 to $7,500 per annum, the House routed the plantation owner's proposal, 172 to 37. At a time when millions of people had their wages cut or lost their jobs, Congress' reluctance to share the losses seemed ill-advised.[44]

Professional iconoclasts and conservatives found Congress the

42 "The Reminiscences of Robert L. Duffus," COHC, p. 114; quoted in William E. Leuchtenburg, *Franklin D. Roosevelt and the New Deal, 1932–1940* (New York, 1963), pp. 30–31; "To Hand F.D.R. the Economy Ax," *Literary Digest*, February 25, 1933, p. 7; New York *Times*, February 10, 11, 1933.

43 Charles Stevenson, "Congress Cashes In," *Liberty*, December 17, 1932, clipping found in Norris MSS; Charles Albert Billings, "Statesmen at the Bier," *North American Review*, CXXXIV (September, 1932): 205–12; New York *Times*, February 12, 1933.

44 The Whittington proposal sounded virtuous but was vehemently opposed for other than personal reasons. The lame duck Fiorello La Guardia pointed out that "it is impossible for any Member of this House to do that which is required of a Member with less than the salary he is getting now." Reducing salaries would turn Congress into a "rich man's club," because only wealthy men could afford to serve. *Congressional Record*, 72nd Cong., 2nd sess., pp. 3391–92; New York *Times*, February 5, 1933.

perfect target for vilification. Much of the commentary was captious, but it mostly centered on Congress' obvious inefficiency and lack of direction. The *Saturday Evening Post* detected a trend by Congress toward "becoming less responsible and coherent as time goes on." The national legislature featured far too many mob scenes and craved devices which would expedite the passage of laws, one writer argued. "We can no longer get along without more parliamentary responsibility than we now have," Newton Baker remarked; "I am a good deal disturbed at the current distrust of representative government. . . ." Many Americans viewed their representatives as gods who failed because they sinned like mortals. Their foibles were too apparent. They talked too much, accomplished too little, acted frivolously, and practiced nepotism. Congressmen, after all, a correspondent proclaimed, were "just as good . . . mediocre . . . bad . . . hard working . . . lazy . . . earnest [and] stupid . . . as we are who sent them there." People should take Congress not seriously but as "the big, lovable, overgrown hobbledehoy it is."[45]

Some commentators asserted that Congress was not puerile but senile. Its procedures were antiquated and as a result, Charles Beard said, Congress would "muddle rather than clarify issues." Like any outmoded machine which had not been modified in keeping with technological advances, Congress could no longer perform effectively. "Congress is so crowded with measures and bills that endless delays are inevitable," Beard declared. Debate was too often "banal, personal, irrelevant, and partisan in the low sense of the term." Beard's argument suggested that the whole American system had become an anachronism: "The truth is that representative government, which originated in an agricultural age and was well enough adapted to the simple requirements of an agricultural scene, does not function efficiently in a closely meshed

---

[45] "Unbalanced Government," *Saturday Evening Post*, February 18, 1933, p. 20; Fabian Franklin, "The Impotence of Congress," *Forum*, LXXXVIII (September, 1932): 166–70; Newton Baker to John M. Clarke, August 12, 1932, Baker MSS; Hilton Butler, "The Racket on Capitol Hill," *American Mercury*, XXVIII (February, 1933): 193–201; Katharine Dayton, "Why We Love Politics and—Believe It or Not—Congress," *Saturday Evening Post*, February 18, 1933, p. 21.

technological society." *Colliers* hoped that Congress would "avail itself of the technical resources of this age to expedite its business." But Henry Hazlitt would dispense with Congress altogether and replace it with a modern twelve-member directorate of elected statesmen.[46] All the critics concurred that Congress as they knew it was not Congress as they wanted it.

Alienated conservatives, anticipating reforms, heaped abuse upon the institution; an activist Congress was a bad Congress. Simeon Fess bemoaned the presence of publicity seekers who proclaimed radical nostrums in order to draw attention to themselves. The clash of interests and the errand-boy role foisted upon legislators by favor-seeking constituents annoyed Millard Tydings; most of all, Tydings deplored the outmoded Senate rules which permitted the Long filibuster. After one year in the Senate, a discouraged Josiah Bailey wrote: "I see so much of futility and so much of petty politicians and so much of ignorance in Congress that it is very difficult for me to keep in heart." Joe Shannon, a freshman in the House, ridiculed his colleagues for their inconsistencies, dubbing them "tumblebugs" because they "tumble first one way and then another."[47]

The lame-duck session reinforced this ennui. As expected, it did nothing of enduring value. "In newspaper vernacular, this final session of the 72nd Congress has been a series of 'one-day stories,' " Turner Catledge wrote. "From the very beginning of the session great purposes were announced one day, followed to anti-climax the next and all but forgotten on the third." Editorial writers indulged themselves by creating clever analogies with which to heap scorn upon the ineffectual lawmakers. The last session of the 72nd Congress was, a Los Angeles *Times* editor wrote, "like a war dance around a witches' cauldron"; it reminded the New York

---

[46] Charles A. Beard, "Representative Government under Fire," *Yale Review*, XXII (1932): 35–51; "What's Wrong with Congress," *Colliers*, January 28, 1933, p. 46; Henry Hazlitt, "Without Benefit of Congress," *Scribner's Magazine*, XCII (1932): 13–18.

[47] Simeon Fess to Sumner Fess, January 13, 1933, Fess MSS; New York *Times*, February 5, 1933; Bailey to B. H. Butler, December 12, 1932, Bailey MSS; *Congressional Record*, 72nd Cong., 2nd sess., p. 4280.

Times of "an old lamp gradually going out and making a bad smell as it is finally extinguished."[48]

Congress was buying time. "We're muddling along here with all eyes on the fourth of March . . . ," Hiram Johnson remarked. Senators disparaged themselves and the institution in which they served. The hallowed rule of unlimited debate and the senators' propensity to take full advantage of it served as handy butts for their tired jokes. Alben Barkley apologized for talking for fifteen minutes, saying he had done it only because "no good is coming out of this session anyway" and debate "may be the least harmful thing that may come out of the balance of the session." When Arthur Vandenberg requested the withdrawal of an objection so that there would be "less debate," Henry Ashurst informed the Michigan Republican that he had erred. "There is no contingency under the sun in the Senate as less debate," said the Arizonan amid the laughter of his fellow senators and the galleries.[49] Even the undaunted Bob La Follette admitted that "the legislative situation has never been in such a hopeless condition." Democrats feared that the chaos of the lame-duck session would carry over to the special session of the 73rd which Roosevelt was sure to convene. Congress had neither leadership nor a program. The 72nd Congress was a lost cause; it had performed, Arthur Capper commented, "a Fiddler's Job."[50]

Progressives and Democrats maintained that Congress' infirmities would not show once GOP lame ducks departed in March. They always conceded its faults but insisted that these were outweighed by its accomplishments. "Lousy as Congress may be," Tom Amlie declared, "I cannot help but believe that it is something of a safeguard insofar as the people are concerned." Thus, it functioned well in its role in the delicate system of checks and balances. Admittedly, many of its politicians were not saints;

[48] New York *Times*, February 26, 11, 1933; quoted in Washington *Post*, January 23, 1933.

[49] Johnson to McClatchy, January 29, 1933, Johnson MSS; New York *Times*, February 15, 3, 1933.

[50] New York *Times*, February 2, 1933; Key Pittman to Raymond Moley, February 15, 1933, Pittman MSS; *Capper's Weekly*, March 11, 1933, in scrapbooks, Capper MSS.

Kenneth McKellar assured a Methodist pastor that they were no more dishonest than the ordinary man. Shown an article describing the financial excesses of congressmen, George Norris conceded that part of it was true but insisted much of it was either falsehood or "very greatly exaggerated."[51]

Sometimes its defenders wondered if there existed a conspiracy to discredit Congress. It seemed that all the woes of the nation were blamed on Congress; "the House and the Senate are damned for every known affliction from Bank closings to athlete's foot," a correspondent wisecracked. Of course, there were "representatives in Congress who no sane person would ever select to do a modestly important personal commission," Newton Baker told Walter Lippmann. Still, Baker cogently observed, Congress was no more confused than the American people.

> In recent years there has been too much talk about fear of Congress—fear to have it in session lest it disturb business. Much of this talk has come from people whose business ought to have been disturbed. There is too much talk now, I think, about Congress making a spectacle of itself in the present uncertainties. The fact is, Congress is not any more uncertain than the country and its muddling impotence is not greatly different from the cross purposes, hesitancies and lack of conviction which one hears in the very best of circles of private life.[52]

Indeed, Congress did nothing because it mirrored the drift of the American people. "Congressional government has not broken down," the *Nation* declared; rather it craved direction. Although

---

[51] Tom Amlie to Max W. Heck, June 1, 1932, Amlie MSS; Kenneth McKellar to Dr. Hubert D. Knickerbocker, December 20, 1932, McKellar MSS; George W. Norris to Dr. E. E. Cone, December 21, 1932, Norris MSS.

[52] Paul Y. Anderson, "In Defense of Congress," *Nation*, CXXXVI (June 28, 1933): 720–22; Baker to Walter Lippmann, May 13, 1932, Baker MSS.

Apropos of Baker's latter point, Secretary of Commerce Roy Chapin told General Motors' Alfred P. Sloan, Jr., "Between you and me, I am fearful of the effect of the business leaders coming down to appear before Congress, every one of whom is liable to have different ideas.

"Can't you and some of the group in New York try to unify a few basic policies for these men who are coming, so that they will not give to the country a picture of business apparently up in the air without any definite policies upon which there is an agreement[?]" February 9, 1933, Chapin MSS.

Huey Long served as a convenient scapegoat for some who explained the lame-duck session's inertia, journalist Paul Y. Anderson noted that "the disgraceful fact was not that a few men blocked consideration of a general program of relief and rehabilitation, but that no such program existed." Both Hoover and Roosevelt preferred no legislation to any which the dying 72nd would pass. Congress, said R. L. Duffus, required command and was "now looking to the executive to furnish that leadership."[53] Holdover legislators riveted their attention on the president-elect and wondered what he had in store for them. Franklin Roosevelt was "a new Moses," Andrew May of Kentucky told the House, and America would experience new greatness "if we will but follow." Anderson believed that Congress would follow "almost blindly" if he presented it with a program for action.[54] The stage was set for a transfer of power. At 11:21 A.M. on March 4, the 72nd Congress adjourned; at noon the Capitol would witness the inauguration of the new president and perhaps a new era.

[53] "Do We Need a Dictator?" *Nation*, CXXXVI (March 1, 1933): 220; Paul Y. Anderson, "Filibusters and Futility," *ibid.* (February 1, 1933): 118; R. L. Duffus, "Congress Gropes in Doubt," *New York Times Magazine*, February 26, 1933, p. 3.
[54] *Congressional Record*, 72nd Cong., 2nd sess., p. 5662; Paul Y. Anderson, "The Company Roosevelt Keeps," *Nation*, CXXXVI (February 15, 1933): 171.

☆ ☆ ☆ ☆ ☆

9

BETWEEN THE NEW ERA
AND THE NEW DEAL

THE HOOVER YEARS had been tremulous for all Americans. The
nation's best minds and leaders felt nearly powerless to deter the
disaster which had so suddenly concluded the New Era. Exclamations like "Never have I witnessed such despair and hopelessness"
were commonplace in Washington, Wall Street, and almost every
other center of political and economic power throughout the
country. The collapse, coming at this particular juncture in time,
sharply defined the third and fourth decades of the twentieth
century in the American psyche. Closed banks and breadlines became as symbolic of poverty in the thirties as the stock ticker and
the automobile had been of the twenties' apparent abundance. It
had been an incomprehensible reversal. Viewing the human
wreckage about him from the perspective of a community leader,
Newton Baker suspected that "practically every man in Cleveland who was rich three years ago is poor now." "Men worth
from ten to one hundred million dollars three years ago are dis-
charging most of their servants, shrinking their office employees
into skeleton organizations and struggling to get extensions of
large bank loans, so that each day seems to bring a fresh revelation
of distress in an unexpected quarter. . . . I suppose some day there
will be a lot of rich men again, but they do not seem likely to be
the same men who were rich a short time ago."[1] For those who
had little to begin with, there was even less now. Frank Keeney,

[1] Bernard Baruch to Frank Kent, June 1, 1931, Baruch MSS; Newton Baker
to John H. Clarke, April 22, 1932, Baker MSS.

president of the West Virginia Mine Workers Union, complained strenuously that despite "wages so low that those working are near starvation," coal companies were still reducing pay rates.[2] The crisis went beyond all experiences and against the nation's destiny. "In the past it has seemed that the Almighty Father has kept His eye on America," a pietistic North Carolina congressman wrote; "we can only hope and pray that in His own good time He will show us the way out of this unprecedented, tragic situation."[3]

The bewildered sought in vain for guidance. "Where, oh, where are the brave leaders of 1929?" Bernard Baruch inquired with the smugness of one who had anticipated adversity and had insured himself against it.[4] Yet this query was often repeated by many congressmen who keenly felt the absence of leadership. While a few legislators mused about the desirability of totalitarian command, others simply wished for a charismatic personality to develop a cohesive sentiment behind a firm national policy. Panaceas abounded; missing was a common thread that unified them or a great personage to persuade a majority that he possessed a compelling course of action. "There was never such a call for leadership by one individual in high place . . . ," Cordell Hull affirmed.[5]

Since most people agreed upon the need for leadership, any debate centered upon the nature of the course of action. Implicit in that debate was the understanding that a laissez faire political economy was moribund if leadership emanated from Washington. Accordingly, each scheme for recovery depended upon the schemer's perspective of the proper relationship between the federal government and the economy; or, for many legislators, it depended upon their willingness to put philosophical considerations aside in favor of what appeared to be practical. After dismissing laissez faire and reaching a consensus that Washington

[2] Frank Keeney to Robert F. Wagner (telegram), April 3, 1931, Wagner MSS.
[3] Edward W. Pou to Josephus Daniels, September 16, 1931, Daniels MSS.
[4] Baruch to Kent, June 1, 1931, Baruch MSS.
[5] Cordell Hull to Colonel E. M. House, December 31, 1932, Hull MSS; also see Josiah W. Bailey to Bion H. Butler, December 12, 1932, Bailey MSS.

had a legitimate role to play in reconstruction, Congress, with its statute-making authority, became a yardstick which measured federal intervention in the economy. In this way, congressional action early in the depression became a standard for the nature and energy of the Hoover leadership.

The lack of any substantial reconstruction legislation by Congress during the first two years of the depression testifies to the quasi–laissez faire nature of Hoover's policies. This does not mean that the president followed a deliberate do-nothing course of inaction; rather, he confined federal action to the limits of executive powers, used persuasion instead of coercion, and excluded Congress from any major remedial function. In part, he did this because he distrusted Congress; poor relations with the national legislature through most of his public career made him uneasy in its presence. More important, however, he was truly devoted to the ideals of voluntarism and community cooperation, espousing them as more representative of a democracy than its government.

On Capitol Hill and perhaps in the nation, a consensus had approved Hoover's laissez faire type of activism. The Democrats had more courage for dealing out verbal abuse upon Hoover than for fighting his program. They still preferred that the legislative initiative be assumed by the administration. Both parties were comforted by the president's preference for handcuffing Congress in order to permit natural economic forces to develop a new momentum. Conservatives were apprehensive when Hoover cajoled industry to sustain production, wage, and price levels; they tolerated his acceleration of federal works projects and committees to organize relief. Although they chafed against the president's avuncular policies, they admired the spirit of industrial organization which was so vitally a part of the times and implicit in Hoover's schemes. Conservative congressional leaders appreciated the president's way of celebrating and preserving individual initiative. Thanks to this understanding, the president reassured businessmen in 1931 that they had only themselves to fear and not legislative meddling.

But community organization proved to be weak, cooperation occasional, voluntarism rare, and, as Hoover had suspected, the businessman his own worst enemy. The president had offered the American community an opportunity to save its body and soul without the collectivistic influence of Washington. By late 1931, it seemed evident that he had suffered a momentous defeat; the American community, particularly the leaders of big finance who should have been examples of self-reliance, craved federal assistance regardless of the price on their souls. Hoover's policies perhaps had not been in operation long enough to have a fair test, but, although many rugged individuals in business still preferred them, panic had set in to produce a contagion of fear. Only legislative activity could still the anxiety. Hoover reluctantly became obliged to give Congress assignments beyond its revenue and appropriation functions. Voluntarism was no longer the sole desideratum.

The second Hoover program ended the community dream. When Hoover agreed to the Wall Street bankers' demands for the Reconstruction Finance Corporation, he opened the floodgates to a torrent of demands for federal relief legislation. He had admitted that the means of reconstruction was less important than the objective. Also, by giving relief to capital institutions, he had sanctified the claims of other sectors of the community to federal relief. Moreover, he had given Congress a license for legislating recovery and relief. Before the RFC, laws could no more change the business cycle than Congress could alter the weather; in 1932 they became as effective as medical science against disease. Metaphors were significant in depression psychology.

Hoover had been confident that the Democrats lacked the principles needed to defy the consensus of approval for his leadership. He was correct. With the collaboration of Democratic leaders Garner and Robinson, the president showed a fair legislative virtuosity during the first three months of the 72nd Congress. Instead of conflict with the acutely divided 72nd Congress, Hoover enjoyed more cooperation than he had had from the Republican 71st Congress. On key roll calls in the Senate of both Congresses, only a GOP core usually voted with the president; several Democrats occasionally enlarged the pro-administration group. On the other hand, when the 72nd Senate voted on key roll calls, several Democrats attached themselves to that Republican core usually in support of the White House and an even larger number of Democrats occasionally voted for the president's position.[6] What these data do not tell us is that the increase in cooperation was contingent upon Hoover presenting a legislative program which promised action against the crisis. When Hoover's visible action slackened in the spring of 1932, congressional initiatives and the president's hostile response produced the sharpest conflicts of the session. Ironically, Democratic expediency, which worked in Hoover's favor earlier, turned against him with the approach of the electoral campaign.

The confining limitations of the second Hoover program became evident during the writing of the revenue bill. The administration handed the congressional leadership the nebulous responsibility of balancing the budget without suggesting how it could accomplish that dubious task. The Democratic leadership convinced itself of the necessity of maintaining the Hoover consensus by balancing the budget with a sales tax. But the waves of letters that inundated Congress washed away the aura of popularity attached to "fiscal responsibility." It was romantic to think that voters would accept further taxation in a depression simply because the levies balanced the federal budget. Politicians cannot afford to be romantics in an election year. Hoover, on the other hand, unwisely insisted upon the budget principle to maintain business confidence. Moreover, by promoting the bland proposition of a balanced budget and not directly committing himself to the sales tax device, he forfeited the legislative leadership of Congress to Doughton and La Guardia. Nobody doubted that Hoover wanted the sales tax, but not until it was beaten did he fully communicate his wish to Congress.

In March, 1932, the second Hoover program had been stripped

6 See Tables I and II in Appendix.

down to homilies on a balanced budget and economy in government. The sales tax revolt signalled congressional restlessness and
despair; what had been done would not be enough. Congressmen
were being pressed by their homefolks to exact less and succor
more. The Hoover consensus for legislative inertia except at presidential direction was in retreat; a new one calling for action for
the sake of action had begun to develop. This growing passion
for action confronted Congress with an agonizing paradox: most
legislators continued paying lip-service to the twin shibboleths of
a balanced budget and government retrenchment while killing
taxes that overburdened their constituents and demanding job-
producing public works which wrecked the budget.

In the spring of 1932, federal spending for public works, with
the dual objectives of pump-priming and vote-gathering, replaced
the shell of Herbert Hoover's program. For several months Senators La Follette and Costigan had patiently documented the abject
collapse of the president's relief schemes. Voluntarism had failed.
Private and local welfare agency officials testified that the need
for relief had sharply inflated while their funds had shriveled. The
time for massive federal aid, they urged, had come. La Follette
and Costigan used these data to buttress arguments for their relief
bill in February, 1932; at this juncture, however, the Senate still
clung to the Hoover master plan. The erosion of confidence in
Hoover's methods over the following months dramatically altered
Congress' attitude. By May the two progressive senators almost
were relegated to roles as spectators while congressional leaders
vied for consideration of their own relief bills. The Hoover consensus verged upon disintegration.

Still, the conservative Democrats had not lost their hold upon
legislating. The lawmakers craved affirmative injunctions such
as Hoover had given them earlier on the debt moratorium, RFC,
and Glass-Steagall bills. But many legislators felt trapped between
a president who dispensed aphorisms and an angry electorate
which demanded legislation. The moment for tractable politicians
had arrived and found Robert Wagner, Joe Robinson, and John
Nance Garner prepared. The New York senator was a proven

master of legislative timing who understood his colleagues' whims; the Senate majority leader, with the counsel of Bernard Baruch, sought to control inevitable spending; the Speaker was the sullen head of a victory-starved pack of Democrats which had led him on a previous occasion, something that made him determined to avoid its repetition. Without any practical alternatives, the Democrats for months had seconded Hoover. Now, as it became clear that the president had nothing more to offer, the Democrats decided they would spend and elect.

Congress assumed the initiative against the depression. The tenets of the New Era, which downgraded the legislative role, went the way of voluntarism. The business attitude that militated against congressional tinkering was of no value in the crisis. Hoover's economic and social theories may have been correct, but nobody had time to wait and see. Hunger and poverty were conditions which demanded greater attention than the president's postulates. Hoover endeavored to curtail the legislative initiative through Senator Barbour and the Old Guard but failed to stall the relief impetus. The more practical Democrats could not understand why the president and his advisers were so needlessly obstinate and unyielding on public works legislation.[7] Nevertheless, the Democrats had to be grateful for the way in which Hoover elaborated upon his image as a modern Nero. His veto of the Wagner-Garner bill and acceptance of the ensuing Emergency Relief and Construction Act were Pyrrhic presidential victories. The Democrats, belatedly and perhaps undeservedly, had earned a reputation for legislative action against the depression.

Indeed, that was the way Democrats represented themselves in the 1932 campaign. The leading congressional activists were prominent in Franklin Roosevelt's drive for the presidency and he, in turn, enjoyed and sought this identification with them. In the course of the campaign he enunciated the new consensus by pledging "action to make things better"[8] without specifying the

[7] Joe T. Robinson to Baruch, May 27, 1932, Baruch MSS.
[8] Quoted in J. Joseph Huthmacher, *Massachusetts People and Politics, 1919–1933* (New York, 1969), p. 248.

nature of the action. There was no apparent contradiction in most minds when the Democratic candidate assured voters that he would give them a balanced federal budget and practice economy in government along with action. It was comforting that the New Deal meant new laws.

Conservatives who feared new laws reduced the lame-duck session of the 72nd Congress to an abomination. Moreover, the inherent problems of a lame-duck session aided their elaboration upon the vices of congressional government. The selfish maneuvering, the Long filibuster, the peregrinations over Barry's sinecure, all tended to substantiate tory arguments for a new Cromwell instead of a New Deal. Yet the exhibitionism of the old Congress could not thwart action by the new Congress if the president commanded it. What really mattered was the yearning of most holdover legislators for a creative, fruitful, junior partnership with Roosevelt during a special session of the 73rd Congress. Here was a longing for tangible leadership which assigned lawmakers a productive role.

In the New Era of the twenties it had been understood that legislative inertia encouraged public confidence; in the New Deal of the thirties it was understood that legislative action boosted public confidence. The despair of 1932 had occasioned a turning point in the relationship of the federal government and the economy. Many incumbents of the 73rd Congress were anxious to avoid repeating the nightmarish dilatoriness of the 72nd. A consensus for action ruled in 1933. But this was also due to the apparent wrath of the electorate. Of those representatives elected to the last Congress of the New Era, 55.4 per cent would not return for the New Deal Congress; 37.5 per cent of the 73rd Senate had not served in the 71st. Inexperience and constituent restlessness may have made this sizable group of tyros amenable to an assertive leadership.

The historiography of the New Deal is too Roosevelt-oriented; a legislative history of the period might give balance by illustrating the program-making function of Congress. It is apparent, for example, that the National Industrial Recovery Act owed its inception in great measure to the concern of Senators Black and Wagner. The insistence of Wagner, La Follette, Costigan, and numerous others in both houses made public works an automatic consideration in 1933. When FDR balked at action, the excesses and perseverance of congressional schemes spurred him to assume leadership. The Senate drive for inflation, for instance, accelerated passage of the Agricultural Adjustment Act. Norris' years of educating colleagues on the wisdom of public power facilitated their acceptance of the Tennessee Valley Authority. The movement for federal insurance of bank deposits came from Congress; Roosevelt simply went along with the demands which had originated during debates on the RFC. The second hundred days, the 74th Congress, highlighted by social security, unemployment insurance, and the National Labor Relations Act, owed a great deal to a Congress which had overcome presidential timidity and to the cautious spadework of Wagner back in the 72nd Congress.

By no means, however, does the action of the successor Congress indicate that the New Deal would have been enacted in 1932 had the Chief Executive been a Democrat and not Hoover. A consensus of Congress and the nation trusted in Hoover's voluntarism and his curtailed federal activity. Only the practical failure of Hoover's program obliged Congress to assume a new tack. Suddenly the men in Congress responded to the human predicament in defiance of former conceptualizations of their institution. The national legislature ceased to function in an institutional vacuum and began to reflect the anxieties of the electorate. Events had produced a chain reaction based upon a subtle human equation: despair had induced vacillation which reinforced despair; the appearance of momentum would restore hope which might, in turn, reinforce momentum.

APPENDIX

Usually Voting with President Hoover

Score 11

Bingham, R-Conn.	Reed, R-Pa.
Fess, R-Ohio	Smoot, R-Utah
Hastings, R-Del.	Walcott, R-Conn.
Hebert, R-R.I.	Watson, R-Ind.
Moses, R-N.H.	

Score 10

Goldsborough, R-Md.	Kean, R-N.J.
Hale, R-Me.	Metcalf, R-R.I.

Score 9

Dale, R-Vt.	Patterson, R-Mo.
Keyes, R-N.H.	Vandenberg, R-Mich.

Score 8

Townsend, R-Del.

Occasionally Voting with President Hoover

Score 7

Capper, R-Kans.	Hawes, D-Mo.
Glass, D-Va.	Tydings, D-Md.
Hatfield, R-W.Va.	

Score 6

Carey, R-Wyo.	Morrison, D-N.C.

239

Glenn, R-Ill.
Harrison, D-Miss.
McNary, R-Ore.

Oddie, R-Nev.
Shortridge, R-Calif.

Score 5

Broussard, D-La.
King, D-Utah

Steiwer, R-Ore.

Score 4

Barkley, D-Ky.
Borah, R-Idaho
Bulkley, D-Ohio
Connally, D-Tex.
Copeland, D-N.Y.
Couzens, R-Mich.
Davis, R-Pa.

Jones, R-Wash.
Pittman, D-Nev.
Robinson, R-Ind.
Robinson, D-Ark.
Wagner, D-N.Y.
Walsh, D-Mass.

Usually Voting against President Hoover

Score 3

Ashurst, D-Ariz.
Black, D-Ala.
Caraway, D-Ark.
George, D-Ga.
Hayden, D-Ariz.

Kendrick, D-Wyo.
Smith, D-S.C.
Thomas, R-Idaho
Trammell, D-Fla.
Walsh, D-Mont.

Score 2

Blaine, R-Wis.
Cutting, R-N.M.
La Follette, R-Wis.
Norbeck, R-S.D.

Sheppard, D-Tex.
Shipstead, R-Minn.
Stephens, D-Miss.

Score 1

Bratton, D-N.M.
Brookhart, R-Iowa
Dill, D-Wash.
Fletcher, D-Fla.
Frazier, R-N.D.

Howell, R-Nebr.
McGill, D-Kans.
Schall, R-Minn.
Swanson, D-Va.
Wheeler, D-Mont.

Score 0

Johnson, R-Calif.
McKellar, D-Tenn.
Norris, R-Nebr.

Nye, R-N.D.
Thomas, D-Okla.

Appendix

Usually Voting with President Hoover

Score 8

Austin, R-Vt.*	Keyes, R-N.H.
Bailey, D-N.C.*	Metcalf, R-R.I.
Bingham, R-Conn.	Moses, R-N.H.
Dale, R-Vt.	Patterson, R-Mo.
Fess, R-Ohio	Reed, R-Pa.
Goldsborough, R-Md.	Vandenberg, R-Mich.
Hale, R-Me.	Walcott, R-Conn.
Hastings, R-Del.	Watson, R-Ind.
Hebert, R-R.I.	White, R-Me.*
Kean, R-N.J.	

Score 7

Barbour, R-N.J.*	Smoot, R-Utah
Capper, R-Kans.	

Score 6

Glass, D-Va.	Hull, D-Tenn.*
Hatfield, R-W.Va.	Morrison, D-N.C.
Hawes, D-Mo.	Tydings, D-Md.

Occasionally Voting with President Hoover

Score 5

Byrnes, D-S.C.*	Harrison, D-Miss.
Carey, R-Wyo.	McNary, R-Ore.
Coolidge, D-Mass.*	Steiwer, R-Ore.
Gore, D-Okla.*	

Score 4

Broussard, D-La.	Logan, D-Ky.*
Bulkley, D-Ohio	Oddie, R-Nev.
Connally, D-Tex.	Robinson, R-Ind.
Copeland, D-N.Y.	Robinson, D-Ark.
Couzens, R-Mich.	Townsend, R-Del.
Dickinson, R-Iowa*	Trammell, D-Fla.
Glenn, R-Ill.	Wagner, D-N.Y.

Score 3

Ashurst, D-Ariz.	Jones, R-Wash.
Bankhead, D-Ala.*	Kendrick, D-Wyo.
Barkley, D-Ky.	Pittman, D-Nev.
Black, D-Ala.	Shortridge, R-Calif.
Caraway, D-Ark.	Smith, D-S.C.
Davis, R-Pa.	Walsh, D-Mass.
George, D-Ga.	Walsh, D-Mont.

Usually Voting against President Hoover

Score 2

Blaine, R-Wis.	King, D-Utah
Borah, R-Idaho	La Follette, R-Wis.
Costigan, D-Colo.*	Lewis, D-Ill.*
Cutting, R-N.M.	Sheppard, D-Tex.

Score 1

Bratton, D-N.M.	Neely, D-W.Va.*
Brookhart, R-Iowa	Norbeck, R-S.D.
Dill, D-Wash.	Schall, R-Minn.
Fletcher, D-Fla.	Shipstead, R-Minn.
Frazier, R-N.D.	Stephens, D-Miss.
Howell, R-Nebr.	Wheeler, D-Mont.
McGill, D-Kans.	

Score 0

Bulow, D-S.D.*	Nye, R-S.D.
Johnson, R-Calif.	Swanson, D-Va.
McKellar, D-Tenn.	Thomas, D-Okla.
Norris, R-Nebr.	

Roll Calls Selected for Tables from *Congressional Record*

1. Nomination of John J. Parker to the Supreme Court; May 7, 1930; 71st Cong., 2nd sess., p. 8487.
2. Conference Report on Muscle Shoals; February 23, 1931; 71st Cong., 3rd sess., p. 5716.
3. Hoover veto of veterans' bonus; February 27, 1931; 71st Cong., 3rd sess., p. 6320.

4. Moratorium on foreign debts from World War I; December 22, 1931; 72nd Cong., 2nd sess., p. 1126.

5. Amendment to permit the Reconstruction Finance Corporation to lend to municipal governments; January 11, 1932; 72nd Cong., 1st sess., p. 1686.

6. Reconstruction Finance Corporation; January 11, 1932; 72nd Cong., 1st sess., p. 1705.

7. La Follette–Costigan relief bill; February 16, 1932; 72nd Cong., 1st sess., p. 4052.

8. Blaine amendment to Glass-Steagall banking bill; February 19, 1932; 72nd Cong., 1st sess., p. 4331.

9. D. I. Walsh amendment to revenue bill; May 31, 1932; 72nd Cong., 1st sess., p. 11664.

10. Moses amendment to public works bill; June 23, 1932; 72nd Cong., 1st sess., p. 13781.

11. Conference Report on public works bill; July 9, 1932; 72nd Cong., 1st sess., p. 14957.

BIBLIOGRAPHY

Manuscript Collections

Thomas R. Amlie MSS, Wisconsin State Historical Society.
Josiah W. Bailey MSS, University of North Carolina Library.
Newton D. Baker MSS, Library of Congress.
Alben W. Barkley MSS, University of Kentucky Library.
Bernard M. Baruch MSS, Princeton University Library.
John J. Blaine MSS, Wisconsin State Historical Society.
William E. Borah MSS, Library of Congress.
Walter F. Brown MSS, Ohio State Historical Society.
Robert J. Bulkley MSS, Western Reserve Historical Society.
Arthur Capper MSS, Kansas State Historical Society.
Roy D. Chapin MSS, Michigan Historical Collections, University of Michigan.
Edward Tracy Clark MSS, Library of Congress.
Thomas Connally MSS, Library of Congress.
Royal C. Copeland MSS, Michigan Historical Collections, University of Michigan.
Edward P. Costigan MSS, University of Colorado Library.
Bronson M. Cutting MSS, Library of Congress.
Josephus Daniels MSS, Library of Congress.
Norman H. Davis MSS, Library of Congress.
Charles G. Dawes MSS, Northwestern University Library.
Democratic National Committee MSS, Franklin D. Roosevelt Library.
Robert L. Doughton MSS, University of North Carolina Library.
Simeon D. Fess MSS, Ohio State Historical Society.
Carter Glass MSS, University of Virginia Library.
George L. Harrison MSS, Columbia University Library.

Pat Harrison MSS, University of Mississippi Library.
Herbert Hoover MSS, Herbert Hoover Presidential Library.
Edward M. House MSS, Yale University Library.
Cordell Hull MSS, Library of Congress.
Hiram Johnson MSS, University of California Library.
Wesley L. Jones MSS, University of Washington Library.
Edward F. Keating MSS, University of Colorado Library.
John B. Kendrick MSS, University of Wyoming Library.
Frank Knox MSS, Library of Congress.
Fiorello La Guardia MSS, Municipal Archives, New York City.
James Hamilton Lewis MSS, Library of Congress.
Breckenridge Long MSS, Library of Congress.
Ralph F. Lozier MSS, University of Missouri Library.
William Gibbs McAdoo MSS, Library of Congress.
Kenneth D. McKellar MSS, Memphis Public Library.
Charles L. McNary MSS, Library of Congress.
J. J. McSwain MSS, Duke University Library.
Ogden L. Mills MSS, Library of Congress.
Ewing D. Mitchell MSS, University of Missouri Library.
George H. Moses MSS, New Hampshire Historical Society.
William Starr Myers MSS, Princeton University Library.
John M. Nelson MSS, Wisconsin State Historical Society.
Peter Norbeck MSS, University of Missouri Library.
George W. Norris MSS, Library of Congress.
Key Pittman MSS, Library of Congress.
Henry T. Rainey MSS, Library of Congress.
Daniel A. Reed MSS, Cornell University Library.
Lawrence Richey MSS, Herbert Hoover Presidential Library.
Franklin D. Roosevelt MSS, Franklin D. Roosevelt Library.
Henrik Shipstead MSS, Minnesota State Historical Society.
Jouett Shouse MSS, University of Kentucky Library.
Frederick Steiwer MSS, University of Oregon Library.
Henry L. Stimson MSS, Yale University Library.
French Strother MSS, Herbert Hoover Presidential Library.
Claude Swanson MSS, University of Virginia Library.
John Taber MSS, Cornell University Library.
Arthur H. Vandenberg MSS, Clements Library, University of
   Michigan.
Robert F. Wagner MSS, Georgetown University.

Bibliography

Frederic C. Walcott MSS, Yale University Library.
David I. Walsh MSS, Holy Cross College Library.
Frank P. Walsh MSS, New York Public Library.
Thomas J. Walsh MSS, Library of Congress.
William Allen White MSS, Library of Congress.
Colonel Arthur Woods MSS, Herbert Hoover Presidential Library.
Robert W. Woolley MSS, Yale University Library.
Thomas Yon MSS, University of Florida Library.

Reminiscences, Oral History Research Office, Columbia University

Horace M. Albright   H. L. Mitchell
Henry Bruere   Robert L. O'Brien
Harvey H. Bundy   Henry L. Stimson
Robert L. Duffus   Thomas Thacher
Florence J. Harriman   James W. Wadsworth
Marvin Jones   Stanley Washburn
Arthur Krock   Roy Wilkins
Marie La Guardia   M. L. Wilson

Government Documents

Congressional Record. 71st Congress; 72nd Congress.
U.S. Senate. *Hearings on a Bill to Establish a National Economic Council.* Subcommittee of the Committee on Manufactures, 72nd Cong., 1st sess., 1932.
————. *Hearings on Federal Aid for Unemployment Relief.* Subcommittee of the Committee on Manufactures, 72nd Cong., 1st sess., 1932.
————. *Hearings on Federal Cooperation in Unemployment Relief.* Subcommittee of the Committee on Manufactures, 72nd Cong., 1st sess., 1932.
————. *Hearings on Federal Emergency Measures to Relieve Unemployment.* Subcommittee of the Committee on Manufactures, 72nd Cong., 1st sess., 1932.
————. *Hearings on Unemployment in the United States.* Subcommittee of the Committee on Commerce, 71st Cong., 2nd sess., 1930.
————. *Hearings on Unemployment Relief.* Committee on Banking and Currency, 72nd Cong., 1st sess., 1932.
————. *Hearings on Unemployment Relief.* Subcommittee of the Committee on Manufactures, 72nd Cong., 1st sess., 1932.

————. *Investigation of Economic Problems.* Committee on Finance, 72nd Cong., 2nd sess., 1933.

Books

AFL-CIO Research Department. *State and Local Taxes.* Washington, D.C., 1958.

[Allen, Robert S., and Drew Pearson]. *Washington Merry-Go-Round.* New York: Horace Liveright, 1931.

————. *More Washington Merry-Go-Round.* New York: Horace Liveright, 1932.

American Institute of Public Opinion. *The Gallup Political Almanac for 1948.* Princeton, N.J., 1948.

Bailey, Stephen Kemp. *Congress Makes a Law.* New York: Vintage Books, 1964.

Barkley, Alben W. *That Reminds Me—.* Garden City, N.Y.: Doubleday, 1954.

Barnard, Harry. *Independent Man: The Life of Senator James Couzens.* New York: Charles Scribner's Sons, 1958.

Baruch, Bernard M. *The Public Years.* New York: Holt, Rinehart and Winston, 1960.

Bernstein, Irving. *The Lean Years: A History of the American Worker, 1920–1933.* Boston: Houghton Mifflin, 1960.

Blakey, Roy G., and Gladys C. Blakey. *The Federal Income Tax.* New York: Longmans, Green, 1940.

Brown, Josephine C. *Public Relief, 1929–1939.* New York: Henry Holt, 1940.

Burner, David. *The Politics of Parochialism: The Democratic Party in Transition, 1918–1932.* New York: Alfred A. Knopf, 1968.

Burns, James MacGregor. *Roosevelt: The Lion and the Fox.* New York: Harcourt, Brace, 1956.

Byrnes, James F. *All in One Lifetime.* New York: Harper and Brothers, 1958.

Chamberlain, Lawrence H. *The President, Congress and Legislation.* New York: Columbia University Press, 1946.

Childs, Marquis W. *I Write from Washington.* New York: Harper and Brothers, 1942.

Conkin, Paul K. *The New Deal.* New York: Thomas Y. Crowell, 1967.

Costigan, Edward P. *Public Ownership of Government.* New York: Vanguard Press, 1940.

Cuneo, Ernest. *Life with Fiorello.* New York: Macmillan, 1955.

Doan, Edward N. *The La Follettes and the Wisconsin Idea.* New York: Rinehart, 1947.

Douglas, Paul H. *The Coming of a New Party.* New York: McGraw-Hill, 1932.

Feis, Herbert. *1933: Characters in Crisis.* Boston: Little, Brown, 1966.

Freidel, Frank. *Franklin D. Roosevelt: The Triumph.* Boston: Little, Brown, 1956.

Galbraith, John Kenneth. *The Great Crash 1929.* Boston: Houghton Mifflin, 1954.

Gayer, Arthur D. *Public Works in Prosperity and Depression.* New York: National Bureau of Economic Research, 1935.

Goldman, Eric F. *Rendezvous with Destiny.* New York: Alfred A. Knopf, 1952.

Hicks, John D. *Republican Ascendancy, 1921–1933.* New York: Harper and Brothers, 1960.

Hinshaw, David. *Herbert Hoover: American Quaker.* New York: Farrar, Straus, 1950.

Hooker, Nancy Harvison. *The Moffat Papers.* Cambridge, Mass.: Harvard University Press, 1956.

Hoover, Herbert. *Memoirs.* Vol. II: *The Cabinet and the Presidency, 1920–1933.* New York: Macmillan, 1952.

———. *Memoirs.* Vol. III: *The Great Depression, 1929–1941.* New York: Macmillan, 1952.

Hoover, Irwin Hood. *Forty-two Years in the White House.* Boston: Houghton Mifflin, 1934.

Howe, Mark DeWolfe. *Holmes-Laski Letters.* New York: Atheneum, 1963.

Hull, Cordell. *Memoirs.* Vol. I. New York: Macmillan, 1948.

Huthmacher, J. Joseph. *Massachusetts People and Politics, 1919–1933.* Cambridge, Mass.: Belknap Press, 1969.

———. *Senator Robert F. Wagner and the Rise of Urban Liberalism.* New York: Atheneum, 1968.

Ickes, Harold L. *The Autobiography of a Curmudgeon.* New York: Reynal and Hitchcock, 1943.

Israel, Fred L. *Nevada's Key Pittman.* Lincoln: University of Nebraska Press, 1963.

James, Marquis. *Mr. Garner of Texas.* Indianapolis: Bobbs-Merrill, 1939.

Johnson, Claudius O. *Borah of Idaho.* New York: Longmans, Green, 1936.

Joslin, Theodore G. *Hoover Off the Record.* Garden City, N.Y.: Doubleday, Doran, 1935.

Keller, Morton. *In Defense of Yesterday: James M. Beck and the Politics of Conservatism, 1861–1936.* New York: Coward-McCann, 1958.

Kimmel, Lewis H. *Federal Budget and Fiscal Policy, 1789–1958.* Washington, D.C.: Brookings Institution, 1959.

Leuchtenburg, William E. *Franklin D. Roosevelt and the New Deal, 1932–1940.* New York: Harper and Row, 1963.

———. *The Perils of Prosperity, 1914–1932.* Chicago: University of Chicago Press, 1958.

Lief, Alfred. *Democracy's Norris.* New York: Stackpole Sons, 1939.

Limpus, Lowell M., and Burr W. Leyson. *This Man La Guardia.* New York: E. P. Dutton, 1938.

Link, Arthur S. *American Epoch: A History of the United States Since 1890.* New York: Alfred A. Knopf, 1967.

Lippmann, Walter. *Interpretations, 1931–1932.* New York: Macmillan, 1933.

———. *Men of Destiny.* New York: Macmillan, 1928.

Longworth, Alice Roosevelt. *Crowded Hours.* New York: Charles Scribner's Sons, 1935.

Lubell, Samuel. *The Future of American Politics.* New York: Harper and Row, 1963.

McCormick, Anne O'Hare. *The World at Home.* New York: Alfred A. Knopf, 1956.

McCoy, Donald R. *Angry Voices: Left-of-Center Politics in the New Deal Era.* Lawrence: University of Kansas Press, 1958.

———. *Calvin Coolidge: The Quiet President.* New York: Macmillan, 1967.

McGeary, M. Nelson. *Gifford Pinchot: Forester-Politician.* Princeton, N.J.: Princeton University Press, 1960.

McKenna, Marian C. *Borah.* Ann Arbor: University of Michigan Press, 1961.

Mann, Arthur. *La Guardia: A Fighter against His Times, 1882–1933.* Philadelphia: J. B. Lippincott, 1959.

Mason, Alpheus Thomas. *Harlan Fiske Stone: Pillar of Law*. New York: Viking Press, 1956.

Mayer, George H. *The Republican Party, 1854–1964*. New York: Oxford University Press, 1964.

Merrill, M. R. *Reed Smoot*. Logan: Utah State Agricultural College Monograph Series, 1953.

Mitchell, Broadus. *Depression Decade*. New York: Rinehart, 1947.

Moos, Malcolm. *The Republicans*. New York: Random House, 1956.

Morison, Elting E. *Turmoil and Tradition*. Boston: Houghton Mifflin, 1960.

Myers, William Starr (ed.). *The State Papers and Other Public Writings of Herbert Hoover*. 2 vols. Garden City, N.Y.: Doubleday, Doran, 1934.

————, and Walter H. Newton. *The Hoover Administration: A Documented Narrative*. New York: Charles Scribner's Sons, 1936.

National Industrial Conference Board. *Federal Finances, 1923–1932*. New York, 1933.

National Tax Association. *Proceedings of Fourteenth National Conference 1921*. New York, 1922.

————. *Proceedings of Twenty-second National Conference 1929*. Columbia, S.C., 1930.

————. *Proceedings of Twenty-third National Conference 1930*. Columbia, S.C., 1931.

Nelson, Carl, Gladys C. Blakey, and Roy G. Blakey. *Sales Taxes*. Minneapolis: League of Minnesota Municipalities, 1935.

Nelson, Daniel. *Unemployment Insurance: The American Experience, 1915–1935*. Madison: University of Wisconsin Press, 1969.

Neuberger, Richard L., and Stephen B. Kahn. *Integrity: The Life of George W. Norris*. New York: Vanguard Press, 1937.

Nicolson, Harold. *Dwight Morrow*. New York: Harcourt, Brace, 1935.

Norris, George W. *Fighting Liberal*. New York: Collier Books, 1961.

Odum, Howard W. *Southern Regions of the United States*. Chapel Hill: University of North Carolina Press, 1936.

Paul, Randolph E. *Taxation in the United States*. Boston: Little, Brown, 1954.

Peel, Roy V., and Thomas C. Donnelly. *The 1932 Campaign: An Analysis*. New York: Farrar and Rinehart, 1935.

Proceedings of a Conference of Progressives. Washington, D.C., 1931.

Quint, Howard H., and Robert H. Ferrell (eds.). *The Talkative President: The Off-the-Record Press Conferences of Calvin Coolidge.* Amherst: University of Massachusetts Press, 1964.

Ratner, Sidney. *American Taxation: Its History as a Social Force in Democracy.* New York: W. W. Norton, 1942.

Robinson, Edgar Eugene, and Paul Carroll Edwards (eds.). *The Memoirs of Ray Lyman Wilbur.* Stanford, Calif.: Stanford University Press, 1960.

Rollins, Alfred B., Jr. *Roosevelt and Howe.* New York: Alfred A. Knopf, 1962.

Romasco, Albert U. *The Poverty of Abundance: Hoover, the Nation, the Depression.* New York: Oxford University Press, 1965.

Roosevelt, Elliot (ed.). *F.D.R. His Personal Letters, 1928–1945.* New York: Duell, Sloan and Pearce, 1950.

Ross, Martin. *Shipstead of Minnesota.* Chicago: Packard, 1940.

Schlesinger, Arthur M., Jr. *The Crisis of the Old Order, 1919–1933.* Boston: Houghton Mifflin, 1957.

Seldes, Gilbert. *The Years of the Locust.* Boston: Little, Brown, 1933.

Shannon, David A. (ed.) *Progressivism and Postwar Disillusionment.* New York: McGraw-Hill, 1966.

Shoup, Carl. *The Sales Tax in the American States.* New York: Columbia University Press, 1934.

Smith, Rixey, and Norman Beasley. *Carter Glass: A Biography.* New York: Longmans, Green, 1939.

Smothers, Frank (ed.). *The Book of the States.* Chicago: Council of State Governments, 1962.

Socolofsky, Homer E. *Arthur Capper: Publisher, Politician, and Philanthropist.* Lawrence: University of Kansas Press, 1962.

Sparks, George F. (ed.) *A Many-Colored Toga: The Diary of Henry Fountain Ashurst.* Tucson: University of Arizona Press, 1962.

Stokes, Thomas L. *Chip Off My Shoulder.* Princeton, N.J.: Princeton University Press, 1940.

Studenski, Paul, and Herman E. Krooss. *Financial History of the United States.* New York: McGraw-Hill, 1952.

Swanberg, W. A. *Citizen Hearst.* New York: Bantam Books, 1961.

Timmons, Bascom N. *Garner of Texas.* New York: Harper and Brothers, 1948.

Tucker, Ray, and Frederick R. Barkley. *Sons of the Wild Jackass.* Boston: L. C. Page, 1932.

Bibliography

U.S. Department of Commerce. *Planning and Control of Public Works: A Report of the Committee on Recent Economic Changes of the President's Conference on Unemployment.* Washington, D.C.: Government Printing Office, 1930.

Warren, Harris Gaylord. *Herbert Hoover and the Great Depression.* New York: Oxford University Press, 1959.

Watson, James E. *Memoirs: As I Knew Them.* Indianapolis: Bobbs-Merrill, 1936.

Wecter, Dixon. *The Age of the Great Depression, 1929–1941.* New York: Macmillan, 1948.

Wehle, Louis B. *Hidden Threads of History: Wilson through Roosevelt.* New York: Macmillan, 1953.

Wheeler, Burton K., with Paul E. Healy. *Yankee from the West.* Garden City, N.Y.: Doubleday, 1962.

White, William Allen. *A Puritan in Babylon.* New York: Macmillan, 1938.

White, William S. *Citadel: The Story of the U.S. Senate.* New York: Harper and Brothers, 1956.

Wilbur, Ray Lyman, and Arthur Mastick Hyde. *The Hoover Policies.* New York: Charles Scribner's Sons, 1937.

Williams, Edward Ainsworth. *Federal Aid for Relief.* New York: Columbia University Press, 1939.

Wilson, Edmund. *The American Earthquake.* Garden City, N.Y.: Doubleday, 1958.

Zinn, Howard. *La Guardia in Congress.* Ithaca, N.Y.: Cornell University Press, 1959.

Articles

Adams, Mildred. "Huey the Great." *Forum*, LXXXIX (February, 1933): 70–75.

"Advance Planning of Public Construction Receives Federal Government Approval," *American City*, XLIV (March, 1931): 93.

A.F.C. "Backstage in Washington." *Outlook and Independent*, May 14, 1930, p. 60.

————. "Backstage in Washington." *Outlook and Independent*, April 22, 1931, p. 555.

Allen, Robert S. "Texas Jack." *New Republic*, LXX (March 16, 1932): 119–21.

Anderson, Paul Y. "The Company Roosevelt Keeps." *Nation*, CXXXVI (February 15, 1933): 171.
————. "Filibusters and Futility." *Nation*, CXXXVI (February 1, 1933): 118.
————. "In Defense of Congress." *Nation*, CXXXVI (June 28, 1933): 720–22.
————. "Texas John Garner." *Nation*, CXXXIV (April 20, 1932): 134.
————. "Wanted: A Mussolini." *Nation*, CXXXV (July 6, 1932): 9–10.
Atwood, Albert W. "The Limits of Government." *Saturday Evening Post*, December 26, 1931, p. 57.
Ballantine, Arthur A. "The General Sales Tax Is Not the Way Out." *Annals*, XCV (May, 1921): 212–20.
————. "When All the Banks Closed." *Harvard Business Review*, XXVI (March, 1948): 129–43.
Barkley, Frederick R. "The Voice of the Corn Belt." *Outlook*, CLVII (January 14, 1931): 52–54.
Barry, David S. "Over the Hill to Demagoguery." *New Outlook*, CLXI (February, 1933): 40.
Beard, Charles A. "Conservatism Hits Bottom." *New Republic*, LVIII (August 19, 1931): 7–11.
————. "Representative Government under Fire." *Yale Review*, XXII (1932): 35–51.
Bicha, Karel Denis. "Liberalism Frustrated: The League for Independent Political Action, 1928–1933." *Mid-America*, XLVIII (January, 1966): 19–28.
Bielschowsky, Georg. "Business Fluctuations and Public Works." *Quarterly Journal of Economics*, XLIV (February, 1930): 286–319.
Billings, Charles Albert. "Statesmen at the Bier." *North American Review*, CXXXIV (September, 1932): 205–12.
Bingham, Hiram. "Is Wagner Proposal for Federal Employment Agencies Sound?" *Congressional Digest*, X (January, 1931): 12–13.
Blakey, Roy G., and Gladys C. Blakey. "Revenue Act of 1932." *American Economic Review*, XXII (December, 1932): 620–25.
"Borrowing Billions to Turn the Tide." *Literary Digest*, January 30, 1932, pp. 7–8.

Brookhart, Smith W. "Let's Abandon the Gold Standard." *Forum*, LXXXVIII (July, 1932): 10–12.

Brown, E. Cary. "Fiscal Policy in the 'Thirties': A Reappraisal." *American Economic Review*, XLVI (1956): 868–69.

Brown, E. Francis. "Congress Plays Its Part." *Current History*, XXXVI (July, 1932): 464–65.

———. "Roosevelt Takes Control." *Current History*, XXXVIII (April, 1933): 81–82.

Butler, Hilton. "The Racket on Capitol Hill." *American Mercury*, XXVIII (February, 1933): 193–201.

Capper, Arthur. "Curtis and Norris." *North American Review*, CCXXV (May, 1928): 525–29.

Clapper, Raymond. "Senate Leaders and Orators." *Review of Reviews*, LXXXIX (February, 1934): 29.

"Congress Adopts Public Works Planning." *American Labor Legislative Review*, XXI (March, 1931): 95–96.

"Congress's Terrific Blow at the Depression." *Literary Digest*, July 30, 1932, p. 1.

Conley, William G. "How West Virginia Found New Revenue." *Review of Reviews*, LXXXII (October, 1930): 120–22.

Connor, Sennett. "Mississippi Tries the Sales Tax." *Review of Reviews*, LXXXVI (October, 1932): 28–29.

Cook, Louis H. "Brookhart, Insurgent." *North American Review*, CCXXXI (February, 1931): 179–80.

Corwin, Edwin S. "Social Planning under the Constitution—A Study in Perspectives." *American Political Science Review*, XXVI (February, 1932): 26.

Costigan, Edward P. "A National Political Armistice?" *Atlantic Monthly*, CXLVII (February, 1931): 260.

Crisp, Charles W. "Does the Credit of the United States Depend on a Balanced Budget?" *Congressional Digest*, XI (May, 1932): 140.

Davenport, Walter. "Fighting Blood." *Colliers*, April 23, 1931, pp. 10–11.

———. "The Man Who Grew Up." *Colliers*, September 10, 1932, p. 10.

———. "Pay as You Go." *Colliers*, November 19, 1932, pp. 10–11.

Dayton, Katharine. "Why We Love Politics and—Believe It or Not—Congress." *Saturday Evening Post*, February 18, 1933, p. 21.

Degler, Carl N. "The Ordeal of Herbert Hoover." *Yale Review*, LII (June, 1963): 563–83.

Dennis, Alfred Pearce. "The Diligent Senator Smoot." *World's Work*, LIX (May, 1930): 62–64.

Dewey, John. "The Need for a New Party." *New Republic*, LXVI (March 18, 1931): 115–17.

———. "Politics for a New Party." *New Republic*, LXVI (April 8, 1931): 205.

———. "Who Might Make a New Party?" *New Republic*, LXVI (April 1, 1931): 177–79.

"Doles for Industry." *Nation*, CXXXIV (February 3, 1932): 131.

Douglas, Paul H. "The Prospects for a New Political Alignment." *American Political Science Review*, XXV (November, 1931): 906–14.

"Do We Need a Dictator?" *Nation*, CXXXVI (March 1, 1933): 220.

"The Drive to Shatter the Glass Bank Bill." *Literary Digest*, April 9, 1932, p. 12.

Duffus, R. L. "Congress Gropes in Doubt." *New York Times Magazine*, February 26, 1933, p. 3.

Edmonds, Richard Woods. "A New Source of State Revenue." *Current History*, XXX (November, 1930): 244.

Fess, Simeon D. "Party Heads Discuss Republican Record." *Congressional Digest*, IX (October, 1930): 240.

Fite, Gilbert C. "Peter Norbeck: Prairie Statesman." *University of Missouri Studies*, XXII (1948).

Flannagan, John W. "Does the Credit of the United States Depend on a Balanced Budget?" *Congressional Digest*, XI (May, 1932): 139.

Franklin, Fabian. "The Impotence of Congress." *Forum*, LXXXVIII (September, 1932): 166–70.

Garner, Alfred W. "A Note on the Mississippi Sales Tax." *Southern Economic Journal*, I (January, 1934): 24–27.

"The Gathering of Progressives." *World Tomorrow*, XIV (April, 1931): 9.

Gayer, Arthur D. "Financing the Emergency Public Works Program." *American Labor Legislative Review*, XXII (June, 1932): 71–75.

The Gentleman at the Keyhole [Clinton Gilbert]. "Anti-Knock Charlie." *Colliers*, January 25, 1930, p. 40.

————. "Big-Town Bob." *Colliers*, March 21, 1931, p. 38.

————. "Capitol Chatterbox." *Colliers*, April 2, 1932, p. 16.

————. "Glass Edges." *Colliers*, April 18, 1931, p. 38.

————. "Oregon Trader." *Colliers*, February 21, 1931, p. 53.

————. "The Pennsylvania Blues." *Colliers*, October 5, 1929, p. 66.

————. "Put Your Best Foot Forward." *Colliers*, January 19, 1929, p. 47.

————. " 'A Real Republican.' " *Colliers*, October 10, 1931, p. 28.

————. "Simeon Pure." *Colliers*, September 27, 1930, p. 55.

————. "With But a Single Thought." *Colliers*, August 30, 1930, p. 38.

Gilbert, Clinton W. "American Representative." *Colliers*, May 14, 1932, p. 22.

————. "The Laugh Cure." *Colliers*, August 6, 1932, p. 21.

————. "The People against Pork." *Atlantic Monthly*, CL (August, 1932): 134.

————. "Private Party." *Colliers*, May 7, 1932, p. 19.

————. "Reward of Virtue." *Colliers*, April 8, 1933, p. 24.

————. "The Roosevelt Convention." *Colliers*, June 4, 1932, p. 24.

————. "Sound Effects." *Colliers*, June 14, 1933, p. 34.

————. "West Winds." *Colliers*, January 21, 1933, p. 9.

Gilfond, Duff. "Americans We Like: Congressman La Guardia." *Nation*, CXXVI (March 21, 1928): 319.

————. "La Guardia of Harlem." *American Mercury*, XI (June, 1927):152–58.

————. "A Superior Person." *American Mercury*, XIX (March, 1930): 307–13.

"Great Expectations." *Nation*, CXXXIV (February 24, 1932): 216.

Hallgren, Mauritz A. "Progressivism Turns to the Left." *Nation*, CXXXII (March 25, 1931): 320–21.

————. "Third Party Fantasy." *American Mercury*, XXIII (May, 1931): 38–46.

Hamilton, Marty. "Bull Moose Plays an Encore: Hiram Johnson and the Presidential Campaign of 1932." *California Historical Society Quarterly*, XLI (September, 1962): 212–21.

Hard, William. "Leadership in the House." *Review of Reviews*, LXXIV (August, 1926): 160.

————. "Nicholas Longworth." *Review of Reviews*, LXXI (April, 1925): 370–73.

Harris, S. E. "Banking and Currency Legislation, 1932." *Quarterly Journal of Economics*, XLVI (May, 1932): 546–57.

Hazlitt, Henry. "Without Benefit of Congress." *Scribner's Magazine*, XCII (1932): 13–18.

Herring, E. Pendleton. "American Government and Politics." *American Political Science Review*, XXVI (October, 1932): 868–72.

———. "First Session of the Seventy-third Congress, March 9, 1933 to June 16, 1933." *American Political Science Review*, XXVIII (February, 1934): 65–83.

———. "Second Session of the Seventy-second Congress, December 5, 1932–March 4, 1933." *American Political Science Review*, XXVII (June, 1933): 404–22.

"Hoover's 'Plan to Keep the Dinner-Pail Full.'" *Literary Digest*, December 8, 1928, pp. 5–7.

"Huey Long's Rampage." *Literary Digest*, January 28, 1933, p. 8.

Hull, Cordell. "Call Off the Tariff War!" *Nation*, CXXXIII (December 16, 1931): 668–69.

Isakoff, Jack F. "The Public Works Administration." *University of Illinois Bulletin*, XXIII (November 18, 1938): 9-16.

"Is Mr. Hoover Inevitable?" *Nation*, CXXXIII (September 30, 1931): 322.

"Johnson's Slam at Hoover." *Literary Digest*, December 5, 1931, p. 8.

Jones, Weimar. "North Carolina's New Senators." *Nation*, CXXII (January 7, 1931): 11.

Kent, Frank R. "Senator James E. Watson: The Professional Public Servant." *Atlantic Monthly*, CXLIX (February, 1932): 184–87.

Kiplinger, W. M. "Indirect Relief." *Forum*, LXXXVII (June, 1932): 351.

La Follette, Robert M., Jr. "The President and Unemployment." *Nation*, CXXXIII (July 15, 1931): 133.

"La Follette Routs the 'Old Guard.'" *Literary Digest*, January 25, 1930, p. 13.

La Guardia, Fiorello H. "Government Must Act." *Nation*, CXXVI (April 4, 1928): 378–79.

———. "Is the Sales Tax a Sound Method of Raising Federal Revenue?" *Congressional Digest*, XI (May, 1932): 145.

Lawrence, David. "Station USA." *Saturday Evening Post*, May 16, 1931, p. 33.

Link, Arthur S. "What Happened to the Progressive Movement in the 1920's?" *American Historical Review*, LXIV (July, 1959): 833–51.

"Listening in on the Debt Debate." *Literary Digest*, January 30, 1932, p. 9.

McArthur, Lucille. "Idle Moments of a Lady in Waiting." *Saturday Evening Post*, September 19, 1931, pp. 3–5.

McCormick, Anne O'Hare. "Hoover Looks Back—and Ahead." *New York Times Magazine*, February 5, 1933, p. 1.

McKee, Oliver. "Reconstruction Finance Corporation." *World's Work*, LXI (March, 1932): 36.

Macmahon, Arthur W. "First Session of the Seventy-first Congress." *American Political Science Review*, XXIV (February, 1930): 38–59.

———. "Second Session of the Seventieth Congress." *American Political Science Review*, XXIII (May, 1929): 364–83.

———. "Second Session of the Seventy-first Congress." *American Political Science Review*, XXIV (November, 1930): 913–46.

———. "Third Session of the Seventy-first Congress." *American Political Science Review*, XXV (November, 1931): 932–55.

Mallery, Otto T. "A Program of Public Works." *Survey*, LXV (March 1, 1931): 605.

Mencken, H. L. "What Is Going on in the World." *American Mercury*, XXVII (December, 1932): 385.

Milburn, George. "The Statesmanship of Mr. Garner." *Harper's*, CLXV (November, 1932): 669–82.

"Mississippi Trying the Sales Tax." *Literary Digest*, May 21, 1932, p. 9.

"The Month in Congress." *Congressional Digest*, XI (June, 1932): 182.

"Moratorium Debates Reveal Attitude of Congress on Foreign Debt Revision." *Congressional Digest*, XI (January, 1932): 16–24.

Moses, George H. "Death—and Taxes." *Saturday Evening Post*, June 27, 1931, p. 97.

———. "Speaking of the Senate." *Saturday Evening Post*, July 25, 1931, pp. 8–9.

Murphy, William C., Jr. "Borah—Now or Never." *Nation*, CXXXIV (March 2, 1932): 247–49.

———. "Progressive Politics." *Commonweal*, XIII (April 8, 1931): 632–33.

————. "Senator Reed." *North American Review*, CCXXXI (May, 1931): 419–21.

Myers, William Starr. "Looking toward 1932." *American Political Science Review*, XXV (November, 1931): 925–31.

Nash, Gerald D. "Herbert Hoover and the Origins of the Reconstruction Finance Corporation." *Mississippi Valley Historical Review*, XLVI (December, 1959): 455–68.

Norris, George W. "Hope for Progressives." *Nation*, CXXVII (December 19, 1928): 679–80.

"Nicholas Longworth." *Nation*, XXXII (April 22, 1931): 441.

"Parochial Politics." *Saturday Evening Post*, July 12, 1932, p. 20.

Petrie, John Clarence. "Sales Tax Hailed as State-Saver." *Christian Century*, L (March 8, 1933): 338.

"Party Perplexity after Longworth." *Literary Digest*, April 25, 1931, p. 11.

"Playing Brookhart Out with a Steam Calliope." *Literary Digest*, June 18, 1932, p. 5.

"Political Effects of the Hoover Adventure." *Literary Digest*, August 1, 1931, pp. 5–6.

"President Hoover's Great Action." *Nation*, CXXXIII (July 1, 1931): 4.

"President Hoover's One Year Moratorium Plan—Developments to Date." *Congressional Digest*, X (October, 1931): 236.

"The Progressive Conference." *New Republic*, LXVI (March 25, 1931): 138.

"The Progressives Bid for Power." *Literary Digest*, March 28, 1931, pp. 7–8.

"The Progressives of the Senate." *American Mercury*, XVI (April, 1929): 385–93.

"Progressivism Awakes." *Nation*, CXXXII (March 25, 1931): 316.

"Public Works for Periods of Depression Stabilize Prosperity." *American Labor Legislative Review*, XVIII (December, 1928): 414–16.

Raine, William McLeod. "Costigan of Colorado." *Nation*, CXXXI (October 29, 1930): 465–66.

"A Ratification with a Sting in It." *Literary Digest*, January 2, 1932, p. 7.

"Relief by Public Works." *New Republic*, LXIX (December 23, 1931): 164.

Bibliography

"The R.F.C. to the Rescue." *Literary Digest*, February 13, 1932, p. 9.

"A Roosevelt Boom for President, 1932." *Literary Digest*, May 10, 1930, p. 12.

"Roosevelt 'Out in Front.'" *Literary Digest*, April 18, 1931, p. 10.

Schwarz, Jordan A. "John Nance Garner and the Sales Tax Rebellion of 1932." *Journal of Southern History*, XXX (May, 1964): 162–80.

Shepherd, William G. "Save Smoot and Watson." *Colliers*, September 3, 1932, pp. 14–15.

Smoot, Reed. "Our Tariff and the Depression." *Current History*, XXXV (November, 1931): 365–68.

"The 'Soak-the-Rich' Drive in Washington." *Literary Digest*, April 2, 1932, pp. 8–9.

Soule, George. "Hard-Boiled Radicalism." *New Republic*, LXV (January 21, 1921): 261–65.

"Squabbling over Maine's Election." *Literary Digest*, September 20, 1930, pp. 7–8.

"Talk of the Nation." *New Outlook*, CLXI (February, 1933): 57.

"They Stand Out from the Crowd." *Literary Digest*, May 4, 1935, p. 22.

Thurston, Elliot. "Senator Joseph T. Robinson." *Forum*, LXXXVI (October, 1931): 254–56.

Tindall, George B. "Business Progressivism: Southern Politics in the Twenties." *South Atlantic Quarterly*, LXII (Winter, 1963): 92–106.

"To Hand F.D.R. the Economy Ax." *Literary Digest*, February 25, 1933, p. 7.

"Tossing in Mr. Hoover's 1932 Hat." *Literary Digest*, January 2, 1932, p. 6.

T.R.B. "Washington Notes." *New Republic*, LXII (February 26, 1930): 46.

Tucker, Ray T. "Borah Tells the World." *Outlook*, CLIX (November 11, 1931): 348.

———. "Faithful Fess." *Outlook*, CLXI (September 10, 1930): 43–45.

———. "Leader of the Status Quo." *Outlook*, CLIII (December 25, 1929): 649–51.

———. "The Senate's Bad Boy." *Outlook*, CLVI (October 22, 1930): 294–95.

261

———. "Tiger from Texas." *Outlook and Independent*, CLVI (November 26, 1930): 492–94.

Tugwell, Rexford G. "F.D.R. on the Verge of the Presidency." *Antioch Review* (Spring, 1956), p. 62.

"Unbalanced Government." *Saturday Evening Post*, February 18, 1933, p. 20.

Villard, Oswald Garrison. "Congress, Debts, and Bankers." *Nation*, CXXXIII (December 30, 1931): 717–18.

Wagner, Robert F. "Is Wagner Proposal for Federal Employment Agencies Sound?" *Congressional Digest*, X (January, 1931): 12–13.

———. "The Problem of 25,000,000." *New Outlook*, CLXI (October, 1932): 35–37.

———. "Rock-Bottom Responsibility." *Survey*, LXVIII (June 1, 1932): 222–24.

"Wagner: 'Thorough' Senator Has Known Fear of Insecurity." *News-Week*, February 2, 1935, p. 21.

Watson, Richard L., Jr. "The Defeat of Judge Parker: A Study in Pressure Groups and Politics." *Mississippi Valley Historical Review*, L (September, 1963): 213–34.

Wharton, Don. "Give 'Em Hell, Carter." *Outlook*, CLX (April, 1932): 219.

"What's Wrong with Congress." *Colliers*, January 28, 1933, p. 46.

White, Owen P. "Member of Both Clubs." *American Mercury*, XXV (February, 1932): 182–89.

———. "When the Public Needs a Friend." *Colliers*, June 2, 1934, p. 18.

"Why North Carolina Drops Her 'Little Giant.'" *Literary Digest*, June 21, 1930, pp. 10–11.

Williamson, K. M. "The Literature on the Sales Tax." *Quarterly Journal of Economics*, XXXV (August, 1921): 618–33.

Wilson, Charles Morrow. "Mighty Like a Giant." *Outlook*, CLX (January 6, 1932): 11–12.

Wilson, Edmund. "An Appeal to Progressives." *New Republic*, LXV (January 14, 1931): 234–38.

———. "A Senator and an Engineer." *New Republic*, LXVII (May 27, 1931): 36.

Wolman, Leo. "Unemployment." *Yale Review*, XX (December, 1930): 241–43.

Bibliography

Woolf, S. J. "A Senator Asks Security for Workers." *New York Times Magazine*, January 11, 1931, p. 6.

Unpublished Doctoral Dissertations

Berman, Averill. "Senator William Edgar Borah: A Study in Historical Agreements and Contradictions." University of Southern California, 1955.

Carlson, Earland I. "Franklin D. Roosevelt's Fight for the Presidential Nomination, 1928–1932." University of Illinois, 1955.

Dollar, Charles M. "The Senate Progressive Movement, 1921–1933: A Roll Call Analysis." University of Kentucky, 1966.

Duke, Escal F. "The Political Career of Morris Sheppard." University of Texas, 1958.

Forth, William S. "Wesley L. Jones: A Political Biography." University of Washington, 1962.

Greenbaum, Fred. "Edward Prentiss Costigan: A Study of a Progressive." Columbia University, 1962.

Moore, John R. "Josiah W. Bailey of North Carolina and the New Deal, 1931–1941." Duke University, 1962.

Neal, Nevin E. "A Biography of Joseph T. Robinson." University of Oklahoma, 1958.

Savage, Hugh J. "Political Independents of the Hoover Era: The Progressive Insurgents of the Senate." University of Illinois, 1961.

Schwarz, Jordan A. "The Politics of Fear: Congress and the Depression during the Hoover Administration." Columbia University, 1967.

Symonds, Merrill A. "George Higgins Moses of New Hampshire— The Man and the Era." Clark University, 1955.

Waller, Robert A. "Congressman Henry T. Rainey of Illinois: His Rise to the Speakership, 1903–1934." University of Illinois, 1963.

INDEX

Index

Index

180; works for FDR candidacy, 181, 182, 183–84; characterization of, 181–82; notes need for uniting force in Congress, 231

Hyde, Arthur M., 48, 72

Ickes, Harold, 87, 193, 199*n*
Income tax, 65

Johnson, Rep. Albert, 125
Johnson, Sen. Hiram: forecasts defeat of Parker nomination, 9; on 1930 Lewis-McCormick Senate race, 19; on committee unemployment hearings, 26; notes confusion on remedial legislation, 33; on Hoover's internationalism, 47; on debt moratorium, 81, 87; on Vandenberg, 94; derides Democrats, 101; notes increase of partisanship, 104; on sales tax rebellion, 122; on Democratic revolt, 133; on congressional session, 157, 158, 175; on economy in government, 165*n*; on first Wagner relief bill, 168; on Hoover-Robinson advocacy of federal relief, 173; and Hoover's renomination, 193; and FDR, 199, 200; on Long, 217, 218; on lame-duck session, 227
Johnson, Hugh, 117, 161–62
Johnson, Pyke, 140–41
Joint Committee on Unemployment, 160
Jones, Rep. Marvin: praises McNary, 58; on Garner, 65–66, 125*n*; on Democratic cooperation with Hoover, 100–101; on sales tax for states, 130
Jones, Sen. Wesley L., 205; career of, 57; introduces public works bill, 143; in 1932 election, 200
Joslin, Theodore: as Hoover press secretary, 48; notes end of nonpartisanship, 104; and Hoover's ideas on relief, 145; quotes Hoover on Congress, 220

Kahn, Rep. Florence, 85
Kaltenborn, H. V., 38
Keating, Edward F., 199*n*
Keeney, Frank, 230–31
Kellogg, Paul U., 38*n*, 151–52
Kelly, Rep. Clyde, 164
Kendrick, Sen. John B., 75–76, 157, 183*n*

Kennedy, Joseph P., 191
Kent, Frank R.: on Hoover, 6, 11; on Baruch, 69, 70; on effect of debt moratorium, 79; on Garner's revenue bill statement, 124; notes Democratic support of FDR, 182; on Garner's leadership, 187
Kenyon, Sen. William S., 142–43
Keynes, John Maynard, 127
King, Sen. William H., 183
Kleberg, Rep. Richard M., 120
Knox, Frank, 47, 222
Krock, Arthur, 104, 206, 207
Ku Klux Klan, 55

Labor: opposition to Parker nomination, 9; and defeat of Allen, 20; and employment exchanges bill, 38, 39; opposes sales tax, 106–7, 140; supports La Follette–Costigan bill, 153; Wesley Jones seeks support of, 200; urges approval of Black's thirty-hour bill, 209
Labor statistics bill, 23, 26–28, 30
La Follette, Robert M., Sr., 70, 199
La Follette, Sen. Robert M., Jr., 172; on Hoover's program, 33–34, 235; appraises 71st Congress, 43; on debt moratorium, 79; urges 1931 special congressional session, 80; opposes sales tax, 137; on need for unemployment relief, 142, 149; characterization of, 147–48; holds hearings for National Economic Council bill, 148; introduces relief bill, 149–50, 164; collects data on relief funds, 150–51; leads fight in Senate, 152; differs with Wagner, 154, 210–11; on federal demand for loan compensation, 154; opposes substitute relief measures, 154*n*; Hoover excludes from relief discussion, 157; on subcommittee considering new relief bill, 160; conservative relief plan as victory for, 163; on first Wagner relief bill, 168; proposes increased funds for public works, 168–69; charts new role for Washington, 173; prefers public works to veterans' bonus, 174, 238; praises FDR, 198; agitates for relief, 210; advises FDR against relief amendment, 212–13; on Finance

273

1928 presidential nomination, 47; opposes League of Nations, 47; and Hoover, 49, 67; rejects Hoover's congressional organization plan, 54–55; career of, 55, 56; opposes debt moratorium, 80, 83, 84; denies necessity for special congressional session, 81; supports Hoover's banking proposals, 95; seeks veterans' bonus, 107; opposes additional taxes, 113; on La Follette–Costigan bill, 151; confers with Hoover on relief, 157; assails Democratic relief plans, 164; forecasts veto of Garner-Wagner bill, 170; gives no assistance to Hoover in 1932, 196; and 1932 election, 200, 202; supports filibuster, 219, 220

Webb, Sidney, 25

Wheeler, Sen. Burton K., 70, 181, 191, 192, 199n

White, William Allen, 120; on 1930 elections, 20, 21; on Hoover's enigmatic personality, 40; on sales tax, 135; on urgent mood for relief, 146, 147; pessimistic view of depression, 159–60; on Garner relief bill, 165; notes public hostility to Republican candidates, 196

White, William S., 26

Whittington, Rep. William, 224

Wiggin, Albert H., 148n

Wilbur, Ray Lyman, 48, 72, 218

Wile, Frederic William, 177

Willard, Daniel, 148n, 160

Williams, Rep. Clyde, 127n

Willis, H. Parker, 96

Wilson, Woodrow, 46, 68, 69, 148, 207

Wise, Stephen S., 38n

Wolcott, Rep. Jesse P., 130–31

Wolman, Leo, 144n, 148n

Wood, Rep. Will R., 19, 81, 82, 202

Woods, Arthur, 30, 31, 32, 35, 36, 40

Woodward, George, 108–9

Woolley, Robert W., 184

Young, Owen D., 144n, 180, 189

Young, Roy A., 94–95, 98

"Young Turks," 94

A NOTE ON THE AUTHOR

Jordan A. Schwarz is associate professor of history at Northern Illinois University, De Kalb. He received his B.A. from City College of New York in 1959 and his Ph.D. from Columbia University in 1967. His first book, *1933: Roosevelt's Decision: The United States Leaves the Gold Standard*, was published in 1969.

UNIVERSITY OF ILLINOIS PRESS